THE U.S. CONGRESS

Men Who Steered Its Course

1787-1867

BY THE AUTHOR OF

The Supreme Court In American History

The Bill of Rights: Its Impact on
the American People

THE U.S. CONGRESS

Men Who Steered Its Course,
1787-1867,

MARJORIE G. FRIBOURG

Macrae Smith Company

[c1972] *Philadelphia*

ACKNOWLEDGMENT

The author wishes to thank Mr. William P. Cochrane, Assistant Parliamentarian for the United States House of Representatives, for his invaluable advice and assistance in reviewing this manuscript.

Copyright © 1972 by Marjorie G. Fribourg
Library of Congress Catalog Card Number 72-1751
Manufactured In The United States of America

Published simultaneously in Canada by George J. McLeod,
Limited, Toronto.
ISBN: 0-8255-3410-0

7208

Foreword

This remembrance of things past is an instructive journey through the early evolution of the Congress. Marjorie Fribourg has resurrected for us glimpses of a usable past—one in which we may find clues to the present predicament of the Federal legislature and encouragement for its future. A concerned public, as well as the 535 members of today's Congress, can, so to speak, better understand the man by studying the child. The author helps us in this undertaking.

The agendas of the early Congresses, as the book tells us, seem surprisingly contemporary. There were those fierce legislative struggles over the role of the Congress in foreign-policy making, as epitomized by the imbroglio over the Jay Treaty. The Congress clashed with the Supreme Court over the extent of the judicial power, as illustrated in the instance of Marbury v. Madison. The matter of internal public improvements pitted Southern states against Western. Extended debate erupted over the scope of the "implied powers" of the Constitution, as these involved the legislative and executive branches of the fledgling government. Nearly two centuries later, comparable struggles still occupy the Congress. From the beginning, it is obvious, the legislative and executive branches have regarded each other with mutual suspicion.

Marshaling the battalions during those early conflicts between headstrong Presidents and stubborn Congresses were public men who still loom large in the national consciousness—Madison and Monroe, Jefferson and Hamilton, Webster and Calhoun, John Randolph and Fisher Ames, John Quincy Adams and Jackson, and not least, that unrelenting proponent of congressional supremacy, Henry Clay of Kentucky. Clay succeeded for many years. Ultimately, however, Jacksonian populism dethroned the Congress for nearly three decades. Thereafter, the Congress would again enjoy periods of dominance offset by periods of decline.

Referring to this pendular movement, Mrs. Fribourg writes: "Always, in the past, when their authority was at a low ebb, they have rallied and freshly asserted themselves. Perhaps they will again."

Let us hope so. Thirty years of marathon warfare have very nearly transformed the Presidency into a Caesardom. Should that exalted role remain unchallenged by a subservient Congress, the American Republic will go the way of Rome.

Frank Church

(May 12, 1972)

Senator Church (D-Idaho) is a member of the Foreign Relations Committee, and of the Interior & Insular Affairs Committee, and Chairman of the Special Committee on Aging, United States Senate

Contents

Introduction

This book is dedicated to anyone who wants to influence the future of the Congress of the United States. It is being written at a time when Congress has become the target of a host of reformers who intimate that our national legislature has lost its initiative and its ability to cope with our modern problems.

Members of Congress also are taking a critical look at the origins and purposes of long-revered congressional traditions.

As difficulties are aired and proposals made, the members of Congress find that the lessons learned by their predecessors are an essential ingredient of the decisions of tomorrow. If our elected spokesmen must look at their history before they dare touch the present, so must the voters who hold the reins.

Here is the history of the men who designed and guided the Congress from its inception until the end of the Civil War. I have chosen to cover this period for two reasons. First, these years produced the basic decisions that shaped our modern Congress. Secondly, the leaders of that time recorded their actions and reactions with a frankness which is most useful to anyone wishing to examine the arts of legislative leadership.

The story unfolds as Senators and Representatives find or invent methods with which to resolve the issues they face. As they surmount an unending succession of emergencies, the impact of their means, as well as of their aims, molds the legislative environment in which they function. To list all their major decisions and accomplishments would require a complete review of American history and lots more. This book is not that. I have picked events which show the giants of the past meeting their problems and influencing their world. Much of their philosophy is still helpful and many of their techniques are still valid. Their mistakes are at times worth remembering.

Often they worked through periods as disturbing as our own, when each day's decisions were pregnant with tomorrow's worries and when, time and again, the members of Congress believed they were experiencing a bloodless revolution.

Faced with the challenge of clashing wants and beliefs, and with a host of members each with a will to be effective, Congress had to seek ways to preserve order. It took organization and rules of procedure to dispose of all the proposals and complete all the work. But before long it was evident that these very instruments of order could be the weapons of control for a powerful faction. Meanwhile, in the House particularly, abuse of privilege led to a succession of limitations on freedom.

Later, the admitted need for order was offered as an excuse for suppression. By then, it was obvious that to preserve the rights and prerogatives through which a Congressman can protect the interests of his constituents would take constant vigilance. Men saw that the battle to keep Congress what it was intended to be — "the people's branch," the voice of all the citizens, and the nations's great deliberative body, where the wisdom inherent in the minority, as well as the majority viewpoint, would not be lost—would have to be waged without letup.

At the same time, Congressmen faced threats other than those infringements of their rights caused by their fellow members. In those early years, they learned that power planted in the area of the executive branch tended to grow and flourish, depleting the influence of Congress.

The origins of that cycle can be seen in the events presented in this volume. At the same time we see the amazing ingenuity of those who led the Congress and the heartening flexibility of the legislative institution and its leaders. Always, in the past, when their authority was at a low ebb, they have rallied and freshly asserted themselves. Perhaps they will again. If they do, they will act with more caution and more foresight if both they and we first take a look at the record.

THE U.S. CONGRESS

Men Who Steered Its Course

1787-1867

This cartoon, published by Benjamin Franklin before the Revolution, had lost none of its relevance when the designers of Congress met in Philadelphia. They were still desperately in need of an effective union.

Join or Die   *The Historical Society of Pennsylvania*

Part I

Designing the Congress of the United States

The Congressional Scene

The designing of the Congress of the United States and the Constitution in which it was embodied was one of the triumphs of the ages.

In 1787 American freedom and self-government, so gloriously won, appeared to be ingloriously doomed. Thirteen separate sovereign States were tugging their flimsy union apart. By violating the foreign treaties negotiated by their Continental Congress, they were endangering the peace. By conducting commercial wars against each other they were making havoc out of the economy, filling the prisons with debtors and setting riots and rebellion in motion. By not paying their quotas into the Continental treasury they were leaving the Congress of their Confederation helpless in the face of the problems they had created.

History had taught that chaos breeds a despot, and that weakness invites invading armies. Men who knew their history persuaded the Continental Congress to authorize a constitutional convention. Delegates were picked by all of the proudly independent States except Rhode Island, which found itself too proudly independent to do so.

In May of 1787 the convention convened in Philadelphia. There the creators of the Congress of the United States worked to devise a system of government and write a Constitution that not only would rescue the tottering union but would also have at least a chance of being accepted. Fearing that their plans would be rejected before they could be fully formulated, the delegates worked in secret. The notes taken by the

3

different participants do not always agree exactly as to what was said, but from them we can ascertain the obstacles and fears and the near-despair that attended the formulation of our national legislature.

In the delegates' recorded words lie the preludes to the later dramas of American history and to the major issues we still face today. The delegates decided that the President should see to it that the laws were faithfully executed but that the Congress, or the people's branch, should hold the purse strings. Here was a separation of functions more easily put on paper than into practice, creating a saga of its own that is still not finished. When they faced the problem of sectional difficulties, delegate George Reed of Delaware predicted: "Too much attachment is betrayed to the State governments. We must look beyond their continuance." His contemporaries considered him impractical, but more than a few of his descendants are still haunted by his prophecy.

Finally, the delegates wanted a vigorous government but one so limited in power and so hemmed in with checks and balances that it could never abolish freedom. Since what they wrote was a broad basic structure of government and not a detailed code of laws, they bequeathed to their followers unending questions as to when and how Congress could properly show its muscle. That part of history must start with what Congress was intended to be. This introductory chapter describes the creation of the national legislature and, therefore, the beginning of the evolution of Congress.

"The Fundamental Defect Is in a Want of Power in Congress"

"Good God! who, besides a tory, could have foreseen, or a Briton predicted . . . the disorders which have arisen in these States." The words flowed from the quill pen of General George Washington. Exclamations of surprise and horror filled the pages as he leaned over his desk pouring out his concern to friends and fellow veterans.

"What a triumph for our enemies . . . to find that we are incapable of governing ourselves . . ." he wrote. Living in retirement as he was, Washington was unaware how many other

Americans, during the mid-1780s, shared his sentiment. Again and again their diagnosis was the same as his. "The fundamental defect is in a want of power in Congress."

Perhaps no public figure was blunter or more persistent on this point than Alexander Hamilton of New York, a brilliant economist sent by his State to the Continental Congress.

"States," he said, "show a jealousy of all power not in their own hands, and this jealousy has led them to exercise a right of judging . . . the measures recommended by Congress, and of acting according to their own opinions. . . ." Congress, Hamilton complained, was left without funds, credit, or influence with which to preserve the Republic from harm.

This observation was reinforced when he served in the Continental Congress as collector of continental taxes. Congress sent out requisitions to the States begging them to pay their quotas into the Federal Treasury, and there were always States who made no response.

When Hamilton's own home State was among the offenders, he took it on himself to have a notice printed in the *New York Packet* announcing to all who might be concerned that Congress "has received nothing on account of the quota of this State for the present year."

No thinking man could sit in Congress and not be concerned when funds were not forthcoming from the States and when, consequently, money owed to France, Spain and Holland went unpaid. Here was a dangerous grievance to make available to crowned heads who loathed Republicanism and longed for fresh territories to plunder. The weakness of the Confederation was no secret abroad. England, while trying to protect the property rights of British creditors and her American Tories, had discovered that the States did not necessarily honor a treaty negotiated by Congress. In London, the King's ministers had informed American Ambassador John Adams that henceforth His Majesty's Government would deal only with the separate States. This affront was particularly unsettling, as it came at a time when England was insisting on retaining her bases south of the Canadian border.

The day would come when Hamilton, in an essay addressed

to the people of New York, would devise deliberately embarrassing, rhetorical questions to keep the British insult from being forgotten. "Have we valuable territories and important posts in the possession of a foreign power which . . . ought long since to have been surrendered? . . . Are we in a condition to resent or repel the aggression?" he asked, and then he answered for the reader: "We have neither troops, nor treasury, nor government."

Congress had neither the authority to draft an army nor the means to equip one. It could depend only on the reluctant States. As Hamilton saw it, Congress could not even "remonstrate with dignity" in the face of a broken treaty. There was also the matter of freely navigating the Mississippi. Spain excluded us from it. She was entrenched across the mouth of that great water route and Congress sat by helplessly. Hamilton did not need to add that neither the English nor the Spanish were above exciting the Indians against the population. There were others who had that in mind. The New Yorker, instead, pointed to the shocking chaos in the domestic economy.

Here too, Congress had no control. Connecticut commercially warred with Massachusetts. Virginia law exacted a port tax from ships coming from Massachusetts, Maryland, Pennsylvania and elsewhere in the country, as if sister States were foreign countries. New York maintained a custom house, exacting ruinous tariffs from the merchants of neighboring communities. There was no uniform system of weights and measures agreed to between the States. Each State issued its own currency, much of it worthless. Poverty spread across the land like a plague.

For a long time Hamilton's readers, although aware of much of what he described, told themselves that the States had not fought a bloody war against a tyrannical Parliament only to place themselves under a domineering Congress. Many of his contemporaries saw Hamilton as an innovator; a lean, stiff, intellectual; and perhaps a snob. He had written the article under a pen name, but many surmised the identity of the author. They would have gone on ignoring the point of view he represented had they not been frightened by recent political developments in Massachusetts.

In an effort to pay off old debts Massachusetts had heaped heavy taxes on her already depressed economy. Veterans of the Revolution now swelled the population of the debtors' prisons. Farmers watched their cattle being seized by the sheriff to satisfy lucky creditors holding court orders. In 1786, the Massachusetts debtors rebelled. Mobs took possession of the courthouses. When they chose a leader for their campaign, he was Captain Daniel Shays, a veteran of Bunker Hill. People who had so recently fought a revolution and vanquished the authorities ruling over them could easily repeat the process.

Massachusetts appealed to Congress for help but Congress was unable to send any. Two anxious members of Congress, Henry Lee and John Jay, wrote to General Washington. In the past it had been the universal respect for the General that had held the American people together.

Now, in 1786, though troubled by current events, Washington saw no reason to come out of retirement. He was busy with his Mount Vernon plantation. His diary was filled with plans to improve his groves, plant hemlocks, clean the underbrush out from under the pines, and grow berry bushes and ivy. "Nor could it be expected that my . . . opinions would have much weight in the minds of my countrymen," he told a friend.

He was absorbed with his agricultural chores when he received John Jay's letter. Jay, a one time president of the Congress, wrote, "I am uneasy and apprehensive, more so than during the war . . . What I most fear is, that the better kind of people, by which I mean the people who are orderly and industrious . . . will be led . . . to consider the charms of liberty as imaginary and delusive."

Washington, in reply, conceded that matters were coming to a crisis. "I do not conceive we can exist long as a nation, without lodging, somewhere, a power which will pervade the whole Union," he said. He then added: "To be fearful of investing Congress . . . with ample authority for national purposes, appears to me the very climax of popular absurdity and madness."

When a veteran of the Revolution wrote to Washington suggesting that influence be used to quiet the rebels in Massachusetts, Washington did not think that using influence was the solution. In his answer he said: "Influence is not government.

Let us have a government by which your lives, liberties, and properties will be secured."

The words ring with the confidence of command, but in a note to James Madison of Virginia, Washington described his own mood as melancholy.

Fortunately, at about this time Virginia and Maryland needed to come to an agreement. Washington, among others, had long been interested in developing the Potomac River as a portal to the western territory, thus tying the settlers more closely to the Republic. As the river ran between the two States, Maryland and Virginia appointed commissioners who met with General Washington to discuss the formulation of a bi-State program for regulating commerce and navigation. The outcome of the meeting unquestionably reflected the General's able guidance. The commissioners reported back that if the water route was to tie in to more westerly waterways, Pennsylvania's commercial interests were involved. Delaware also had an interest, situated as she was so near the Chesapeake Bay that she could one day be linked to it by canal. In fact, this might well be the time for all the States to meet and face the whole uncomfortable issue of their abominable lack of commercial cooperation. Consequently, an invitation went out from Virginia to all the States to send representatives to Annapolis, Maryland, to confer on questions of trade.

The result was disturbing. Only delegates from Virginia, Pennsylvania, Delaware, New Jersey and New York appeared. So small a group could do nothing. Madison and Hamilton, who were both present, looked at each other. The national crisis called for their contrasting talents. Madison was a gentle, soft-spoken, scholarly attorney and a well-liked veteran of Virginia politics. He had used his influence to bring about this meeting. Hamilton was bolder and more impatient. It was Hamilton who took command at Annapolis.

After obtaining the consent of the representatives present, he drafted a message addressed to the legislatures of their respective States urging that another meeting be called at Philadelphia "to devise . . . provisions . . . to render the Constitution of the Federal Government adequate to the exigencies of the Union."

He begged the legislatures to induce more States to participate. Several of the States helped carry this message to the Continental Congress.

If it had not been for Shays' rebellion, the Continental Congress might never have agreed to such a conference, or if it had agreed, the States might have failed to give their support.

Congress, however, did authorize a meeting of State delegates to consider revising the Articles of Confederation, and to report their proposals to Congress and the several State legislatures. Delegates were to assemble in Philadelphia on the second Monday in May of 1787.

In Philadelphia a world-famous philosopher, scientist and statesman named Benjamin Franklin eagerly awaited their arrival. He was by now eighty-one and so crippled with gout that he had to be carried through the streets in a sedan chair. Franklin was, nonetheless, still politically astute and active. He was, moreover, President of the Executive Council, which governed the State of Pennsylvania. In addition to being one of the delegates to the convention, he intended to be cordially hospitable to the group. An impressive array of America's greats, including delegate George Washington, would walk down Market Street, to pay their respects to Mr. Franklin at his home.

Before the convention met, Franklin wrote to Thomas Jefferson in Paris: "Indeed, if it does not do good it must do harm, as it will show that we have not wisdom enough among us to govern ourselves; and will strengthen the opinion of some political writers, that popular governments cannot long support themselves."

Here, then, was the awesome responsibility faced by the delegates. Not only the infant American republic but the hopes of all men who wanted a say in their own destinies hung in the balance. It was to be a long, anxious summer in Philadelphia.

Madison arrived early. His absence from Congress, which was meeting in New York, would be noticed, but the Virginian had ample reason for leaving his duties there. He was convinced that what the delegates were authorized to do—merely revise the Articles of Confederation—was not sufficiently drastic to save the country. The Confederation was only a league to which sovereign and independent States belonged. What Madison wanted to see come out of the convention was a supreme Federal Government.

Nobody knew better than he did how unlikely it was for such a proposal to succeed. First the delegates, who had not been authorized to go that far, would have to agree on a suitable plan for the new supreme government. Then Congress, in spite of having limited their authority, would have to approve their having gone beyond it and accept their recommendations. States that would necessarily be losing much of their jealously guarded independence under the new system would have to ratify it— ". . . a series of chances which would inspire despair in any case where the alternatives were less formidable," as Madison wrote to a friend.

Madison had work to do. The Virginia delegation of seven must meet and hammer out a draft of a possibly suitable plan of government and be ready to present it to the convention. As other delegates arrived, Madison must consult with them and gain their cooperation.

Even before the convention met, it was evident what trouble lay ahead. George Read of Delaware was convinced that the convention would provide an opportunity for the large States to swallow up the small ones. His State credentials forbade him to accept any change in the voting system of the Continental Congress. Under the Articles of Confederation each State had one vote and one vote only, regardless of the size of a State's population. Virginia wanted that changed; so did Pennsylvania. Obviously, they must not get embroiled in so inflammatory an issue too early in the proceedings.

Slowly, the delegates drifted into the convention city. Hamilton arrived from New York, and on meeting Rufus King of Massachusetts, filled the plump, kindly attorney's ear with all that Hamilton hoped the convention would achieve.

Finally, they assembled in the State House, presented their credentials, adopted their own rules, agreed to keep their deliberations secret, and elected George Washington President of the convention.

At last, they listened to Virginia's Governor Edmund Randolph, six feet tall, with a gentle face framed by his soft black hair. What was lacking was an effective government that could secure the country against foreign invasion, check the quarrels between the member States, regulate for the common good, and enforce its mandates. The Congress of the Confederation could do none of these things. To be effective, the central government needed to be superior to the local governments. In short, as Randolph would propose later, a national government ought to be established with a supreme legislature, judiciary and executive. In essence, Virginia was proposing to change the league of separate States into a nation.

There was no immediate discussion of Randolph's speech. The delegates decided they had heard enough of this revolutionary idea for one day. They agreed only to turn themselves into a committee of the whole (including all the delegates). Whatever was agreed on in committee could later be formally presented to the convention for a final vote. The Virginia plan was to be referred to this committee of the whole, which would meet to begin discussing it the next day.

It must have been a long night in the life of James Madison. The next day, Wednesday, May 30, Washington gave up the presiding officer's seat to Nathaniel Gorham of Massachusetts, the chairman of the Committee of the Whole.

The proceedings started off as might be expected. Young Charles Pinckney of South Carolina wanted to know if Randolph intended to abolish the States. Randolph reassured him. Only those State powers which clashed with the powers to be granted the new government would be yielded.

As the discussion progressed, another Virginian, George Mason, contributed an important explanation. The articles were weak because Congress could not punish uncooperative States. Sovereign States could not easily be coerced. A government was necessary which could make its rules apply directly to the individuals in the States and punish those whose guilt required it. That was what Madison also wanted—a national government.

Then the inevitable happened, with Robert Yates of New York recording it in great detail. General Charles Pinckney— the cousin of young Charles—had the floor. With the speech and manner of an elegant gentleman, Pinckney stated that if the delegates accepted Randolph's premise (that a mere confederation of the States would never suffice to provide for the common defense, the general welfare, or the security of liberty), "their business was at an end." In other words, they might as well go home, for they had no authority to do anything more than revise the Articles of Confederation.

Yates wrote, "This remark had its weight."

More than a few delegates felt the need for caution as they directed their attention toward Gouverneur Morris of Pennsylvania. Morris was a large man whose impressive poise was undiminished by a wooden leg. Hamilton, sitting among the other delegates, watched Morris with approval. They were both alumni of King's College (now Columbia University). Of the two, Morris was more of a social mixer, a witty man who loved convivial merrymaking. Today, he was anything but frivolous. He was vehement.

"A federal agreement which each party may violate at pleasure cannot answer the purpose," he warned. "We had better take a supreme government now than a despot twenty years hence—for come he must."

Throughout the debates no one in the room was taking more complete notes than James Madison. He sat close to the presiding officer's chair, eagerly writing down all that he heard. Finally, with profound relief, he heard the passage of the resolution: "A national government ought to be established consisting of a supreme Legislative, Executive and Judiciary."

The wording would later be altered, but the essence of the decision would remain. Here was the first triumph for the Virginia plan. Thus it was decided that a national legislature was to be established. What that legislature would be like was another problem.

"Groping . . . in the Dark to Find Political Truth"

The awful moment had now come when the Virginians must confront the committee of the whole with their most inflammatory resolve. From now on, the bigger, more populated States must have fair representation.

First Randolph tried, without success, to offer methods of allotting representation in the new Congress. Then Madison rose, smoothly omitting the details of any method; he merely asked the assembly to vote; "that the equality of suffrage established by the Articles of the Confederation ought not to prevail in the national legislature . . . an equitable ratio of representation ought to be substituted."

Gouverneur Morris from big Pennsylvania happily seconded Madison's motion. With that, Delaware threatened to secede.

Letting any State walk out of the convention this early would be disastrous. The delegates voted to postpone the question. That saved the convention for the time being, but obviously they could not postpone the question forever.

On Thursday, May 31, the delegates agreed that the legislature should have two branches. Randolph's plan called for letting the people select the members of what he called the first branch. (Later it would be called the House of Representatives.)

Roger Sherman of Connecticut objected to giving the people so much influence. He had been coping with city, State, and national political problems for a long time. The people "want information and are constantly liable to be misled," he said.

Elbridge Gerry of Massachusetts agreed with Sherman. "The people . . . are the dupes of pretended patriots . . . They are daily misled into the most baneful measures . . . by designing men." No one doubted that Gerry, a well-to-do Boston merchant and ship owner, was referring to the mobs of Massachusetts debtors.

Mason of Virginia, while not exactly disagreeing with Gerry and Sherman, pointed out that superior classes could be indifferent to the needs of humanity. "We ought to attend to the rights of every class of the people," he said. This could only be done by giving them a voice in the government. He wondered that men forgot how quickly their prosperity could disappear. Every selfish motive should recommend adopting Randolph's proposal to let the people select one house of the legislature, regardless of a delegate's present fortune. It was a bold position taken at a time when most States limited the franchise to men with at least some type of property.

Madison believed that the people would have more affection for the central government if they elected one branch. Allowing them this right was essential to every plan of free government, he thought.

New Jersey, which was a small State, saw the proposal as a possible step in the direction of depriving her of her equal representation with her more populated neighbors. She was against it. If most of the delegates seemed ready to accept the idea, the small States had no intention of letting the matter rest. They were determined to bring it up again.

The makeup of the second branch of the legislature was discussed, but then the delegates postponed the topic while they considered the matter of a national executive. It appeared that the question of whether the chief executive should be a single person instead of a council was also a trying issue. Being oppressed by an autocrat would be worse than putting up with anarchy. Nothing was keeping the delegates shut up in this humid hall, secretly planning a central government to impose over their beloved States, but the realization that in earlier republics disorders such as the recent ones in Massachusetts had led to the rise of a Caesar. A majority of the delegates emphatically voted against giving the executive an absolute veto over laws passed by the legislature.

In this they were encouraged by Franklin. He remembered the days when no good law had been able to pass the Colonial Assembly of Pennsylvania until the Governor obtained a favor. When news had arrived that Indians were scalping people to the

West, the Governor had demanded a tax exemption before any means of self-defense could be put into action.

Mason was fearful of giving the executive too much authority, but later he announced: "If . . .[the members of] the Legislature are able to raise revenues and make . . . war; I shall agree to a restraining power [over the legislature]."

He shuddered to think of the nation's purse and sword being left in the same unfettered hands. With these conflicting fears in mind, the details of the veto power were left to be worked out later.

On Wednesday, June 6, young Charles Pinckney had arranged to interrupt the proceedings. He wanted the delegates to reconsider and let the first branch of the legislature be elected not by the people but by the State legislatures. He argued that then the State governments would be more willing to ratify the new government.

James Wilson of Pennsylvania did not want to change his position. "The government ought to possess not only first the *force*, but second the *mind* or *sense* of the people at large," he said. He had made a study of the republics of old. As he saw it, a delegate or a congressman, or any kind of representative, "is made necessary only because it is impossible for the people to act collectively." The people, not the States, were the legitimate source of all authority.

Mason again provided the clarifying explanation of why the new government should not include Pinckney's proposal. "Under the existing Confederation, Congress represents the *States*, and not the *People* of the States," he said; "acts operate on the *States*, not on the individuals." Then he said, "The case will be changed in the new plan of government. The people will be represented; they ought therefore to choose the Representatives. . . . Representatives should sympathize with their constituents, should think as they think and feel as they feel."

After hearing all this, a very excited George Read of Delaware predicted that the State governments would be swept away. He did not see how they could continue to function under a national government that represented all the people.

Sherman of Connecticut was calmer. He suggested they narrowly limit the functions and powers of the central government.

More trouble lay ahead as the delegates tried to plan for the second branch, or Senate. Reared in the tradition of the British House of Lords, they automatically looked to a strong Senate to keep a restraining check on the popular branch. They wondered how to provide for this in a republic. They debated and then voted to make the Senators independent of outside influences by giving them a long term in office. Eventually the Constitution would give the Senators a six-year term while Representatives would have to seek reelection every two years. Thus it was expected that the latter would be the more closely responsive to the electorate.

The delegates decided that the Senators should be at least thirty years old and should be elected by their States' legislatures, not by the people. Then, inevitably, they had to return to the problem of how much representation each State should have.

Seeing the trend toward letting some States have more representation than others, William Paterson of New Jersey, an able advocate, called for a reading of the act passed by the Continental Congress which had instigated the convention "for the sole and express purpose of revising the Articles of Confederation . . ."

His motive was clear, but he stated it anyway. "Can we on this ground form a national government? I fancy not . . . We have no power to go beyond the [present] federal scheme," he said. As to the Virginia plan, "the small States would never agree to it." He was riled by Wilson. The Pennsylvanian had evolved the happy theory that since the convention had no authority other than to make recommendations, it could recommend whatever it pleased. Wilson had once hinted that delegates might try to start a general government by first uniting the large States.

"Let them unite," Paterson said, "but let them remember that they have no authority to compel the others to unite." He would oppose the Virginia plan here and when he returned to New Jersey.

In reply, Wilson was equally unyielding. If the small States would not accept this plan, Pennsylvania and, he presumed, some other States would not accept any other.

In that case they would achieve nothing. Tension blanketed the room. Franklin decided that he must take the floor. Troubled by his gout, which was making him too uncomfortable to stand and speak, he wrote out what he had to say on a piece of paper.

Before Franklin was ready to be recognized, Rutledge and Butler, both of South Carolina, championed another scheme that would benefit the large States. Suffrage in the legislature, they said, ought to be in proportion to a State's contribution to the National treasury. "Money is strength," Butler argued. Many delegates felt the large contributors needed protection.

Before the quarrel could again reach a deadlock, Franklin asked to have his paper read to the assemblage by Wilson.

Tactfully, the paper did not mention Paterson or Wilson by name. Franklin merely remarked: "It has given me a great pleasure to observe that till this point . . . our debates were carried on with great coolness and temper. If anything of a contrary kind, has on this occasion appeared I hope it will not be repeated . . . Positiveness and warmth on one side, naturally beget their like on the other . . . I now think the number of Representatives should bear some proportion to the number of the Represented." He ended with an anecdote to help everyone relax.

Humors did improve for a while, but still no solution was reached. On the nineteenth of June, Luther Martin of Maryland —a large, slovenly man—took the floor and ranted. He could never accede to a plan that would introduce an inequality and lay ten States at the mercy of Virginia, Pennsylvania and Massachusetts. "Slavery," he called it. On the twenty-seventh of June, and again on the twenty-eighth, he was to repeat much of the same argument, always with the same vehemence.

Madison tried again to explain. "It is not necessary to secure the small States against the large ones," he pleaded. Pennsylvania, Virginia and Massachusetts had no interests in common that threatened the others.

Wilson added that the small States were not entitled to the same number of votes as the large ones, any more than a deserted borough would be entitled to the same number of votes as a large city bustling with humanity.

When no progress was made, Franklin tried again to calm the

atmosphere. He addressed himself to the Chair. "The small progress we have made after four or five weeks . . . is methinks a melancholy proof of the imperfection of the Human Understanding. We indeed seem to feel our own want of political wisdom . . .

"In this situation of this Assembly, groping as it were in the dark to find political truth . . . how has it happened, sir, that we have not hitherto once thought of humbly applying to the Father of lights?" Franklin suggested that they start each morning with a prayer.

The delegates considered the motion. Hamilton and others felt that the public would sense the extent of their difficulties if people saw a chaplain being brought in at this late date.

Then Hugh Williamson of North Carolina pointed out that they had no money to pay a chaplain. The motion was dropped. The quarrel continued.

Now the conversation veered to the danger of their reaching no agreement. Madison reminded the assembly that separate States had, "rendered the old world the theater of incessant wars." Hamilton pointed to the danger of separate States' forming separate alliances with the European nations who had territorial interests on this continent. [They] are and must be jealous of us . . . We are weak . . . It is a miracle that we [are still] here exercising our tranquil and free deliberations . . . It would be madness to trust to future miracles," he said.

The larger States had repeatedly insisted that they had no interest in menacing their smaller neighbors. Perhaps Hamilton's warning inadvertently provoked the terrible threat that followed.

Captain Jonathan Dayton of New Jersey, young, daring and impetuous, retorted that "when assertion is given for proof, and terror substituted for argument," he presumed they would have no effect.

Then Gunning Bedford of Delaware took the floor. He did not disguise his anger. He quoted the assurances tendered by the larger States, adding: "I do not, gentlemen, trust you . . ." The small States could certainly never accept the Virginia plan, he made clear; yet it was still being urged. "We have been told that this is the last moment for a fair trial in favor of good Government . . ." he said. He charged that insistence on this inequitable scheme was what was destroying the Confederation.

"The large States," he warned, "dare not dissolve the Confederation. If they do the small ones will find some foreign ally . . . who will take them by the hand and do them justice."

The delegates had time and again postponed topics that were too explosive to debate calmly. This time they adjourned for the day.

On the second of July Sherman said, "We are now at a full stop." Nothing was being accomplished.

At a loss as to how to resolve their conflicts, but unwilling to go home with nothing solved, the delegates tried one more approach. They selected a small committee to work out a compromise and present it after the July 4 holiday. Franklin was on the committee, which carefully weighed everyone's demands.

Earlier, John Dickinson of Delaware had suggested that even if one branch of the legislature represented population, at least the other branch could give each State an equal vote. The large States then could not rule the rest. Sherman of Connecticut had recommended that the Senate be the branch where the States would be equally represented. At the time the delegates had not been ready to accept this compromise. Now, under Franklin's guidance, it was proposed again with modifications.

The committee decided that each State should be allowed to send one member to the House of Representatives for every 40,000 of its inhabitants, but that no State, no matter how small its population, should have less than one representative. (The 40,000 figure would later be changed to 30,000.) In the Senate each State would have the same vote as every other State, but only the House, or people's branch, could originate bills raising revenue.

On Thursday, the fifth, the committee presented its recommendations. Madison felt as if he was being asked to give up fundamental principles for expediency, to conciliate the small States. Gouverneur Morris called the scheme objectionable. It gave no influence to property.

In the days that followed, the convention was truly on the

verge of dissolution. Hamilton, who lacked Madison's endless patience, had already left Philadelphia. On July 10, the other two New York delegates departed, adding to the general feeling of futility.

Washington wrote Hamilton that the situation was alarming. "I almost despair . . . I wish you were back."

So prodded, Hamilton did later return. He was vitally interested in everything that affected the country's future.

Sometime during his stay at the convention, Hamilton and Madison went for a long afternoon walk and laid the foundation of a later American drama.

They had talked over one of Hamilton's favorite subjects before. He had very definite ideas on how to cope with the nation's financial difficulties. He wanted the United States to take over the debts the States had incurred during the Revolution, letting all the States function on the same sound basis.

It was this point that concerned the two men during their summer afternoon stroll in Philadelphia. According to Hamilton, "[W]e were perfectly agreed in the expediency and propriety of such a measure; though we were both of the opinion that it would be more advisable to make it a measure of administration than an article of Constitution . . ." It seemed highly inadvisable to multiply the obstacles in the way of getting the new government accepted.

After this happy addition to their previous encounters, Hamilton went away with the impression that "I should have the firm support of Mr. Madison in [my] general course . . ." This impression was later to be the basis of a very unpleasant surprise.

Meanwhile, the delegates had faced the unpleasant question of how the slaves were to be counted in relation to representation, should the committee's recommendations be adopted. Pierce Butler of South Carolina made it clear that the South would have to be sure that "their negroes may not be taken from them which some gentlemen within or without doors have a very good mind to do."

There were indeed many such gentlemen, both in the hall and in the population at large, who loathed and condemned the institution of slavery. Others thought the practice of holding slaves would die out in time. Their feelings were almost immaterial, since it was obvious that no government could be formed without the approval of those who were economically dependent on slavery. That issue would have to wait until there were more free States in the Union. The delegates finally agreed to count slaves at three-fifths of their actual numbers.

Both Randolph and Mason called for a periodic census, as the size of the population might change in the future. The delegates agreed. Until a census could be taken, they temporarily would have to fix the number of Representatives to which each State was entitled.

By now more delegates were ready to concede that the small committee had solved the problem of giving wealth its fair share of influence. They had given only the people's branch the right to originate bills raising money. The areas with the most population and the areas with the most wealth were approximately the same.

On Monday, July sixteenth, the delegates decided to take a final vote on the committee's compromise formula. The great question must be settled: should they have a two-branch legislature—one representing the States, and one representing the people—with the people's branch having the tighter hold on the purse strings?

At this point they were no longer in the committee of the whole. They were in convention with Washington in the Chair. Five of the States were for the committee's great compromise. Four were opposed. Massachusetts' delegation was divided. On this narrow margin the great compromise was carried.

Obviously, they could not form a union without the opposing States. Randolph said it was useless to come to so important a decision with a bare majority on either side. He wished they would adjourn. Paterson thought Randolph meant to adjourn the convention. Paterson was willing. The majority were relieved when Randolph corrected the impression. He wanted to adjourn only for the day.

The big States then had an awesome decision to make. Should they accept the verdict, or should they withdraw and create a separate union of their own? The delegates from the large States talked it over. When they decided not to withdraw, the worst of the crisis was over. A nation was in the making.

Shortly thereafter, the delegates were ready to select a committee on detail and instruct the committee members to draft a constitution for the United States. The committee was to bring its draft before the delegates on August sixth with the expectation that the delegates would discuss, amend and pass upon it. This the committee did. Then the delegates worked until September 17, perfecting the proposed Constitution. By the time they were through they had given the Senate the right to propose amendments to money bills coming from the House. More important, they had tightened the Congressional hold on the nation's purse strings. "No money," they said, "shall be drawn from the Treasury, but in Consequence of Appropriations made by Law."

It was to Congress that they gave the authority to lay and collect taxes, and duties, "to pay the Debts and provide for the common Defense and general Welfare of the United States." In addition Congress alone was to have the right to borrow funds on the credit of the United States. With these provisions the delegates optimistically believed they had given the lawmakers absolute ultimate control over the Federal pocketbook.

Nor was this all. The delegates decided to give Congress the power

> *To regulate commerce;*
>
> *To establish rules to naturalize new citizens;*
>
> *To coin money and regulate its value and fix the standard of weights and measures;*
>
> *To establish post offices and post roads;*
>
> *To promote the progress of science and useful arts by providing patent and copyright legislation;*
>
> *To establish the lower courts (the Supreme Court was established by the Constitution);*
>
> *To declare war;*
>
> *To raise and support armies and a navy and make rules for the government of these forces;*

To call forth the militia from the various States for repelling invasion, suppressing insurrection or executing the laws of the union;

To buy land and erect needed forts, arsenals, dockyards and other federally needed buildings;

To make all laws which shall be necessary and proper for carrying into execution the foregoing powers.

Furthermore, the Constitution and the laws and treaties of the United States were to be the supreme law of the land, and all laws passed by Congress in accordance with the Constitution were to have supreme status. After so stating, the delegates listed a few things Congress was not to do. The reasons for adding restrictions were clear enough. An elective despotism was not the government for which they fought.

Congress was not to pass an *ex post facto* law penalizing citizens for acts that were not illegal at the time when they were committed.

Except in times of rebellion or invasion, Congress was not to suspend the right of *habeas corpus* (the right of anyone imprisoned to be taken before a judge to challenge the legality of the imprisonment).

Congress was not to use its legislative powers to declare individuals guilty of crimes, for this was a court function. Such "bills of attainder," as they were called, had had a shabby history as instruments of oppression.

The delegates never actually put in writing their decision that if Congress passed an unconstitutional law, the Justices of the Supreme Court could declare it void. During the debates, King of Massachusetts had assumed that the Justices would stop the operation of any law repugnant to the constitution. Gerry also thought that judicial duties included deciding the constitutionality of a law. In Massachusetts judges had already assumed that responsibility.

Later, when Virginians were wondering whether they should accept and ratify the Constitution, a young lawyer named John Marshall assured everyone that the Justices would save the Constitution from being violated by the legislature. Not surprisingly, when Marshall became Chief Justice he asserted this authority for the Court. Since 1803 it has been firmly established that the Justices can overrule an unconstitutional act of Congress.

This check on their activities did not leave the Congressmen helplessly bound by the Court. The delegates had given Congress (like the States) the right to propose amendments to the Constitution. When a suggestion for a constitutional amendment originated in Congress, it first needed the concurrence of two-thirds of each House. Then if three-fourths of the States ratified the proposal, it was to become part of the Constitution. Pointedly, the delegates saw no need to have proposed constitutional amendments approved by the Chief Executive.

The relationship between the Chief Executive and Congress was carefully planned. The President was to see to it that the laws were faithfully executed. That is, once a law was duly made he was to carry it out. He was to give Congress information on the state of the Union and recommend measures for its consideration. He was to ask it for the money he needed and the laws he wanted. He was to obtain the advice and consent of two-thirds of the Senators before he concluded a treaty. He was to need the Senate's consent to confirm the men he would choose to hold appointive offices. If his conduct warranted it, the House of Representatives could formulate charges against him and the Senate would sit as an impeachment court with the Chief Justice presiding.

After long debate, the delegates had given the President a limited check, or veto power, over the legislature. He should not be able to duplicate the mischief of the royal governors, but on the other hand he needed to be able to protect his executive interests. Laws passed by Congress should bear his signature, the delegates decided.

If, instead of signing an act passed by the legislature, the President returned it to the House where it had first been proposed, the lawmakers were to reconsider their act. It could still become a law.

After the President, instead of signing a measure, returned it to that House where it was first proposed, it was to be reconsidered, first by that House and then by the other.

Then, if two-thirds of those present in each house (always provided that a quorum of over half the members was on hand) voted to override the veto, the measure would become law. If he neither signed nor returned it for ten days, then too it would become law, unless Congress had adjourned in the meantime. In that case the bill died. The President's refusal to sign it became known later as "a pocket veto."

In short, the President was to be a vigorous executive of the laws, but he was to have limited powers. The foundations of conflict were etched into the blueprint. Missing from the plan was the extent to which time and problems and the focus of public attention would magnify the leadership role of the executive, shifting initiative into his hands. In spite of all precautions, one day Congressmen would wonder what had happened to their rightful role.

They had been given the right to fashion rules for their own proceedings. With the exception of letting the Vice President preside over the Senate, the delegates had left it up to Congress to discipline its own members and pick its own leadership. Here again lay the beginning of a bitter and significant struggle. Through many disputes, Congress was long to seek a formula whereby it could provide for its members democratic freedom, and at the same time keep them effectively led and organized for action.

Here, then, was the essence of the design for the Congress of the United States, proposed as an integral part of a newly written Constitution. Madison's preplanning, Franklin's tact and good humor, Washington's influence, and the forebearance of most of the others had made it possible.

It was to become effective if it was ratified in nine States. The voters in the States were to choose representatives who would meet in convention and there discuss and accept or reject the new Constitution.

There was one thing the delegates had not done. The omission was to cause such protest in the months ahead that all their labors would be in jeopardy. They had not affixed to the Constitution a bill of rights protecting the liberties of the people against congressional usurpation.

"Preposterous and Dangerous"

As soon as all the delegates who favored it had signed the proposed Constitution, it was sent to the city hall in New York. There, in an upstairs meeting room, the members of the Continental Congress sat wondering what to expect.

The press was equally curious. A few lucky journalists already had copies of the Constitution and were setting the startling document into type. American readers would soon be thunderstruck—and some dismayed—by the bold words that the delegates had placed in the preamble. Far from relying on the authority of the States, the opening phrases read: "We, the People of the United States, in order to form a more perfect union, . . . do ordain and establish this Constitution . . ."

Ten exhausted delegates, James Madison among them, headed for the Congress in New York. By the time Madison reached there, the opponents of the Constitution were already at work.

Richard H. Lee delivered their opening blow. This Constitution called for a new Union that could start functioning after only nine States had accepted it. Congress had no authority to accept any such plan.

Madison reminded everyone that the Congress itself had called the convention because of the need for a more effective national government. Lee then argued that Congress should insert a bill of rights.

At this moment the idea was appalling: for if Congress revised the Constitution, some groups would accept only its proposal, and others would cling to the convention's version. Then neither form of the Constitution would gain enough support to be adopted. Madison and the other Federalists said as much.

Finally the discussion ended with the old Congress gallantly providing for its own doom. It passed the resolution sending the

Constitution to the State legislatures, letting each State submit the document to its own convention to be made up of delegates chosen by its own people, as the authors of the Constitution had planned.

This design left it to each State legislature to set up a general election for the selection of delegates. Their words, uttered in convention, would ever after carry weight, for while debating whether to accept or reject the proposed plan of government, the convention members would leave for future lawmakers a guiding record of their fears and expectations concerning the Constitution and the Congress.

Difficult months lay ahead, and the Federalists knew it. A lot of explaining would have to be done. The country would now have to be convinced—as the Federal Convention had needed to be convinced—of the wisdom of a supreme government.

In Virginia the opposition was gathering fast, and at this point Randolph was no help in stemming their progress. He had his own misgivings about the new plan and indeed had refused to sign the proposed Constitution before he left Philadelphia. Mason had returned to Virginia in a terrible mood. Less than a week before adjournment he had tried and failed to get the convention to add a bill of rights to their summer's work. Now he was determined to keep the Constitution from being adopted. Virginia Federalists desperately needed their most able spokesman, James Madison, but Madison was trapped in New York coping with the problems of the dying Continental Congress.

The Treasury Board was in despair and Madison wrote to Jefferson: "Without money, the offices must be shut up, and the handful of troops on the frontier disbanded, which will probably bring on an Indian War . . ."

As Madison watched the old government crumble, he saw the opposition to the new government swell. At one point he was forced to admit to Randolph that the newspapers in the northern and middle States teemed with criticisms. As Madison analyzed it, "The attacks seemed to be principally leveled against the organization of the government, and the omission of the provisions . . . in favor of the press and juries, etc."

Not surprisingly, journalists wanted a bill of rights guaranteeing freedom of the press. Madison did not think the proposed Congress had the power to muzzle the press. As far as juries were concerned, the Constitution did not provide for them in civil cases but it had provided for them in criminal cases.

Evidently Hamilton had decided that unless an informed defense of the Constitution was circulated the public could be misled and the cause lost. He was thinking of a series of newspaper editorials written for the New York press and he had discussed the idea with John Jay and wanted Madison's help.

At the same time demands for Madison's help were coming from his home State. Washington, among others, wanted him to come to Virginia, run for State convention delegate, and above all, debate down the fearful misconceptions being spread by the Anti-Federalists.

Despite SOS signals coming at him from all directions, Madison remained in Congress. Somehow he also found time to collaborate in Hamilton's project, writing a large number of the wanted articles. They were addressed to the people of the State of New York and signed Publius.

At first they reviewed the weakness of the Confederation and expounded on the blessings of union. Later columns described the future Government and its lawmaking body. As they piled up they developed into one of the great political classics of all time, *The Federalist* papers.

Finally Madison picked a batch of these articles and shipped them to Washington to be reprinted in Richmond. Thus, though in New York, he campaigned for Virginia's ratification of the Constitution. Winning her support caused him considerable anxiety. If Virginia went Anti-Federalist she could lead away the States further south.

Meanwhile, there was trouble in Pennsylvania, where the Federalists tried to settle matters before their opposition had time to organize. A mere eleven days after the convention closed, George Clymer rose in the State assembly. Everyone in the hall knew Clymer, a Philadelphia businessman. He had signed the Declaration of Independence, had fought in the Revolution, and had represented his commonwealth in the Continental Congress and in this newly finished constitutional convention.

He proposed that a ratifying convention be called. The back country members objected to being rushed, and before the question could be decided, nineteen Anti-Federalists had disappeared. Pennsylvania's legislature lacked a quorum. The Speaker sent the Sergeant at Arms to fetch the truants. He failed to corral them, but the next day a house-breaking mob captured two of the assemblymen and dragged them to the Statehouse.

In this inauspicious atmosphere the assembly had a quorum and proceeded to authorize a general election to pick delegates for a convention to consider the Constitution. When that convention met, James Wilson found himself on his feet in the meeting room, defending the omission in the Constitution of a bill of rights that would protect the people from abuse by the Congress.

"Such a measure would be not only unnecessary but preposterous and dangerous . . ." he argued. "A bill of rights," he explained, "is an enumeration of the powers reserved [to the people] . . . everything that is not enumerated is presumed to be given . . . [to] the government."

Wilson contrasted this with the Constitution as proposed. Here the government possessed only its enumerated powers, and "the people never part with their power."

As he saw it, a list of the citizens' rights would imply that the people had no rights that were not listed. The Constitution would then read as if Congress could do anything to a citizen which was not forbidden by the bill of rights. The prerogatives of Congress would thus be increased.

Wilson gave an illustration. "We are told that there is no security for the rights of conscience," he said, "I ask . . . what part of this system puts it in the power of Congress to attack those rights? When there is no power to attack, it is idle to prepare the means of defense."

Wilson's sentiments on this subject were similar to other Federalists who insisted that they had given the Congress only certain stated and limited powers. This arrangement was in itself a bill of rights. Many of their contemporaries realized that, of necessity, the responsibilities given to Congress would carry with them implied or unwritten powers.

The anxiety men felt over the possibly hidden powers of

Congress was best illustrated in the North Carolina convention by delegate Henry Abbot. Abbot told the convention chairman "It is feared, by some people, that, by the power of making treaties, they [the Executive with the consent of two-thirds of the Senate] might make a treaty engaging with foreign powers to adopt the Roman Catholic religion in the United States . . ."

The Constitution said that no religious test was to be required as a qualification for public office. This might prove, as delegate Iredell claimed, that the men who framed the Constitution wanted religious freedom. However, in the generations ahead, it would not be the framers but others who would be implementing the powers of Congress.

Iredell was nearer the point when he said, "If any future Congress should pass an act concerning the religion of the country, it would be an act which they are not authorized to pass . . ."

Delegate Joseph M'Dowall still felt that "A bill of rights ought to have been inserted . . . I say trial by jury is not sufficiently secured . . ."

He then pointed to what he thought was another hidden power of the national legislature. "By the power of taxation, every article capable of being taxed may be so heavily taxed that the people cannot bear the taxes necessary to be raised for the support of their State governments." This he feared could happen even though Congress had no written power to abolish the State governments.

In short, the proposed plan did not satisfy North Carolinians. The year 1788 came and went, and so did much of 1789, and they had still not ratified the Constitution.

"Gentlemen Have . . . Their Doubts"

Delaware ratified, even before the close of 1787. Much to Wilson's delight, so did Pennsylvania, and then New Jersey. On January second, 1788, Georgia ratified. Intently, Madison watched the trend.

Thirty-nine of the Publius articles had been printed by mid-January. Hamilton had already made a sizable contribution. Jay was ill and only one more article would come from his pen.

Madison had to write fast. The Massachusetts convention was already in session. Already the delegates were looking askance at the power of Congress to raise huge armies, and with them, it was feared, "produce a dissolution of the States."

James Madison was not unsympathetic to the civilian horror of standing armies. It was Rome's army that had brought about the downfall of her liberties, a fact known to educated men of the day.

There was, however, another source of danger, and Madison felt he must discuss it. "With what color of propriety," he wrote, "could the force necessary for defense, be limited by those who cannot limit the force of offence?" Congress could not limit the size of an aggressor's army. It could only try to match it. Only the existence of a mighty union would give adequate protection from foreign invasion. To save the Republic from overthrow from within, the Constitution had wisely provided that Congress could never appropriate funds for the support of the armed forces for more than two years at a time. Thus the military establishment could never become too independent of Congress. It would always be under the control of the elected representatives of the people.

As Madison went on to answer other objections being raised to the proposed Constitution, he again restated his principal argument. Congress could be trusted not to abuse its authority, because members of the House of Representatives would be running for election every two years.

Massachusetts delegates were not easily convinced. Delegate Abraham Holmes pointed a finger at what he thought was missing from the Constitution. There was no provision for a grand jury, assuring that a man must be indicted by reasonable men before he could be made to stand trial. The document gave the accused no protection from being forced to furnish evidence against himself, and no right to counsel or to meet his accuser face to face. There was no check on the power of Congress to invent the most cruel and unusual punishments.

Holmes summed up the picture as "dark and gloomy." Congress, he asserted, was possessed of powers enabling it to institute tribunals as evil as that diabolic institution the Inquisition.

Abraham Holmes was not alone. Samuel Adams, whose reputation as a Revolutionary patriot added weight to his words, admitted, "I have had my doubts . . ." and added, "Other gentlemen have had their doubts."

Delegate Heath had noticed the same thing. "Many gentlemen appear opposed to the system," he said.

The Federalists had finally won over Adams, but they were not sure they could persuade John Hancock, the President of the Massachusetts convention, to support their cause. Hancock, a former President of the Second Continental Congress and signer of the Declaration of Independence, at first was conspicuous by his absence from convention sessions. He pleaded "indisposition," but not everyone believed him.

Political discussions went on, inside and outside the hall. Then as the month was ending, Hancock made an unusual move. He proposed to the convention that they ratify the new government with a request that amendments be added to the system. This, after much discussion, the delegates did, trusting that their suggestion would be accepted after the government was operating.

In New York, on the other hand, there was talk of calling another general meeting of all the States to revise the entire plan. Governor George Clinton said he was a friend of a strong government but not obliged to accept a dangerous one.

His political colleague Thomas Tredwell was blunt. "Our lives, our property, and our consciences are left wholly at the mercy of the legislature," he said.

New Yorkers, like citizens in their sister States, feared the powers of Congress. They pointed to the clause giving Congress the authority to "lay and collect taxes . . . to pay the debts and provide for the common defense and general welfare of the United States." People asked, "What limitation, if any, is set?" Congress seemed to have unlimited authority to tax and spend. Others quoted Publius and denied that unlimited powers were intended. Congress could only spend for the subjects covered in her named powers.

In New York, as elsewhere, citizens objected to the slavery provisions in the Constitution, but for the time being nothing could be done on this issue.

While New York's decision still remained uncertain, Virginia's State convention met. Here, Madison could count on help from a political veteran and friend, Edmund Pendleton; from a fellow member of the Continental Congress, Henry Lee; from a young lawyer and former soldier of the Revolution, John Marshall; and from an able Federalist named George Nicholas. He could also count on facing opposition as fierce as any he had encountered in Philadelphia.

Patrick Henry, who could hold any audience entranced, was determined to frighten his fellow delegates out of accepting this new federal scheme. Henry's questions to the Federalists were not inquiries but angry arguments.

"What right had they to say 'We the people?' . . . Who authorized them to speak the language of We the people, instead of We the States?" From inquiry Henry went on to accusation. "The control given Congress over the time, place, and manner of holding elections, will totally destroy the end of suffrage," he claimed.

In essence, Madison answered that the Congress needed this control over elections to protect their plan for a people's government. The time of elections must be uniform throughout the land and in no State should the people be deprived of their right to participate. He might have added that each State still had the power to limit the franchise in Federal elections to those who were eligible to vote in State contests.

Henry's alarmist tactics were inexhaustible. Early in the debate he objected to the power of Congress to enforce the laws by calling forth the militia.

"Our only defence, the militia, is put into the hands of Congress," he warned. Later he again returned to this theme. "It will result . . . that this is to be a government of force," said he.

Madison answered, "There never was a government without force . . . to make people do their duty." As Madison saw it, giving Congress the power to call out the militia provided the nation with a citizen's army, thus protecting the Republic from being dependent on professional soldiers remote in their interests from the people.

Henry went on repeating the objections to the Constitution that had been voiced elsewhere and adding his own. He was helped by Mason. Together they made much of the fact that Congress was to have exclusive control over a ten-mile-square capital city area. Here Federal courts would sit, tyrants would be protected. Law-breaking officials would be safe from justice. Plain citizens would be hanged.

Madison was astonished. It seemed incredible that either of them could have forgotten how the Continental Congress had moved homelessly about, and how it had on one occasion been chased out of Pennsylvania by a riot. Congress had to control its own home.

Beyond all this, Henry fired his heaviest ammunition when he harped on the fact that the document contained no bill of rights protecting the people from abuse.

To handle this issue, George Nicholas made a recommendation for the Federalist side. Henry had claimed that the other States also wanted a bill of rights. In that case, Nicholas said, a bill of rights could be added by subsequent amendments. "We shall find the other States willing to accord with their own favorite wish," he said.

Here, for all practical purposes, was a promise. It was a promise that the friends of the Constitution repeated when they called for a vote to ratify the document. Amendments would be planned and recommended to Congress, they said.

On the basis of this promise, Virginia delegates voted on June 26, 1788, to adopt the Constitution. The Union would have had little chance of success without Virginia. She had a bigger population than any of her sister States.

A month later, New York ratified, with an even more ominous threat to the Constitution than asking for subsequent amendments.

New York's popular Governor, George Clinton, who had presided over his State's convention, wrote a message to accompany the convention's announcement adopting the Constitution: "Nothing but the fullest confidence of obtaining a revision by a general convention . . . could have prevailed upon a sufficient number to ratify it . . ." he said.

New York wanted another meeting of the States, such as the one which had originally framed the Constitution in Philadelphia. To Madison this was a lot more disturbing than letting Congress make a few changes in the new government. "The Congress . . . will probably be careful not to destroy or endanger it," he wrote to a friend. A Convention, on the other hand—meeting in the then existing state of national excitement, and manned by characters who dreaded giving up their State authority, or their control over commerce, or their port taxes—was all too likely to make chaos out of the hard-won new Constitution. At the very least such a Convention would probably so weaken the document as to make it virtually ineffective.

Eleven States were now in the union—two more than were needed to make the Constitution operative—but New York's suggestion held a dangling weapon over the infant nation. Unfortunately, Anti-Federalists elsewhere could count on Henry's powerful help. As Madison campaigned to become a member of the first Congress, the followers of Henry and Clinton campaigned for their new Federal Convention. It was at this point that candidate Madison was approached by a Baptist minister named George Eve.

Mr. Eve wanted Mr. Madison to refute political charges that the candidate was opposed to amending the Constitution and that he had ceased to be a friend to religious freedom, which Madison was known to have vigorously championed in Virginia.

Candidate Madison gave the minister the following statement. "I freely own that I have never seen in the Constitution,
as it now stands, those serious dangers which have alarmed
many respectable Citizens." What Madison had most feared
were conflicting demands for changes, which could be used to
prevent the new plan of Government from ever being adopted.

"Circumstances are now changed," he wrote, ". . . amendments, if pursued with a proper moderation and in a proper
mode, will be not only safe, but may serve the double purpose
of satisfying the minds of well meaning opponents, and of providing additional guards in favour of liberty."

Madison then made his future position clear. ". . . it is my
sincere opinion that the Constitution ought to be revised, and
that the first Congress meeting under it ought to prepare and
recommend to the States for ratification the most satisfactory
provisions for all essential rights, particularly the rights of conscience in the fullest latitude, the freedom of the press, trials by
jury, security against general warrants, etc."

No one knew better than Madison that the first Congress
would have its time filled establishing and organizing the new
Government and correcting the deplorable state of the Federal
finances. The threat of an Indian war and of foreign powers
taking advantage of such an event had not diminished. What lay
ahead was a race to get all the needed work done and also draft
and propose a bill of rights, before the Anti-Federalists could
scream betrayal and overturn the Government of the United
States.

Part II

The Men Who Put the Plan Into Action

The Congressional Scene

The first leaders of Congress found the launching of the new United States Government difficult enough. Hindered and delayed by a lack of precedents, they were forced to devise ways and procedures for doing business.

The impatient wanted to speed their methods; the thoughtful spoke of gaining more information to guide their acts. Inevitably, as they struggled along, viewpoints clashed. Men who feared the domination of the executive branch sparred with men who dreaded a weak Government. State interests and sectionalism fanned the flames of discord, and threats of secession had been hurled at Congress before its second session adjourned.

Meanwhile the men read different meanings into the Constitution. They disagreed as to the extent of the privileges vested in Congress. They differed also as to the dangers to be found in legislative might. By the end of their first session Congress had changed. Led by James Madison, members had forever limited their own authority by the constitutional amendments they proposed to the States in the Bill of Rights.

Two sessions later a faction of the members, encouraged by Alexander Hamilton, had won the first battle in a long fight to pass legislation based on the "implied" but unwritten powers of Congress. And Congress was changing again—reaching for the flexibility to survive.

In the course of all this controversy likeminded men gathered together and political parties emerged. The Federalists were the first to control a majority in Congress. Led by Alexander Hamilton, they narrowed the separation between themselves and the Executive. This, plus their victories, spurred their opposition. Ultimately, however, it was their own autocratic attempts to silence their critics that brought about their defeat and the end of their era.

In this period, extending from the beginning of Congress through the Federalist contribution and demise, we can see the beginnings of practices and problems that foreshadow later events.

Getting Organized in Order to Establish a Government

It should have been the glorious fourth of March of 1789. It should have been the date of the first meeting of the Congress of the United States. The former government had so resolved.

Carpenters and painters had helped to revamp New York's City Hall into Federal Hall. Massive doors opened into the House of Representatives chamber. A chair had been carefully placed on the dais for the as yet unselected Speaker of the House. The galleries were ready to hold the eager visitors. And below the tall windows, the empty seats and desks stood in two neat crescent-shaped rows awaiting fifty-nine newly elected Representatives.

Also waiting for the gentlemen of Congress were a host of national problems. There was no money with which to get the new Government started. There was no treasury department, no department of foreign affairs, no war department. They would have to be created. A system of lower courts had to be established. A permanent home for the Government had to be selected, but on that first day neither a quorum of Senators nor a quorum of Representatives appeared.

For travelers to be long overdue was hardly unusual. Rain turned the dusty roads into sticky mud, slowing the wheels of the stage coach. A fallen tree across the route halted the horse and rider. Unfavorable winds fought back the sailing ship or ice blocked her passage. No interstate gathering seemed able to start on time.

This time the whole month slipped away without a quorum. Members trickled into the city. Elias Boudinot, a former president of the Continental Congress, did not arrive from neighboring New Jersey until March 23. In his case it was the eighteenth of the month by the time his Governor could declare him elected, and even then not all the State's polls were closed. Boudinot and the three other New Jersey Representatives would soon find their elections being contested. Meanwhile, they were neither the first nor the last to claim their seats.

Madison was among the arriving Virginians. Roger Sherman was in the Connecticut delegation. Gerry came from Massachusetts. George Read of Delaware was now a Senator; so was Paterson of New Jersey. Rufus King, who had moved away from Massachusetts, was a Senator from New York. In fact, except for North Carolina and Rhode Island, who had not yet ratified and joined the Union, every State was sending at least one veteran of the Federal Convention. In addition, men who had worked together in the former government met again in this Congress. The hall abounded with reunions.

Experienced though the members were, the task before them was staggering. Before they could even begin to examine legislative issues, they had to formulate at least a few operating procedures, and the House had to select its Speaker.

As Boudinot had been a president of the Continental Congress, he was not an illogical choice for Speaker and he mulled over what he considered were the demands of the position. He pictured himself having to maintain a "proper" New York household in order to do the social entertaining that he judged appropriate to the office. If he did not get the speakership, Boudinot decided he would visit with a relative and not be burdened with an expensive city dwelling. He would miss his wife, but unlike other Representatives he would not have to tolerate the discomforts of a local boarding house during the months when Congress was in session.

He waited. April approached and the hall filled. On the first of the new month the House had a large enough attendance to hold its election. It selected as its Speaker Frederick A. C. Muhlenberg of Pennsylvania, a modest man who in his youth had been ordained a Lutheran minister. After turning to politics Muhlenberg had held many offices, including that of speaker of his Pennsylvania State house of representatives. Thinking he knew the job, the ex-minister viewed it without ambition. He made no plans to run a pretentious household.

Muhlenberg rightly expected that on each meeting day, at the hour set by the House, he would settle himself in the presiding officer's chair, call the members to order, direct that the journal be read, and serve as moderator of the ensuing discussion.

Those who wished to be heard would stand and address him. At the suggestion of the rules committee no private conversations would be allowed while the Speaker was addressing the House. Perhaps the chair would be stating some question to be voted upon. Since every man present must vote, every man present must hear the question. Beyond that, no one would be permitted to walk between the Speaker and a member who had the floor.

This much respect Muhlenberg commanded. He gave no indication, however, that he ever envisioned how the Speaker's office could one day be used to direct the destiny of a nation.

Muhlenberg had been in the chair almost a whole week when on Monday, April 6, Oliver Ellsworth, the Senator from Connecticut, entered the House chamber. At that moment Ellsworth was serving as an official messenger boy. "Mr. Speaker," he announced, "I am charged by the Senate to inform this House that a quorum of the Senate is now formed."

There must have been sighs of relief from those who had waited a whole month wondering if the new Government would ever get under way.

Senator Ellsworth then explained that the House members were now expected to attend their first joint session with the Senate. The Senate was ready to count the votes cast by those men who had been chosen in each State to be the electors of the President and the Vice President.

Without a Vice President, the Senate had no presiding officer, but John Langdon of New Hampshire had been picked to serve as President pro tempore and to open and announce the content of the ballots.

Ellsworth suggested that the House appoint one or more of its members to sit at the clerk's table, along with one of the Senators, "to make a list of the votes as they shall be declared." To this the House agreed.

Thereafter the Speaker left the chair, and the entire assemblage followed him to the Senate Chamber. Before they returned to their own quarters, they had seen President George Washington and Vice President John Adams officially elected.

On Tuesday the House members went back to the task of getting organized. Chairman Boudinot brought in the report of his committee on rules. The Clerk, John Beckley, who was seated at his table near the Speaker, read the report aloud. The Representatives then agreed that no member should speak more than twice to the same question without the permission of the House. No one should even speak a second time until all those wishing to be heard had been given the floor.

The Speaker was given the authority to appoint small committees of three members or less. No one, as yet, imagined that any major legislation would be planned in small committees. That job, they thought, had to be done by the entire membership of the House sitting as the Committee of the Whole. Once a policy was favored, the members of a small committee could work out the details and the wording of a measure or bill and report it to the House.

Later, the members would find that even after a bill was reported to the House, it was usually sent back to a Committee of the Whole, further amended, and again reported to the House, where the new amendments would be read and reread and perhaps voted to adoption. The next day the entire bill, along with the adopted amendments, would again be read by the Clerk. This time, if it passed the House, it would be sent on its way to the Senate.

Under this system almost none of the committees were permanent or standing committees. The House appointed them for only limited periods of time to fulfill only certain well-defined obligations. How well this method of keeping all responsibility in the hands of the entire membership was going to function only the months and years ahead would tell. For the time being this was the only way the first Congress wanted to work.

Without waiting for any further procedures to be established, James Madison on Wednesday, April 8, started the debate on what he considered a pressing matter. He knew the new Government was not fully formed but he wanted the House to pass at least a temporary revenue bill.

"The union," he said, "by the establishment of a more effective government, having recovered from the state of imbecility that heretofore prevented a performance of its duty, ought, in its first act, to revive those principles of honor and honesty that have too long lain dormant."

In other words the nation should prepare to pay its bills. He could have added what they all knew: Without an income the Government could not stay in existence. Now that they were organized, it was time to tackle the nation's problems.

"We Have So Little Time to Spare"

Optimistically, Madison proposed putting duties on imports right away to relieve the Government's desperate financial situation. Then he realized that the Pennsylvanians Hartley and Clyner, although they wanted tariffs on imports, wanted them planned to "protect our infant industries," making competing imports expensive. The project would necessarily prove time-consuming.

Madison admitted that it made him apprehensive.

Before Congress could undertake any such program it needed considerable information on the state of domestic manufacture. "The prospect of our harvest from the spring importations is daily vanishing," he warned. "If the committee delays . . . until a system of protecting duties shall be perfected . . . all the spring vessels will have arrived." He would have been justified in reminding them that they still had not established the Executive Departments or the lower courts.

In spite of him the debate continued and became enmeshed in conflicting sectional interests.

Clymer wanted duties laid on imported steel. "A furnace in Philadelphia," he said, "made three hundred tons in two years . . . deserving protection."

Tucker of South Carolina resented the smallest tax on this article: his constituents were farmers and used steel for tools.

Congressman Thomas Fitzsimons said that if gentlemen did not get rid of local considerations, the Committee of the Whole would make little progress. He spoke as a veteran of both the Federal convention and the Continental Congress, but he could, nevertheless, have remembered that it was the duty of these Representatives to provide a voice for the people of their area.

Boudinot was more diplomatic. "What gentlemen have in view is very desirable," he said. However, he felt he needed more information in order to legislate intelligently on protective tariffs. "We have so little time to spare . . ." he said. Like Madison, Boudinot wanted a temporary measure to bring in the badly needed funds at once.

After that the Committee of the Whole put steel into a general low-duty category, and then Parker of Virginia advocated "laying it on molasses." If the duty discouraged the consumption of New England rum, he thought that a very happy consequence.

In no time a lively young bachelor from Massachusetts named Fisher Ames was denouncing Parker's "speculative piety." Ames was not alone in reminding the gentlemen seated around the semicircle that in this new world Great Britain had found burdensome duties hard to collect.

As usual Madison answered in a low, gentle voice. As usual he relied on logic to guide the course of events. The duties he now proposed could be easily born by the commercial interests. Earlier they had paid State taxes, which were not even uniform from port to port.

Ames, although he was not always impressed with Madison, had to admit that Madison was the leader of the House. "He is our first man," Ames told a friend. The tax on molasses stood.

While the Representatives were thus occupied, the Senators were holding their sessions behind closed doors.

Eventually, they would appoint a committee which would recommend that their secretary roll up three pieces of paper and toss them into a box. Langdon, Dalton and Wingate would then draw lots to decide which men might serve six year terms, which men must leave in only two years, and which in four. The Constitution's mandate for Senators, "that one third may be chosen every second year," was thus to be fulfilled.

First, however, the Senators were deciding how to address the new President. "His Highness the President of the United States and Protector of their Liberties" was suggested. Disgusted, Senator Maclay of Pennsylvania wrote in his diary that he was going to try to get Speaker Muhlenberg's help in resisting that. Maclay blamed the Vice President for dreaming of titles. "This whole silly business is the work of Mr. Adams," he said. Most members of the House of Representatives sided with Maclay. The Chief Executive was addressed simply as Mr. President, and the decision quickly hardened into custom.

On April 30, 1789, the first President was escorted from his residence through the happy mobs in the streets and into the Federal Hall, then to the outside balcony, where George Washington took the oath of office.

After reentering the Hall he addressed the two Houses of Congress. It was, as he recalled, his duty to recommend to the Congress such measures as he judged necessary and expedient.

He was well aware that these first Congressmen would have to transform the new Government from an untried plan into an operating system. Nevertheless, before he concluded with his prayerful thanks for that new Government, he felt that he must draw their attention to the remaining "degree of inquietude." All danger to the new form of union had not yet passed, adding to the cares of Congress the responsibility of considering amendments to the Constitution.

Washington then put into words the principal challenge that would face the lawmakers from then on—to wrestle with the conflicting demands of effective government, public harmony, and individual freedom.

For the First Congress this problem did not come from within their own assembly. It came from State legislators and private citizens who were insisting on getting the Constitution amended in order to guarantee their liberties. It was imperative that the bulk of them be dissuaded from insisting on having the Constitution turned over to the tearing claws of sectional interests in another national convention.

Being from Virginia, the President knew the strength of the Anti-Federalists better than many an unwary Congressman. While warning the members of Congress to plan amendments with great caution, he still recognized that the lawmakers would have to act in this area or the work would be taken out of their hands. In this area, also, they had no time to spare.

Launching the Ship and
Appeasing the Captain

"I have never seen an assembly where so little art was used ... There is no intrigue, no caucusing, little of clanning together ..." Fisher Ames was listening to the debates and at the same time writing to his Boston friend, George Minot. His fellow lawmakers, he found, were "very good men, not shining, but honest and reasonably well informed." He was impressed with their "most punctual attendance." Three or four had obtained a leave of absence, but the rest were always there; the Speaker had no need to send the Sergeant at Arms to find them. What amazed Ames even more was the absence of party spirit, for he knew the strong political differences that divided these men.

In order to handle an explosive political difference with the greatest skill, Madison, on May 4, interrupted the discussion on import duties. He announced that at the end of the month he would offer his suggestions on amending the Constitution. He had not spoken too soon. The next day Mr. Theodoric Bland presented the application from the Virginia legislature that

Madison so feared. It was the work of Patrick Henry and the Anti-Federalists.

In it, Virginia delegates were described as having "yielded their assent to the ratification of the Constitution . . . from a full expectation of its imperfections being speedily amended." Virginians feared "the slow form of Congressional discussion." In order to secure their inalienable rights, the applicants demanded "that a convention be immediately called of deputies from the several States."

Bland wanted this application referred *at once* to the Committee of the Whole. Boudinot agreed with Madison. The application had no legal force unless two-thirds of the States made similar proposals. If that happened, Congress would be forced by the Constitution to call the requested convention. Meanwhile, the application was not a matter for the House to discuss.

Bland was not satisfied. "The application," he said, "contains a number of reasons why it is necessary to call a convention."

Gerry reminded him that "The gentlemen [Madison] . . . told us yesterday, that he meant to move the consideration of amendments [to the Constitution] on the fourth Monday of this month . . ."

This was not what Bland wanted, but he had to accept it.

For the time being the House members concentrated on other problems. Eventually they sent their proposed import duties to the Senate. As yet they had no system of collecting these duties, but nevertheless on May 19 they felt they had to tackle the work of establishing the first executive departments—Treasury, War, and Foreign Affairs.

Madison moved that each department be headed by a secretary. Since these would be major officers, the Constitution called for their appointment by the President with the advice and consent of the Senate. When Madison proposed that the officers be removable by the President acting alone, Ames reported, the idea "kindled some sparks."

Bland was horrified. The President would have a tyrant's absolute authority. Representative White supported Bland. The Constitution gave the Senators a voice in the dismissal process, he said, because "the party who appointed ought to judge of the removal . . ."

The debate had thus evolved into how the legislature should interpret the Constitution. Here was a judicial function. But the House could not create the departments without agreeing on the meaning of pertinent Constitutional decrees.

Perhaps, unless Congress specified for how long a Secretary could hold office, he could never be dismissed, except following an impeachment, trial and conviction. This was one way of interpreting Article II section 4 of the Constitution, which called for the impeachment of ". . . all civil officers . . ." for treason, bribery or other crimes.

It was an interpretation that Boudinot disliked. Impeachment was "intended as a punishment for a crime, and not as the ordinary means of rearranging the Departments," he said. He could see the House giving the Constitution such a narrow interpretation as to render it impossible to execute.

Madison saw no need either to rely on impeachments or to give the Senate any say in dismissals, and he argued that neither was wise. "If the heads of the Executive departments are subject to removal by the President," Madison reasoned, "this makes . . . the President responsible to the public for the conduct of the person he has nominated. . . ." Require the Senate's consent and "the President is no longer answerable . . ."

Madison must have felt shaken when, in rebuttal, William Smith of South Carolina read from the Federalist paper Number 77: "The consent of that body [the Senate] would be necessary to displace as well as to appoint."

If Smith looked straight at the gentleman from Virginia, Madison may have been tempted to explain that Number 77 was Hamilton's work. Perhaps he felt rescued by the position Clymer had already taken that removing subordinates was an executive function.

In any case, Madison now argued quietly that all executive functions belonged to the President unless the Constitution said otherwise. The Constitution, although it did let the Senate advise on major appointments, did not set any exceptions to the President's power to remove department heads. Therefore he had that power.

As the men argued over the degree to which the executive and legislative functions were separated, sides formed. To White, the wish for separation was impracticable. "The Constitution is formed, and the powers blended," he said.

Ames wrote to Boston, "A little of the sourness of the party has been produced by the great debate. . . ." If the debaters could have looked ahead and seen how much their words were going to mean to those battling to protect the seventh President of the United States from censure, their division of opinion might have been even more acrimonious. As it was, Madison prevailed, and the House planned the Departments with the understanding that the President had the power to remove his own appointees without the Senate's consent.

Meanwhile, Madison had patiently agreed to postpone taking up his constitutional amendments because there was so much pressing business before the House. On June 8, he tried again to bring them up for discussion. He wanted to go into the Committee of the Whole.

A gentleman from Maryland was the first to express his resentment of such a sudden transition from other concerns. He judged it "extremely impolitic to go into the consideration of amending the Government, before it is organized . . ."

When Jackson of Georgia gained the floor, he started his remark in a more poetic style. "Our Constitution Sir, is like a vessel just launched, and lying at the wharf . . . It is not known whether she will bear with safety the precious freight to be deposited in her hold . . . Will the prudent merchant . . . employ workmen to tear . . . asunder the frame?"

He went on, and suddenly he was making the same blunt point as the Marylander: "In short, Mr. Speaker, I am not for amendments at this time . . . without we pass the collection bill we can get no revenue, and without revenue the wheels of Government cannot move."

Madison maneuvered. "I only wish to introduce the great work, and . . . I do not expect it will be decided immediately . . ." he said, and then he argued: "If we continue to postpone . . . and refuse to let the subject come into view, it may occasion suspicions, which though not well founded, may tend to inflame or prejudice the public mind . . ."

Congressman John Page was also from Virginia and he, too,

had reason to be worried by all the delays. "After they [the amendments] are published, I think the people will wait with patience . . ." he said. "But [now] it must be very disagreeable to them . . . Putting myself into the place of those who favor amendments, I should suspect Congress did not mean seriously to enter upon the subject." He ended with a warning. "Unless you take early notice of this subject you will not have power to deliberate . . ." He would have been justified in adding that the public was the captain of the ship of state Jackson had described.

It was soon obvious that even if they managed to go into the Committee of the Whole, Jackson and Sherman of Connecticut were going to move for an immediate postponement of the question.

Madison was convinced that some discussion of the issue had to take place. The public must be satisfied that its wishes were not being disregarded. He himself was becoming more concerned. He counted among the dissatisfied, who considered their liberties insecure, many who were respected for their talents and patriotism. "We ought not to disregard their inclinations," he told his colleagues.

With that, Mr. Madison withdrew his motion to go into the Committee of the Whole. He proposed, instead, that a select committee be appointed, and very astutely he proceeded immediately to explain what the committee should consider and why.

To satisfy its critics, he said, the Constitution must be made to bar the Government from interfering with the rights of citizens. Freedom of conscience and expression were essential. Those accused must have a fair trial. Search warrants must be limited in scope. In the process of asking for a committee, Madison discussed how these great rights might be jeopardized and what protection must be enacted.

"In our Government it is, perhaps, less necessary to guard against abuse in the Executive Department than any other, because it is not the stronger branch of the system, but the weaker . . ." he said. [Constitutional protection] must be leveled against the Legislature, for it is the most powerful . . ."

That was how the United States Government looked to future

President James Madison. He thought the Executive was weak. It was his opinion that safeguards, guarantees, and declarations of rights should discourage Congressional majorities from legislating away the rights of minorities. Restrictions should be laid against the actions of the national legislature and the States.

Not all the suggestions Madison made that morning were destined to become law. Almost a century would go by before the Constitution contained amendments that were designed to guarantee civil rights against State action.

Nevertheless, the philosopher had outmaneuvered his opponents. The matter of the amendments appeared in the journal. His colleagues respectfully referred the question to the Committee of the Whole for later consideration. For the moment the disgruntled were appeased.

"A Deep, Dark and Dreary Chaos"

The Representatives found it increasingly difficult to undertake all the essential tasks that stretched before them. Before they returned to the subject of the amendments, they found themselves in another tussle.

Madison wanted a provision inserted in the bill that created the Treasury Department. His proposal—which would soon have more impact than he realized—was to make it the duty of the Secretary to "digest and report plans for the management of the public revenue and the support of the public credit."

Page objected. "A dangerous innovation," this. He thought members "might be led by . . . deference. . . . to support the minister's plan . . . it would establish a precedent . . ." Page envisioned all the department heads admitted onto the floor to explain their plans and order them enacted, like ministers in a monarchy.

Thomas Tucker of South Carolina heartily agreed. Mr. Madison's proposal would undermine the authority of the House.

But Ames was impatient. "The Secretary is presumed to acquire the best knowledge of the subject of finance of any member of the community," he said. "It seems to follow logically that the House must obtain evidence from that officer," He then begged the House to consider the condition of the nation's finances. "It presents to the imagination a deep, dark, and dreary chaos; impossible to be reduced to order without the mind . . . commensurate to the occasion," he claimed.

As if to prove his point, a message arrived from the Senate.

The other chamber had at last agreed to the duties the House wanted to impose, *except* for a few items. The Senators asked the Representatives to send delegates to a conference.

More members could now forsee the delays and difficulties that lay ahead. It would be July 1 before full agreement would be reached and a final, or enrolled, bill would be ready to be checked for accuracy by a few members while other members were being appointed to carry it to the President.

And it would be July 31 before a little group of Senators and Representatives would be calling on President Washington with another bill—one to provide for collecting these enacted duties. And even after the President signed both measures, that would only begin the battle to establish the public credit. . . .

When Lawrence of New York joined Ames and Boudinot in defense of Madison's proposal, it was at last agreed to let the Secretary "prepare" recommendations for the House to consider. The way was thus paved for a powerful Secretary, and through him for a melding of Executive and legislative functions in the area of financial planning.

Surprisingly, Ames had not snatched this occasion to deal with another closely related problem. Ames was exasperated by the strain of constantly working in the Committee of the Whole. He wrote to George Minot, "We correct spelling, or erase *may* and insert *shall* . . . in a manner which provokes me . . . Our great committee is too unwieldy for this operation . . . We could not be so long doing so little, by any other expedient."

Though older and a good deal more patient than Ames, Madison could no longer ignore the slow pace of their progress, which meant he could not yet bring up his bill of rights. He blamed it on the newness of the Congress and on the perplexities springing merely from the want of precedents.

In the area of precedents, however, Congress was making progress. A number of joint committees (manned by selected Senators and House members) had been set up to recommend the proper formalities to be used in relation to the President or in dealings between the two Houses. No longer did either the Senate or the House use their own members to carry official messages from one chamber to the other. This chore was now done by Samuel Otis, the Secretary of the Senate, and the Clerk of the House, John Beckley. A start had been made in formulating the rules. But as yet there was only a restricted use of small committees, although there was one standing, or permanent, committee which Congress had established called the Committee on elections, whose existence proved most convenient.

Clymer chaired the group, which immediately assumed a disagreeable task.

The committee was confronted with the unpleasant challenge of the New Jersey elections. Boudinot from that State did a good share of the work. While the investigation was dragging on, he was often being called on to be the chairman of the Committee of the Whole, occupying the seat vacated by the Speaker and keeping order among the sixty-five members. July came. Clymer's committee was still talking about sending to New Jersey for more evidence or possibly going to the State. As a result, all the New Jersey men lived through most of the session with their right to hold their offices in jeopardy. It was September 2 before the House was in a position to rule to uphold the State's Governor and recognized the election of the four men from New Jersey. At least that matter, having been handled by a committee, did not add another agonizing delay to those Madison already faced.

He was still waiting to bring up his planned amendments when on July 20 the Doorkeeper announced, "Mr. Speaker, a message from the Senate." The Senators had passed the House bill establishing the Department of Foreign Affairs—but with amendments. They had also passed a bill creating the necessary lower judicial courts for the United States. The Constitution had established the Supreme Court, directing Congress to create the rest of the judicial system.

While meaning to obey the directive, the Senate nevertheless had widened the Supreme Court's authority, contrary to the limits set by the Constitution. In paragraph thirteen, they had told the Justices to hear cases involving public officials without requiring these suits to go first through the lower courts. Now the Senate desired the concurrence of the House.

First, the House proceeded to read and agree to the bill establishing the Department of Foreign Affairs, which in a matter of months would be called the Department of State. Agreeing made it unnecessary to choose members to send to a conference. The House then considered the bill for organizing the courts. It was twice read by the clerk, and the House ordered it referred to themselves as the Committee of the Whole to be taken up later. Now, somehow, matters appeared a little less hectic. Madison was induced to try again to call for consideration of his Constitutional amendments.

Evidently, he was so troubled by the delay in planning a Bill of Rights that he failed to react to the legal flaw in the Judiciary Act. When the measure became law in September, paragraph thirteen was still there. He was to live to see it change the course of American history. Meanwhile, he drew the attention of the Representatives to his proposed Bill of Rights.

Ames again was in the forefront of the discussion, wanting the debate confined to the recommendations Madison had already made, fearful that the House would act as if it were another Federal convention and subject the Constitution to the ordeal of another total review. Ames wanted a committee appointed with its authority strictly limited. He was strongly opposed by Gerry, but this time the young man convinced the House. A committee of eleven members was set up to work on the amendments to the Constitution, and Madison was on it.

Three days later, Ames had another reason to be pleased. The reason this time grew out of an argument between Gerry and Fitzsimons. Gerry thought that it would require eight million dollars to meet the Government's expenses, and Fitzsimons felt it could be done with three million. Ames must have been delighted to hear Fitzsimons suggest, "If we wish to have more particular information on these points, we ought to appoint a committee of ways and means." As a result the House on July 24 appointed its first committee on ways and means. The group was destined to hold office for only two months, but on that Friday afternoon neither Ames nor the others in the chamber foresaw the powerful influence to be wielded by the first Secretary of the Treasury.

In August the Congressmen took up and settled their own salaries—$6 a day for Senators and Representatives, $12 a day for the Speaker of the House.

It was August 13 before they were back in the Committee of the Whole on the amendments to the Constitution.

Ames wrote to Minot, "We shall make a dozen or two of rights and privileges for our posterity. If I am to be guided by your advice, to marry and live in Boston, it behooves me to interest myself in the affair."

A good part of Ames' interest consisted of trying to keep Tucker of South Carolina from adding a list of new amendments to those already proposed. Among other things, Tucker wanted to let the people at home instruct their Representatives in Congress how to vote.

Faced with suggestions like this and with talk of a recess to start in September, Madison feared the failure of all his efforts to get his amendments considered in time to stop other mischief.

There was still much to be done. Each provision would have to be approved by two-thirds of both Houses . . . then it would have to be proposed to the States. Provisions "of a doubtful nature" might prejudice the States, Madison argued. He added, "The right of freedom of speech is secured; the liberty of the press is expressly declared . . . the people may therefore publicly address their Representatives . . . or declare their sentiments by petition . . ." Tucker's suggestion to let constituents bind their Representatives was, he thought, unnecessary and impractical.

As the discussion continued, all the amendments that would one day make up the great rights of American citizens were weighed. In addition to the freedom of speech and petition provisions, to which Madison had pointed for Tucker's benefit, all the other safeguards were discussed. Every lawyer in the room knew that their effectiveness depended on how well they were worded.

Together they sought to secure rights for the individual. His freedom of conscience must not be abridged. His home must not be searched—nor his papers seized—arbitrarily. The Courts must be forbidden to demand excessive bail, force a possibly innocent defendant to incriminate himself, or deny him a fair, speedy, public trial. A man's right to defend himself before a jury must be preserved.

Before they finished, the members talked about the State militias, which were made up of private citizens. These citizens had to be allowed to keep firearms. There was the matter of not quartering soldiers in private homes in peacetime. Finally, on August 21, they reviewed the provisions that reserved to the people any powers not specifically delegated to the Federal Government.

Then, at last, the material was on its way to the Senate. But by then the session was almost over, and the proposals for the great rights would arrive in the Senate at a time when they would have to compete with other matters demanding the statesmen's attention. Here was one more indication that the quantity and the quality of the work Congress was to do would depend on the procedures it established. However, in this first most hectic period of its life, Congress could only begin to explore that problem.

Things Done and Left Undone

On Saturday, August 22, President Washington had come to the Senate chamber and brought with him the Secretary of War, General Henry Knox. Ostensibly the President wanted to discuss treaty questions involving not only land disputes but also trade and the maintenance of peace with the Creek and Chickasaw Indians.

Senator Maclay fumed. "I saw no chance of a fair investigation of subjects while the President of the United States sat there, with his Secretary of War, to support his opinions and overawe the timid and neutral part of the Senate . . ." he wrote in his journal.

Maclay—as he reported it—leaned over and whispered to his colleague from Pennsylvania, Robert Morris, that the best way was to have the papers under discussion committed (sent to a committee). Morris so moved, and according to Maclay the President answered with sullen dignity, "This defeats every purpose of my coming here."

The papers were not committed. On Monday August 24, the President was back in the chamber. Votes giving him much but not all of what he wanted were cast while he sat there. Neither the President nor the Senate enjoyed the experience.

On Tuesday evening Maclay was still pouring his aggravation into his diary. "Yesterday I could do nothing, for the attendance of the President," he wrote.

"This morning, however," Maclay noted, "I took the first opportunity, and presented the draught . . ." The draft, over which he was most concerned, proposed sites in Pennsylvania for the permanent capital of the United States. By now it was uncertain whether Congress could settle that issue before the end of the session. That morning, the Senate had agreed to the proposal made by the House to adjourn on September 22. Also that morning, the clerk of the House, Beckley, had brought the Senators the House bill to amend the Constitution. The Senators decided to start working on the amendment bill on the following Monday.

The next entry in Maclay's diary tells of a night meeting of the Pennsylvania delegation. The Senators and Representatives of that State met, not on the Bill of Rights, but on the location of the new nation's capital. Three weeks later their bill to make Germantown, Pennsylvania, the nation's capital had passed the Senate. It ran into trouble in the House. No decision had as yet been reached on the amendments to the Constitution.

Monday, September 21 found Beckley carrying a report to the Senate. His message indicated the difficulties both Houses were having with the all important details of the amendments. The House had agreed to the changes numbered 2, 4, 8, 12, 13, 16, 18, 19, 25 and 26, placed by the Senate in the articles to be proposed to the legislatures of the several States as amendments to the Constitution. The House, however, disagreed with the changes numbered 1, 3, 5, 6, 7, 9, 10, 11, 14, 15, 17, and 20 through 24. The Representatives asked for a conference. Not surprisingly, Tuesday, September 22, arrived with nothing concluded on the proposed amendments.

Both the Senators and the Representatives were eager to go home. They had been living and working in temporary quarters for six long months, but when the question of postponing their adjournment came up, they agreed to postpone. The work continued.

Senators Ellsworth, Paterson and Carroll met with the little group of House members to thrash over the amendments. After the conference the House receded on twelve of its disagreements, provided that the Senate would give in on two points, which it did.

The Congress then asked the President to have the proposed amendments transmitted to the Governors of the several States to be acted on by their legislatures. Thus, out from the first session of the first Congress, went a request for changes in the Constitution that would limit the lawmaker's own power.

The exhausted members were ready for their recess. Before them loomed the gigantic questions of locating the capital—pregnant with that sectional strife they had so far managed to keep to a minimum. The "deep dark chaos" which seemed to envelop the national finances was still not dispelled. Solutions would have to be sought later. After deciding to return, not in December as was expected but in January, the first Congress adjourned its first session. It had made its contribution to history. It had not only launched the new Government but also framed a bill of rights for its posterity.

The First Split Came Over Finance

By act of Congress the second session was due to convene on January 4, but only when Maclay took his seat on the sixth was there a quorum. Its speed remained deliberate. On the seventh, the Senate appointed a Chaplain (as did the House). On the eighth, the furniture in the Senate chamber was rearranged for a joint session. House members took seats on one side of the room and Senators on the other. They all arose as both Doorkeepers escorted the President of the United States to the chair.

As soon as the Cabinet Ministers had slipped into seats at the back of the room, President Washington began his speech. First he noted with satisfaction the accession of North Carolina to the Union. Then he called on Congress to raise troops for the common defense, to fix the terms by which foreigners might be admitted to the rights of citizenship, to appropriate funds to defray the expense of the nation's diplomats, to finance the President's own diplomatic obligations, and to establish post roads and a uniform system of weights and measures.

Thus far not one of his proposals was the least bit controversial. House members would assure him of that when within the week they called on him in a body to offer their official response to this, the President's first annual message.

The President also wanted the Congress to further public education. Washington was concerned with "teaching the people . . . to know and to value their own rights . . . [and] to distinguish between oppression and the necessary exercise of lawful authority. . . ."

He suggested helping seminaries of learning already established or starting a national university.

Federal aid to education in the States was a long way off. However, the Representatives of 1790 would soon promise the President that they would not lose sight of so worthy an objective. Senators, too, would note the President's remarks with approval. The President's speech was nearly finished when Washington focused on the main issue, the issue that would leave behind a Congress forever splintered into political parties.

He broached the subject by quoting an earlier resolution by the House that "an adequate provision for the support of the public credit is a matter of high importance to the national honor and prosperity." He heartily concurred. He knew the House had already asked the Secretary of the Treasury to prepare suggestions for improving the national credit. Now, the President said, he relied on the House to devise the necessary measures, and he relied on the cheerful cooperation of the Senate to turn those measures into law.

Barely twenty-four hours after the President's speech, Speaker Muhlenberg gave the House members a message from the Secretary of the Treasury. Responding to a House resolution, Hamilton had prepared a plan for the support of the public credit. Obviously he wanted to be asked to come to the chamber, where he could defend his proposals.

Dissatisfied, Gerry moved that the report he submitted in writing. Others agreed. Hamilton obediently submitted his written report on January 14.

Among other things, the Secretary wanted to redeem the old certificates or promissory notes with which the former government had paid the soldiers of the Revolution and the small farmers and merchants who supplied the Army. It was true that most of these worthy creditors had long since sold their certificates to speculators who paid only 10 or 15 cents for every dollar's worth of the paper. Nevertheless, Hamilton maintained, the Government had to pay the new owners the full value of their certificates. He proposed to pay them by funding; that is, by offering certificate holders new government securities.

Hamilton's plan made intoxicating news. Maclay recorded in his diary: "It is said a committee of speculators in certificates could not have formed it more for their [own] advantage." Hamilton's report, Maclay claimed, explained the recent rise in the price of certificates. The city buzzed with whispers as to who had been buying the paper in expectation of making a profit.

Maclay looked at the serious faces around the temporary capitol and was sure Alexander Hamilton's reputation was damned forever. But Maclay was wrong. The Congress divided . There were those for and those against the Secretary's position.

Sedgwick of Massachusetts, whose constituents included New England businessmen, insisted that the Government did have to pay the full value of these certificates. The Government's credit and its reputation were both at stake. All its certificates would have been worthless if trusting men had not been willing to buy them.

James Jackson of Georgia answered that he had once believed in making no distinction between original owners and later purchasers, but circumstances had occurred to make him change his mind. Unquestionably his voice must have risen as he explained, "Three vessels, Sir, have sailed within a fortnight from this port. . . . They are intended to purchase up . . . securities in the hands of uninformed though honest citizens of North Carolina, South Carolina, and Georgia. . . ."

The speculators would reach his rural constituents and buy away their certificates before the local people learned of the Secretary's report and the price rise.

Jackson wanted to delay funding and so discipline the smart city dealers. Besides, he wanted the members of Congress to consult their State legislatures on Hamilton's other proposals to have the general Government assume State war debts. "The States ought to be consulted," he said. "I should be glad to know the sentiments of the Legislature of the State from which I come."

Sedgwick noticed that the galleries were unusually crowded. Expectant citizens were waiting in suspense to learn the value of their securities. The way to stop excessive speculation, he claimed, was to dispose of the business quickly.

Jackson looked at the packed galleries with disgust and wished aloud that the House had never agreed to sit in the neighborhood of a populous city and so give urban dwellers advance notice of the Treasury's plans.

He called for justice for the disabled veterans living in the wilderness and claimed the soldier's meager reward for distinguished service was being torn away by the insidious city stock jobber. He made an impression which not even Hamilton could ignore.

The Secretary's reaction to his Congressional opposition caught Maclay's attention. "Mr. Hamilton is very uneasy, as far as I can learn about his funding system," the Senator noted in his diary. Hamilton had called on Speaker Muhlenberg and it looked to Maclay as if the Secretary "spent most of his time in running from place to place among the members."

As Maclay would soon realize, Hamilton was busy gathering together the men who would be willing to support his proposals, intending to have them act in unison in the Committee of the Whole. In other words, the Secretary was organizing his followers in Congress into a political party.

Meanwhile, inside the Representatives' hall, Madison was being strangely quiet. Up to now he had been the recognized leader of the House. Up to now he had also been a friend and consultant to the Chief Executive, but he seemed to be taking no part in the debate on funding. It was February 11 before Madison rose and addressed the chair. He was a small man, modestly dressed, and he spoke so softly that the crowd packed into the spectator's seats probably had trouble hearing what he wished to explain.

"My idea is that . . . the highest market price only should be allowed to the purchasers, and the balance be applied to solace the original sufferers. . . . [Their] claims were not in conscience extinguished by a forced payment in depreciated certificates." This was the essence of his position as he reported it himself to Jefferson.

But this was the kind of discrimination against certificate purchasers that Hamilton wanted to avoid. Some of them had already waited years to be reimbursed. Besides, Hamilton wanted government securities to be fully transferable from one owner to another, to provide the new republic with badly needed paper money. In addition, he had another great concern. "Exigencies are to be expected to occur, in the affairs of nations, in which there will be a necessity for borrowing . . ." he said. "To be able to borrow upon good terms, it is essential that the credit of a nation should be well established." For all these reasons he wanted the nation to pay the face value of its pledges.

To lighten the nation's burden, Hamilton was willing to pay off the new pledges very slowly and give the pledge holders only a small amount of interest. Even so, he was doing his utmost to please the rich so as to win their support for the new government.

Madison saw himself as coming to the rescue of the common man.

Boudinot tactfully remarked that he had long been in the habit of paying great respect to Madison sentiments; but he feared, on this occasion that "the gentleman was led away by the dictates of his heart." Boudinot insisted that the certificates could not possibly be traced to their original owners.

When Boudinot finished speaking, the Committee of the Whole voted to stop work and report to the House, after which the members adjourned, with much to think about.

Hamilton's supporters needed time to form their answers to Madison, and the next day the House members digressed briefly from the topic. They had received two memorials (petitions) from abolitionist societies. In spite of Baldwin, who remembered that the Federal Convention in Philadelphia had well-nigh broken up over this issue, and in spite of Tucker, who was alarmed that his constituents would regret their acceptance of the new Government, the abolitionist petition went to a select committee and then to the Committee of the Whole. Ultimately, little came of them because, as the Constitution then read, there was very little that Congress felt it could do about slavery.

Finally, the House members returned to Mr. Madison's motion. On February 22, 1790, it was put to a vote. For some, the decision was easy. They were speculators, counting on Hamilton to make them prosperous. Others were intent on maintaining the nation's borrowing power and hence the value of the Government's securities. Still others, like Boudinot, claimed that Mr. Madison was not being practical. Thus, the hitherto acknowledged leader of the House went down to defeat. His proposed plan lost, 13 to 36.

Some said Mr. Madison's reputation had suffered. Others, including newspaper editors, judged differently. They printed letters from their readers. "Thank God there lives a Madison," said one.

One defeat could not destroy Madison, but the House was nevertheless split. In spite of its fondness for Madison, it kept Hamilton's plan alive. The final outcome of that plan was to depend on the fate of another one of Hamilton's ideas, which would propel the House even further in the direction of dividing into opposing parties. Thus another phase of Congressional development had already begun.

"Mr. Hamilton Is All-Powerful"

The Secretary also maneuvered for the next step in his program. He wanted Congress to authorize Federal assumption of the State war debts. Senator Maclay watched the Secretary's tactics with unabated venom.

When Speaker Muhlenberg returned to his lodging house from one of the President's receptions, he told Maclay that the State debts must be adopted. Sneeringly, Maclay called the President's house "the court." He preferred to listen to the people's Representatives. Much to his satisfaction, they had provided seats in their chamber for any Senators who might wish to visit. Maclay took advantage of this courtesy to follow the Representatives' debate on the assumption bill.

James Jackson of Georgia again voiced his opposition. After assuming all of the debts of the States, "the whole power of taxation may be absorbed," he warned. He reasoned that the States would then be reduced to insignificance. Madison, too, objected that it was unfair to compel the States which had already paid their debts to "contribute toward States who had not equally done their duty."

Hamilton's supporters thought it was imperative to make clear to financial interests at home and abroad that provision would be made to meet the State obligations.

On March 8 Maclay decided, "This is the important week, and perhaps the important day . . . the question will be put on the assumption of State debts. I suspect this from the rendez-vousing of the crew of the Hamilton galley. It seems all hands are piped to quarters." Perhaps the entire crew was on duty. Maclay waited expectantly, but still the Hamilton forces did not demand the taking of the vote.

That night the Pennsylvanians in Congress supped together and Maclay listened to the relaxed chatter of the others to learn what had happened. It seemed the question was to have been put; but then another member, Vining, had arrived from Dela-ware. Calling for a vote was therefore postponed until Vining could be briefed by the Secretary.

The next day Hamilton's crew seemed desperate. According to Maclay, Bland and Huger were carried into the chamber of Representatives—the one lame, the other sick—and Clymer was stopped from going away, though he had previously arranged to be absent. By these methods Hamilton for one brief fleeting period had the majority he needed. Then more North Carolini-ans took their seats, and again the Secretary's program was in trouble.

Maclay looked around the Senate. He later boasted, "I never observed so . . . forlorn an appearance as overspread the parti-sans of the Secretary."

The Senate being small, it was usual for the men to leave their seats and carry on their discussions around the fire. On April 8, Mr. Ellsworth of Connecticut and Mr. Izard of South Carolina left their seats and paced nervously across the room. Paterson of New Jersey and Strong of Massachusetts seemed equally anxious. Rufus King looked whipped. As for New York's Sena-tor Schuyler (Hamilton's father-in-law), his hair was standing on end. All this Maclay recorded in his diary with evident satis-faction.

Worried or not, on April 12 the Hamilton followers risked calling for the question on the assumption bill in the House of Representatives. The vote was duly taken, and they lost.

As Maclay watched, Sedgwick left the room and came back as if he had been weeping. Fitzsimons' face became scarlet, and

Clymer's deadly white. Boudinot's mouth turned down like a horseshoe. All this delighted Maclay. He did not realize that these men were much too concerned to concede defeat.

Within a week Madison was writing to James Monroe. "The eastern members . . . avow, some of them, at least, a determination to oppose all provision for the public debt which does not include this [assumption]. . . . [They] intimate danger to the Union from a refusal to assume." Congress, it seemed, was meeting and adjourning but producing little more than short tempers and threats.

Madison was worried, and so was normally flippant Fisher Ames. Ames wrote to a friend, Thomas Dwight, "[I]f we should not fund at all . . . I can scarcely expect the government will last long."

It was incredible that Congress seemingly did not remember the days of the Confederation and the lesson that a bankrupt government cannot function. Hamilton was near despair.

One day during this troubled period, Jefferson, who had recently returned from France to become Secretary of State, was on his way to the President's house. Hamilton met him in the street, and for half an hour they walked back and forth before the President's door, talking. As Jefferson later recalled, Hamilton pointed to the danger of secession and the end of the Union. Hamilton wanted to bargain. To push assumption through Congress he needed Virginia's votes and to get them he was willing to see the capitol moved out of New York. He asked for Jefferson's help. He won.

Jefferson arranged a dinner party to which Madison came. Two members who wished to see the capital situated on the Potomac also came. They agreed to switch their votes to support the assumption bill. Hamilton's old friend, Rufus King, who thought a cause should stand on its own merit, was heartbroken, but the bargain saved Congress from impotence.

Ames was again his cheerful self. He wrote to Dwight in Springfield, "Yesterday we renewed the battle for assumption . . . Mr. Jackson then made a speech, which I will not say was loud enough for you to hear. It disturbed the Senate, however; and to keep out the din, they put down their windows." He could afford to be merry. On Thursday, when the session ended, both the funding and the assumption bill had passed. Congress had agreed to move temporarily to Philadelphia and then permanently to the banks of the Potomac.

What was almost as important but less noticed, the House had voted to let the Speaker appoint all committees except where the members specifically decreed otherwise. Here was a powerful tool for later and more ambitious Speakers. For the moment it mattered little. Hamilton and his followers were at the height of their power. During the next session Maclay would complain: "Congress may go home. Mr. Hamilton is all-powerful, and fails in nothing he attempts."

The Split Widens

Senator Maclay was disgusted. Having formed a political party, the "crew of Hamilton" now "caucused" or met before the Congressional sessions to agree on their positions. According to Maclay, "Everything . . . is prearranged by Hamilton and his group of speculators." Though Hamilton could not come to the floor of the chamber, there was nothing to stop him from going to his own party meetings, where his word was virtually law. He was, Maclay thought, turning the Congress into a mere ratifying body—abridging the separation of executive and legislative powers established by the Constitution.

As if all this weren't frightening enough, Hamilton demanded that the lawmakers charter a bank. Nothing in the Constitution gave Congress the power to charter a bank, but the Senate passed the bill without even a roll-call vote.

In the House the bill went to the Committee of the Whole, with Boudinot in the Chair, on January 31, 1791. He read the bill very distinctly and deliberately, he thought, giving all the gentlemen the fullest opportunity to come forward with objections. There were none. The bill passed the Committee and was to be acted upon by the House the next day.

When the time came, Vining of Delaware said later, he was congratulating himself. The bill was ready for its third and final reading without the tedious discussion bills usually received. Then suddenly James Jackson and James Madison were asking to have the measure recommitted.

Madison mysteriously insisted that it was not important to determine how it happened that the objections to the bill were not made at the proper time. His point was that the bank was unconstitutional. He was fully aware that gentlemen would argue that Congress had "implied powers" to charter the institution. This was Hamilton's position.

Boudinot would reason that the members had, from the very beginning, held a substantial amount of authority which was not written but was understood. Under their power to regulate commerce they had also built lighthouses and piers. Under their power to establish courts they had assumed the power to legislate punishment for perjury. Had the delegates at Philadelphia needed to list these, and all other necessary future measures, the Constitution would have filled a multitude of volumes.

Having anticipated this argument, Madison was not surprised to hear Sedgwick claim that "the ends for which this Government was established are clearly pointed out; the means to produce the ends are left to the choice of the Legislature." After all, Sedgwick could have been rephrasing that comment in Number 44 of the Federalist papers: "[W]herever the end is required, the means are authorized; wherever a general power to do a thing is given, every particular power necessary for doing it, is included."

These were Madison's own words, but they were now making him anxious. They could be stretched too far. He recalled the vehemence at the ratifying conventions against sweeping Federal power, and he urged that the Representatives "keep close to our chartered authorities."

Hamilton's friends would argue that the bank was a necessary means of exercising Congress's power to borrow money. Madison saw the bank as a mere convenience. Loans could be arranged from small local banks and from individuals. In short, to interpret the Constitution so as to justify this bill would give to Congress an unlimited power. This was what the Anti-Federalists had feared, and it must not come to pass.

Ames attempted to defend the bank and then listened in bored impatience to Madison's latest anti-Hamilton recruit, another Virginian named William Branch Giles. Mr. Giles saw the bank bill as a dangerous Federal power grab. Ames wrote to Dwight. "All appearances indicate that we shall beat them by a considerable majority."

Finally, without recommitting the measure, the vote was taken. It was thirty-nine for the bank and twenty against. In effect, Congress was launching a new controversy. It was declaring its right to select any means not already forbidden by the Constitution to carry out its functions. The smoke of future battles was in the air.

Hamilton had won another victory but this time a costly one. Madison and Jefferson decided they must organize an opposition. "Its object," Jefferson said later, "was to preserve the legislature pure and independent of the executive . . . and not to permit the Constitution to be construed into a monarchy." To this end, they planned to combine malcontents from among the landed gentry with dissatisfied groups in the big cities, blending them together into a new force.

In keeping with their plans, Jefferson wrote to Madison's old college friend, the poet and newspaper editor Philip Freneau. By offering Freneau a part-time Government job, the two statesmen were maneuvering to have at hand a newspaper friendly to their views.

Then, as soon as Congress adjourned on March 3, they left Philadelphia together, heading for a cross country vacation and a bit of politics. A second political party was in the making and the future of Congress would reflect the fruits of its efforts.

Knowledge and the Lack Of It

The leaders of the new Republican party faced a rough fight. They had chosen to challenge the Federalists, who were well organized and well supported. Happily for the newcomers, land-owning farmers were franchised and made good Republican prospects, but the poor ex-soldier and the city laborer, for whom Madison and Jefferson also wanted to speak, often had no ballot. Most States still required voters to be property owners or at least taxpayers.

Along with working to recruit into the party every possible group and individual, the Republicans kept up their fight in Congress against Hamilton.

As 1792 drew to a close and the new year started, a bill was before the House authorizing the President to pay off the whole of a loan obtained from the national bank—by borrowing two million dollars elsewhere. William Branch Giles was on his feet objecting to it. Like Madison, with whom he now shared the leadership of the anti-Hamilton forces, Giles was a Princeton graduate. Like his Virginia-farmer constituents, Giles was antagonistic to banks. Trying to decipher Hamilton's financial reports made him resent the princely arrogance of the author.

Although the bank was only entitled to a small installment of $200,000.00, Sedgwick still supported Hamilton; the bank could be paid off with money borrowed from other sources at a lower rate of interest, he explained. Giles retorted that placing loans was expensive. Furthermore, it looked to him as if money that should have been used to pay foreign debts had been withdrawn from abroad and deposited by the Secretary in the hated bank. He had other questions on sums borrowed and the application of the moneys. "I cannot help remarking, before I sit down" he told the House, ". . . we have been legislating for some years without competent official knowledge of the state of the Treasury."

The short, robust and belligerent Giles demanded more information from the haughty, aristocratic "minister of finance." Congress was entitled to the information and Hamilton knew it. He worked long and late on an answering report. Along with it he recorded his reaction to the Virginian's demand. "The resolutions to which I am to answer, were not moved without a pretty copious display of the reasons on which they were founded . . ." he complained. "They are . . . to excite attention and beget alarm . . ." After not having bothered to inform the legislature fully, he resented being forced to explain himself.

The fact was that Hamilton had assumed Executive latitude, combining funds that belonged to separate appropriations— ". . . a very blamable irregularity," Madison termed it.

Ames considered that Madison had become a desperate party leader. There had been other occasions when Ames was distinctly conscious of Mr. Madison's new attitude. "Virginia moves in a solid column, and the discipline of the party is as severe as the Prussian," Ames wrote to Dwight.

Three days before adjournment, Virginia's aggressive Mr. Giles asked the House to pass a series of resolutions censuring the Secretary. Laws that made appropriations, he said, should be strictly obeyed. ". . . [A] violation of a law making appropriations is a violation of . . . the Constitution." It was Congress that had the power to authorize how the public funds were to be spent. Hamilton was guilty of violating its edict.

The Representatives picked March 1 for their formal debate on the issue. By then copies of the proposed censuring resolution had appeared in the papers. Crowds watched from the galleries as the debate dragged on into the night and the weary men continued arguing by the light of the flickering candles.

Ames made the most startling remark. "It is impossible to keep different funds . . . so inviolably separate as that one may not be used for the object of the other," he contended.

His wild statement did his side no harm. The attack was already doomed, the censure resolution headed for defeat. Jefferson blamed the coming result on the "bank directors and stock jobbers who would be voting on the case of their chief [Secretary Hamilton]."

It was true. William Smith and Fisher Ames and other members of Congress were bank directors or stockholders. They had conflicting interests when they sat in the chamber and listened to proposals affecting Hamilton and the bank. Jefferson's followers called them a "corrupt squadron," but as yet there were no rules of ethics that the Republicans could enforce against the arrangement. While the impact of the attempted censure was blunted by these loyal followers of the Secretary, it was also blunted by Hamilton's impressive self-confidence. After all, he personally was no wealthier because of his financial highhandedness. Moreover, since he was as brilliant an economist as he was an organizer, not one of the Republicans was qualified to challenge his financial judgment. Until that lack could be corrected, Hamilton was virtually invincible. All the Republicans could achieve was to limit the House authorization for the bank to only the two hundred thousand already due. They could not deprive Hamilton of his tremendous influence over their opponents in the House.

Albert Gallatin

When the third Congress opened on December 2, 1793, a challenger competent to fence with the Secretary entered the Senate. Swiss-born Albert Gallatin had been elected a United States Senator by the Pennsylvania State legislature. His knowledge of finance and his "truly Republican principles" were well known. Federalists judged that he had both the will and the ability to imperil their program.

Within minutes after Gallatin took the oath of office the fight to eject him began. Vice President John Adams, presiding over the Senate, read a petition from nineteen Pennsylvanians. Gallatin, they claimed, had not been a citizen of the United States for nine years and therefore was not eligible to serve in the Senate. Adams tabled the petition, but not for long. In less than two weeks, he had referred it to a committee of staunch Federalists.

Seeing that his days in the Senate were likely to be cut short, Gallatin hastened to launch his attack. On January 8, 1794, he called on Hamilton to furnish the Congress with the details of the Government's loans, receipts and expenditures, and its progress in redeeming the debt. Those watching Gallatin saw a thin, narrow-faced man leaning forward toward the presiding officer's chair. To many Federalists, he sounded like a Frenchman and they abhorred the sound. Radical Frenchmen had overthrown the monarchy and instituted a reign of terror. The United States minister to France, Gouverneur Morris, wrote home descriptions of "unchecked murders, in which some thousands have perished."

Besides overturning their Government and beheading their King on the guillotine, French radicals had embroiled their country in war, first with Austria and Prussia and then with England, Holland and Spain. President Washington had declared his country's neutrality, but he could not neutralize the hearts of his countrymen.

The revolutionary slogan "Liberty, equality, and brotherhood" warmed the spirits of American artisans and small merchants. Here were their own aspirations rephrased. Let Federalist stomachs turn at the excesses of the Paris mob. The farmer and the worker and such Republican spokesmen of theirs as Mr. Gallatin could blame the terror, at least in part, on the royalists who sought foreign aid against their own countrymen.

Pro-French democratic clubs sprang into being. The arriving French minister, Edmond Genet, was made giddy by the exuberant welcome he received. Expecting the people to uphold him rather than their President, he commissioned ships and men to war against the British from United States ports. The indignant President demanded that France recall her unruly minister. But political upheavals then made Genet a fugitive, and Washington generously allowed him to remain in America.

Though many Senators might wish to connect all this with Gallatin and reject whatever he said, the majority gave him a fair hearing and voted to pass his resolution. A report was demanded from the treasury, but then the Senators flung their galleries open to the public and debated the charges in the peti-

Steep de Wheels of Government

A Political Sinner.

The artist depicts Albert Gallatin as he must have looked to the Federalist Senators, who would gladly have sent him to the guillotine shown in the rear.

tion challenging Gallatin's right to hold his office. The committee report had gone against him, but at first, the full Senate seemed almost tied. Then, when the vote was taken, the Federalists held a slim majority and Gallatin lost his seat.

Meanwhile, Hamilton complained that he was already too overworked to furnish the wanted information. With Gallatin ejected, the matter was quietly forgotten. Congress was busy passing a neutrality act to support the President. Neither the Federalists nor the Secretary had been weakened, and they had little reason to expect any more trouble from Gallatin for the present.

Gallatin's political future looked even less promising after his constituents in the western hills of Pennsylvania rioted, protesting the tax on whiskey which Congress had passed on Hamilton's recommendation. Gallatin had already spoken out for these people. They were moneyless settlers, dependent on their liquid corn as a medium of exchange. They could get it down the mountainside by pack horse over trails too narrow to accommodate a produce wagon. To them the tax was oppressive; and the collector was a Federal intruder and a menace to liberty.

Congress had authorized the President in April of 1792 to call out the militia to enforce Federal laws. In the summer of 1794 the President reluctantly used the power against "the whiskey boys," and Hamilton rode with the troops. He would have enjoyed seeing Gallatin punished for working with the rioters. By all accounts, however, when the ex-Senator stood before the armed protesters, he had not abetted them but had checked their violence.

To the horror of Republicans, the President charged that the unrest had been fermented by the "self-created societies," as he termed the democratic clubs. In November, when the President included the accusation in his message to Congress, Madison did his best to keep any mention of the slur out of the House answer. Fitzsimons could not see why. "We cannot withhold our reprobation," he objected.

Like Madison, Giles saw the danger. "[T]here was not an individual in America, who might not come under the charge of being a member of some one or other self-created society . . ." He named Baptists, Methodists, Friends, and organizations for Revolutionary veterans. "If the self-created societies act contrary to law . . . let the law pursue them," he told the House. "It is out of the way of the legislature to attempt checking or restraining popular opinion."

To this Madison added that if Congress passed a vote condemning the societies, that condemnation would amount to a severe punishment. Congress, he reminded the assembly, was forbidden to act as a court imposing penalties. The Constitution outlawed such a bill of attainder.

For once, the Republicans won. The House members agreed not to condemn the societies. The Republicans felt like winners again when the 1795 session began. The voters of Pennsylvania had sent Albert Gallatin back to claim a seat in the House, and this time the Federalists could not get rid of him. Last time it had taken a full month before he attacked the Treasury. This time it took him only ten days. This time when he stood up he wanted a committee appointed to examine the public debt, the public revenue, and the public expenditures. Furthermore, he wanted the committee to continue indefinitely superintending the financial operations of the Government.

No subject was in greater need of competent handling, Gallatin told his colleagues. By now the listening House members included a sizable number of Republicans. As a result, the Representatives, on December 21 established a standing committee on ways and means. (Later, the rules adopted in 1802 called for keeping a standing committee on ways and means.) Congress was reaching for its rightful control over the nation's pocketbook.

According to the custom at that time, Gallatin, having suggested the measure, was put on the committee. There, financial proposals coming from the Treasury were submitted to scrutiny. Attention was drawn to economies that might have been made in the past. Above all, Gallatin tried to insist that appropriation bills be more tightly written, so as to state how the sums were to be allocated. Later Congress did not always remember his advice where military appropriations were concerned. Nevertheless, he had started a new trend of thinking in the area of Congressional authority, and the effect of his influence was evident in the years that followed.

The Power of Making Treaties
and the Right to Call for Papers

It was not long before the Republicans plunged into their next battle with the Executive. For some time, Madison had wanted to discriminate against commerce with royalist Britain, indirectly benefiting republican France. Instead, Washington had sent Chief Justice John Jay to London to negotiate a treaty. Britain was to be asked to stop the impressment of American seamen, open the West Indies to U. S. trading ships, evacuate her western fur posts, and redress various other grievances.

Unfortunately, Hamilton talked too much to British minister George Hammond behind Jay's back, disrupting the negotiations. As a result, Jay won few concessions and Washington was appalled. Except for an agreement that various claims and boundary disputes were to be settled by a binational commission, little was gained. Britain did repeat her earlier agreement to give up her fur posts, but she said nothing about impressment. In one clause she put a 70-ton limit on U. S. ships to the West Indies and added a list of articles the traders could not carry to Europe. There were other objectionable features.

For sixteen grueling days in June of 1795 the Senate, fearing the public's reaction, debated the treaty in secret. On June 24 they approved it, but only with the proviso that Britain agree to eliminate the West Indies clause, and even then they were still unwilling to have the document made public. Their policy of concealment was defiantly smashed by Stevens Thomson Mason, a Senator from Virginia, who boldly carried the text of the agreement to a Philadelphia newspaper. Once the story was printed, resentment swept the nation like a tornado. City mobs burned copies of the treaty and burned John Jay in effigy. The people's Representatives caught the message.

In March the treaty rested on the Speaker's desk in the House chamber. In order to carry it into effect, appropriations were needed. Representative Edward Livingston, New York's brilliant new addition to the Republican side, moved that the President be requested to lay before the House a copy of the instructions he gave to Jay and all his other correspondence relevant to the treaty. With that, a storm broke over the House which soon became a constitutional tempest.

Giles resented gentlemen who called an attempt to examine the merits of the treaty "a rebellion", and Gallatin asked his opponents to calm themselves. The motion before the House was merely to call for papers.

Smith of South Carolina was for the Administration. Usually he sounded as if his lines had been written by Alexander Hamilton, although by now the ex-Secretary had left Government to practice law. This time Smith insisted that "The President and the Senate have, by the Constitution, the power of making Treaties, and the House have no agency in them . . ." The members, then, had no need for papers. Smith suddenly wanted a strict construction of the Constitution whereby the House would be required to pass obediently all legislation that implemented a treaty—unless, of course, the implementing act was unconstitutional.

To this Gallatin answered that, since the House had the power to originate money bills, if implementing the treaty required funds, the sanction of the House was necessary before the treaty could become law. Otherwise, he said, "the treaty-making power . . . may extend to every object of legislation, under it money may be borrowed as well as commerce regulated . . . the President and Senate . . . can by employing an Indian tribe pass any law under the color of a treaty."

When Giles, too, expressed concern that the treaty-making power could become limitless, Sedgwick insisted that he would be willing to trust the Senators, who must ratify a treaty. He agreed with Smith. Treaties once ratified were the law of the land, which the House must obey, not question.

The implications of this brought Madison into the argument. The House, he said, must act in a responsible manner whenever it performed one of its functions, in this case making an appropriation. He did not expect the House to be a mere instrument of the Executive.

The House that listened to him had grown to 105 members since the census of 1790. On that March morning in 1796, 99 of them voted and the count was 62 to 37 to demand the treaty papers.

In less than a week the President had as much as told them that the papers were none of their affair. "The assent of the House of Representatives is not necessary to the validity of a treaty." He refused to submit any papers.

The Republicans decided to go on record as having the right to demand the papers, as well as the duty to decide whether to implement the treaty. They had enough strength to put through a resolution to this effect on the floor of the House.

When the papers were still not forthcoming, Fisher Ames hurled himself into the Administration's cause. The House, he warned, must carry out the treaty or risk war with the British, who could utilize their western forts to incite the Indians to massacre. He directed his words as if they were being heard by the settlers. "In the daytime, your path through the woods will be ambushed; the darkness of midnight will glitter with the blaze of your dwellings . . . By rejecting [this treaty] . . . we light the savage fires—we bind the . . . wretches that will be roasted at the stake . . ."

Listening visitors were close to tears, as Ames, pale and unwell, predicted his own death. (He lived another dozen years.) Perhaps hoping that the emotional pitch to which Ames had stirred the House might in time subside, the Republicans rushed through a recess.

It was a worthless maneuver. Ames had already achieved his objective. The House implemented the treaty, voting the necessary funds, without seeing the correspondence or the orders that Jay had received. President Washington never did produce them. And Presidents are still asserting the right to withhold documents relevant to their negotiations with foreign powers. In 1961 Congress passed an act cutting off foreign aid payments in any case where the Executive withholds a document that Congress wants to see. However, the act concedes to the President the privilege of blocking the cutoff by explaining his reasons for ordering the material withheld. In 1972 one attempt to implement the law was aborted by President Nixon's claiming "executive privilege."

The possibility for future clashes in this area between the Executive and members of Congress, particularly Senators, remains.

Hysteria and the End of an Era

The next time the Representatives asked the Executive for papers, the President was John Adams and the year was 1798. Incensed by the Jay Treaty, France had announced that what was contraband for Great Britain was also contraband for her. She too would molest American shipping. The President had sent three envoys to France to seek peace, but he had also asked Congress to pass measures for the national defense. The Federalists fought for appropriations to build frigates, fortify harbors, and increase the militia in an atmosphere of ever-increasing partisan bitterness. While Gallatin accused Smith of wanting war with France, Representative Harper of South Carolina ranted against the French "enemy."

On March 19, 1798, the President, while alluding to "dispatches" from his envoys, announced the failure of his peace mission. The rest of his speech was described by disheartened Vice-President Thomas Jefferson as a war message.

This time Congress wanted to see the relevant dispatches. The President produced the papers the next day. They revealed that while not officially received, the American envoys had been contacted by Messrs "X, Y and Z" demanding money for officials of the French Directorate and a large loan to France.

The House of Representatives cleared its galleries before discussing the documents, but the Senate promptly ordered copies printed and circulated, intending to inflame the country into the anti-French and pro-Federalist camp. In this atmosphere, Republican Congressmen fled the House, Giles among them, and Gallatin was left with insufficient strength to stem the war hysteria. Jefferson, presiding in the heavily Federalist Senate, wrote to Madison, "They will carry what they please." He left for home before the session ended, pinning his hopes on the next election.

Another exodus, which preceded Jefferson's, caused little excitement at the time. A Senator from Tennessee, named Andrew Jackson, resigned his seat.

With their opposition shattered, there was no inhibiting force to make the Federalists cautious, and they were in no mood to act with moderation. Led by their extremists, they rushed through an act empowering the President to deport any dangerous aliens. They lengthened the time needed to become a citizen to keep the immigrant Irish from swelling the ranks of the "Jacobin Republicans." In keeping with their wild mood, Senator James Lloyd of Maryland offered his Sedition Act.

Fines and imprisonment were provided for any person who should write, print, utter, or publish libelous or scandalous matter, defaming the Government of the United States, or either House of Congress, or the President.

On the day of the final vote, according to Stevens Thomson Mason, the trumpets and drums of a Fourth of July parade nearly drowned out the voices of those who wished to comment or urge a postponement. The noise mattered little. The majority of Senators had made up their minds. They looked out of the window and voted for the measure.

In the House, Representative Harrison called for a reading of the First Amendment with the guarantee of free speech.

Harper's answer condemned all the bill's opponents for being in league with the enemy, France.

The debate went on, filling the air with innuendoes and accusations. It was J. A. Bayard who said that a defendant charged with seditious libel should be released if he could prove he spoke the truth. This amendment was substantially all that differentiated the act from earlier tyrannical laws abroad. Finally the measure passed, and President Adams, resentful of slander, failed to veto it.

In practice, the act was enforced against political opponents whose opinions could not be proved. Consequently, arrests were made and Republican editors were fined or jailed. One member of Congress, Matthew Lyon, who had criticized Adams, ran for re-election from inside a prison cell. When he was returned to the House, a motion that he be expelled as a "seditious person" was urged by Bayard. This motion failed only because, under the rules, such a measure needed the support of two-thirds of the members. That left it up to future Congresses to decide whether the members could properly expel a man for conduct prior to his election. (By the eighteen eighties they had decided they could not.)

When Gallatin, Livingston, and Nicholas tried hopelessly to convince the House to rescind the oppressive Sedition Act, they found themselves trying to talk over the sound of other men's voices, coughs, and laughter. Their attempt failed.

During the next Congress, James Ross, a Federalist, suggested the setting up of a Congressional committee to judge the legitimacy of the electoral votes from the States and decide which ones to count. His plan was never passed, but an unfriendly account of the proposal, an insinuation that it had been prepared in caucus and a misstatement that it had passed, appeared in the *Aurora*.

The Senators appointed a "Committee of Privileges" to recommend the measures proper to be adopted. Charles Pinckney insisted that they had no right to discipline the press. He reminded them that the State legislatures had insisted that the Senate open its door to permit its proceedings to be recorded. If a printer could be seized and perhaps imprisoned for what Pinckney described as minor mistakes, ". . . no reporter will certainly attempt to take your debates, and your doors may just as well be shut again."

Mason added a warning. The public mind was already considerably agitated at the unconstitutional exercise of power over the press in the Sedition Act. A flood of petitions against the law supported his claims. The elderly Virginian then said of the Ross bill: ". . . gentlemen . . . seem to consider the . . . declaration of its having passed the Senate as a scandal . . . Well, it might perhaps be a subject of scandal . . . if they had passed it . . ."

In spite of him the Senate voted to censure the editor, though he was never prosecuted.

With the big election coming, prosecutions under the Sedition law increased. Republicans, however, could take some comfort in President Adams' increasing estrangement from the other important Federalists, especially Hamilton. The Federalists would have to campaign as a divided party.

In the midst of all this turmoil the lawmakers moved out of civilized Philadelphia into the near-wilderness of the District of Columbia. The route past the President's new White House was an uninviting ribbon of watery mud. At the far end of this swampy path was a hillside, which the ingenious city planner Pierre Charles L'Enfant had utilized as a natural pedestal for the congressional building.

On that hill, District Commissioner Doctor William Thornton, a famous amateur architect, and construction superintendent J. Hoban had somehow surmounted the shortages of tools and workmen to be expected in this underdeveloped area. One boxlike wing of the capitol was nearly completed. In its columned Senate Chamber the members of both Houses gathered to hear President Adams "congratulate the people of United States on the assembling of Congress at the permanent seat of their Government."

The listening lawmakers did not feel so overjoyed. The shabby village of Washington with its miserable little huts offered almost no place to live. The men could either crowd into the inadequate boarding houses or commute several miles over the bad roads to Georgetown. The Vice President picked a boarding house patronized by Republican Congressmen. There he took meals along with over two dozen others at the common dinner table.

During this period, while eagerly awaiting the election results, Jefferson arranged for the printing of his carefully compiled "Manual of Parliamentary Practices." Here he set down for posterity the courtesies to be observed in congressional debate. Here he decreed—unquestionably with relish as he recalled the pro-Hamilton speculators—"Where the private interests of a member are concerned in a bill or question he is to withdraw."

By December twentieth the newspapers had the results of the balloting by the electors. The Republicans had swept the Federalists out of office. Having disregarded the Bill of Rights, and having quarreled among themselves, the Federalists were defeated. The Representatives of the Republican-minded citizens were to replace the voices of the privileged.

There was only one terrible problem. Every one had expected that in the event of a Republican victory Jefferson would be President and Aaron Burr Vice President, but as yet the Constitution did not provide for a candidate for Vice President. That office was to be filled by the runner-up in the presidential race.

This time there was no runner-up. Jefferson and Burr were tied.

By February 11, when Congress met in joint session to count ballots, the atmosphere in the snow-blanketed Federal city was alive with rumors of intrigue and corrupt deals. There was talk, too, of arming to prevent an usurper from taking office. Jefferson as Vice President presided over the counting by the tellers, and the tie became official. After that, the election was thrown into the House of Representatives, where the votes were counted by States. On the first ballot, early in the afternoon, Jefferson carried eight of the sixteen States. He needed one more. Burr had six. Both the Maryland and Vermont delegations were so evenly divided that they could cast no vote. Eighteen ballots were taken before midnight. The result did not change. No one left the cold, vaultlike chamber. Representative Joseph Nicholson lay on a cot sick and feverish but dared not leave. If he did, Maryland could go for Burr.

The twenty-seventh ballot was taken at 8 A.M. the next morning. Finally, Bayard, the Federalist from Delaware, broke the deadlock and with it the threat of chaos that hung over the nation. On February 17, after verbally endorsing Jefferson, he withheld his vote. What induced his action is still a matter of dispute. In any case, Maryland and Vermont then voted for the winner. Jefferson became President and the first era in the evolution of Congress came to an end.

Never again would the statesmen face so many novel decisions in so short a time. When the first Congress met, the members were a handful of political pioneers. Together they labored to put into practice the Constitution's design for a national legislature. When the Sixth Congress adjourned, rules and precedents had been formed.

A few standing committees were now part of the Congressional structure. More important, the Constitution had been both amended and interpreted in relation to the powers of Congress. The need for one other type of constitutional amendment was also evident, and Congress would soon suggest the Twelfth Amendment to the States ("The electors . . . shall name in their ballots the person voted for as President, and in distinct ballots the person voted for as Vice-President . . ."). Simultaneously,

Congress had asserted, though not finally established, that it possessed "implied" but unwritten powers to give it both the authority and flexibility to adjust to future situations.

The members had repeatedly orated on the powers of Congress to control the national pocketbook, and on its right to be independent of the other branches of Government. In practice, however, the majority of lawmakers had accepted the leadership of the Executive. Herein lay the seeds for future battles and the impetus for the emergence of future leaders.

Part III

Leadership and Disorder

The Congressional Scene

It was a second revolution—or so it seemed. Republican-minded men had captured more than the Presidency. When the Seventh Congress met in December of 1801 they were the new majority. Confidently they expected to usher in a new era.

It happened that out of all the significant events which did take place during the next eight years, nothing had more of an impact on the future of Congress than those plans which did not succeed, those policies which could not be implemented, and, above all, those disorderly scenes in the House.

According to Thomas Jefferson, his followers in Congress had organized originally "to preserve the legislature pure and independent of the executive . . ." As their partisan leader Jefferson had said, "the executive is . . . already too strong."

As President, Jefferson could not remain idle when he considered that Congress lacked the proper leadership. Thus for a time the Executive had more influence over the legislature than before. Here was a situation that would recur repeatedly down through the decades. Whenever Congress lacked effectiveness it tended to delegate its authority to the Executive and permit its role to be diluted.

Among other things, the Jeffersonians had intended to have Congress keep a tight control over public funds. In his first message to the Seventh Congress, the President advised them to state specific sums in their appropriation bills and make these sums applicable to specific purposes. In short, the heads of Government departments should not be granted much discretionary power over money. The Republicans agreed, but they ran into practical problems when they tried to apply these recommendations. Congress, consequently, began its interminable hunt for workable ways to control executive spending.

A more immediate step in the evolution of Congress came about when Republican Congressmen—who earlier had demanded a stricter, more literal interpretation of the Constitution—claimed the authority to add the Louisiana Territory to the Union. Since Representatives from the new acquisition would eventually take their seats in the legislative chambers, the future composition of Congress would be altered. Not all the New England Federalists could be reconciled to that prospect.

However, it was the administration's embargo on trade (adopted to avoid war) which led New England to near-rebellion and led Jefferson's friends in Congress to abandonment of the Executive's leadership. Simultaneously, the chaos in the loosely organized House led the members to think in terms of harnessing their debates with parliamentary procedures. By the time this period closed, Congress was ready to place authority in the hands of a powerful Speaker.

Meanwhile—and this was at least equally important—the Jeffersonian lawmakers had wrestled with the authority of the Judiciary and lost. During this period the Supreme Court Justices were able to establish the right of the Court to void an unconstitutional law passed by the legislature. Consequently, another set of reins was placed on the acts of Congress.

What follows is a picture of the Jeffersonians coming to power, struggling first with the Judiciary and then with themselves and ultimately making of their time on the political stage a period more of transition than of revolution.

A Change of Administration

The Republican victory seemed so secure that later John Quincy Adams failed to understand why the victors constantly trembled, fearing that the Federalists would rise again.

If Adams, the son of the former President, had not still been a Federalist, he might have heard Mason's explanation. "Should an opening be given . . . by an unfortunate schism among ourselves . . . they will come forward . . . taught by the fatal consequences of their late divisions." This was the dread Mason confided to James Monroe. He had ample reason for doing so.

How well the Republicans would work together was most uncertain. Gallatin, now Secretary of the Treasury, could remember that when he was in the House they had caucused on only two major issues. Even then, the members were not bound by the majority decision. It might be thought that since politically congenial men arranged to lodge together, there was ample caucusing in the Washington boarding houses. Dinner table conversation, however, was not the equivalent of discipline, as the new Secretary of State, James Madison, well knew. At the time of the Jay Treaty, Madison had been more upset by the "unsteadiness. . . . of our friends . . . than in the strength . . . of our opponents." What leadership, if any, these friends would follow was a mystery. This especially since their chief was a President who had repeatedly preached the necessity of an independent legislature and insisted, "the Executive is the branch of our government which . . . is already too strong."

Now if Jefferson was going to guide his freedom-loving friends in Congress, he was going to have to devise tactful ways of doing it. They already disagreed with him on one point. Jefferson, hoping to see political parties obliterated, was deliberately limiting the use of patronage as a means of gratifying party supporters.

Giles, back in Congress and intending to lead the Jefferson forces, thoroughly disapproved. He wrote the President, "[A] pretty general purgation of office, has been one of the benefits expected by the friends of the new order of things. . . ."

The idea of wooing the Federalists instead of ousting their appointees seemed foolhardy to other Republicans also. Nevertheless, for the time being, that was the President's plan. A year later Jefferson conceded that he had not eliminated partisan sentiments in Congress. In a note to a future Congressman, he regretfully announced, "[B]esides the slander in their [Federalist] speeches, such letters have been written to their constituents as I shall forbear to qualify by the proper terms."

Along with their other complaints, the Federalists missed the pomp and ceremony of their own regime. Jefferson did not appear in person to deliver his annual message to Congress. He had his Secretary carry the document to the Capitol, which incidentally caused another custom to be abolished. Neither the Senators nor the House members would ever again parade in a body through the streets to the President's mansion to return his call and personally deliver their answer to his address. To Jefferson, their answer would be spelled out in the way they implemented his requests.

He wanted the Alien and Sedition Laws forgotten, the aliens' enforced wait to become a citizen shortened, the size of the armed services cut, the internal taxes repealed, and both the national debt and the Government's expenditure reduced.

To all of this the new Speaker of the House, Nathaniel Macon, a North Carolina planter with a deserved reputation for fairness, gave his attention. He liked the President's plans, but at the same time he considered himself a creature of the House and not its ruler. Macon could remember that Theodore Sedgwick had tried to use the Speaker's office to push his own opinions, which the House had resented. If this was on Macon's mind, he must have been relieved to realize how many members were eager to carry out Jefferson's proposals.

Joseph Nicholson of Maryland wanted to begin looking for ways to "promote economy" by having a committee investigate the management of the funds drawn from the Treasury.

James Bayard, the Federalist from Delaware, acknowledged that if they investigated they would find that money had not always been spent strictly according to appropriations. When "the public service forbade delaying certain measures. . . ." he awkwardly explained, "it had been the custom in cases where money was wanted for one [thing] though appropriated to another, under the same department, to take it from the latter and apply it to the former." This was illegal, he knew, but he thought "it being the custom palliates it."

On hearing that, the House quickly agreed to Nicholson's

motion, and the Speaker at once appointed a committee with Nicholson as chairman. Thus in a matter of weeks the Republicans established legislative goals, abolished the "monarchistic" formalities between the Executive and Congress, and put an investigation into motion. All this was important, but none of it could compare in significance with the outcome of their next undertaking.

Harnessed by the "Court"

The old Federalist Congress had, in its closing days, rushed through an act benefiting the judiciary and also creating a host of new circuit judgeships for defeated President Adams to fill during his last hours in office. The Jeffersonians and their President wanted to be rid of the new judiciary act, the posts it created, and the "midnight" judges who filled those posts.

Senator Breckenridge of Kentucky chose Wednesday, January 6 to propose a bill repealing the 1801 Act. Having been for a long time a close associate of the President's, Breckenridge couldn't resist remarking that since the Sedition Act was no longer operative, "suits were decreasing" and there was no need' for so many judges. The debate that tiggered dragged on for weeks.

At last Federalist Senator James Ross summarized the issues: Whatever its title may be, he said, "the bill itself is nothing less than an act of the Legislature removing from office . . . the judges of all the circuit courts . . . It is a declaration that those officers hold their offices at your will and pleasure.

"This is a direct and palpable violation of the Constitution . . .

"By article third . . . the judges . . . hold their offices during good behaviour."

What was at stake here, as the Federalists saw it, was the independence of the judiciary.

They had listened carefully and heard the "democrats" claim

that independent judges were dangerous, that although the Constitution prohibited the Executive or the Legislature from displacing any judge directly, yet the Legislature might abolish his office and thereby indirectly effect the same end.

Ross felt that Congress was erecting itself into a tyranny that could emasculate the Constitution. Senators should ask themselves, "If you pass laws . . . violating our public faith . . . will our courts have enough courage to obey the Constitution . . . by declaring such acts void? Will the judges dare . . . ? If they do, their doom is certain."

Mr. Breckinridge was shocked. "I did not expect," he said, "to find the doctrine of the power of the courts to annul the laws of Congress as unconstitutional so seriously insisted on." He cautioned his fellow Senators to consider carefully before insisting on a power for the judges which would place the Legislature at their feet.

Gouverneur Morris had considered. Judges were bound by an oath to support the Constitution. To do this, they had to be free *not* to apply unconstitutional laws. Furthermore, if Congress repealed the reform act, the Supreme Court Justices would have to hear the circuit court cases, riding from town to town like post boys instead of remaining at home with their law books.

To a gentleman who said he wanted to keep the Justices thus occupied to keep them out of mischief, Morris answered: "If ever the occasion calls for it, I trust the Supreme Court will not neglect doing the great mischief of saving this Constitution." It was still painful for Morris to remember with what great difficulties that document had been obtained.

As the debate went on, Senator Dayton of New Jersey, an ardent Federalist, realized that the repeal bill might pass by a small majority. Dayton in February, 1802, was no less daring than he had been in 1787 at the Constitutional Convention in Philadelphia. If anything, his assurance had grown since he had been the Speaker of the House in the Fourth and Fifth Congresses. Now he reasoned aloud that since so many gentlemen found the the measure either "bold and violent" or "unconstitutional," it should be referred to a committee for further study. He so moved, but the vote was 15 ayes and 15 nays.

The Senators waited for the deciding vote of Vice President Aaron Burr. Burr said he felt disposed to accommodate the gentlemen voting to commit, in the hope that the bill might be rendered more acceptable to the Senate. While thus voting with the Federalists, he nevertheless wanted to assure his Jeffersonian associates that he was not against their measure. He voted "yes" to send the bill to committee. Perhaps some were prone to forgive him, but he soon added to their distrust when he attended a Federalist party in honor of George Washington's birthday. Meanwhile, following the Senate's vote, a select committee of five members was chosen by ballot. Unlike the Representatives, the Senators selected their committees, thus giving observers a chance to gauge a statesman's popularity and prestige.

For the moment, the prestige of the Republicans in the Senate was in Breckinridge's hands. He soon succeeded in getting another vote to have the committee discharged and the bill to repeal the judiciary act of 1801 brought back to the floor. After that, it passed.

When the Bill arrived in the House, it was well championed by Giles and by one of the most bizarre political leaders ever to strut across the Washington scene.

John Randolph of Roanoke sat in the House wearing his riding boots and spurs and holding his whip in hand. Not infrequently a hunting dog lay by his side. From a distance he looked like a slim, beardless boy rather than a full-grown man. Speaker Macon liked him and had made him, rather than Giles, chairman of the Ways and Means Committee. For the moment, this young second-term Congressman was also on good terms with the President. Being a States' Rights advocate, Randolph was pledged to a strict interpretation of the Constitution. Nevertheless he supported repealing the law and thus unseating the judges.

Bayard tried hopelessly to convince the Republicans that there was more to the question than any of them were considering. "The object," he said, "is to repeal the law of last session. Are there six gentlemen in this House who can . . . tell me even how many sections there are in it . . . ? Is it possible that the blindness of party spirit can say we will repeal a law though we do not know what it is?" He wanted the repeal bill sent to a select committee so that the wholesome features of the judiciary reform act might be kept.

Both Giles and Randolph objected to the loss of time involved. Bayard was sure this was because they had already determined what their positions would be in their caucus meeting.

Randolph indignantly called for order, but Speaker Macon permitted Bayard to finish his speech. The Republican majority then voted to keep the bill in the Committee of the Whole, and debate continued.

Giles thought the Judiciary was becoming dangerously ambitious. There was one situation to which he particularly referred. A last-minute appointee named Marbury had gone before the Supreme Court to sue the Secretary of State. The commission which made Marbury a justice of the peace had disappeared from the Government offices. And Chief Justice Marshall had had the audacity to order Mr. Madison to show the Court why, as Secretary of State, he should not be forced to produce this commission, thus letting Marbury serve out his appointment. As Giles spoke, the case was on the docket waiting to be heard.

Encouraged by Giles, the irate Congressmen did more than repeal the 1801 act. They also postponed the next Supreme Court session, hoping to intimidate the justices.

When the Court finally did convene, Madison pointedly did not appear to answer the Chief Justice's order. Undeterred, the Justices went on with the case, listening to the witnesses and reviewing the law.

The Constitution made the Supreme Court only a court of appeal, except where a State or representative of a foreign power was involved. Marbury had, nevertheless, started his suit against Madison in the Supreme Court because he relied on an extension of the Court's authority which had been passed as part of the Judiciary Act of 1789. This was the basis on which he lost his case. Chief Justice Marshall, speaking for the Court, ruled that Congress had violated the Constitution. It cannot extend the Court's authority beyond constitutional limits. An unconstitutional act passed by the Legislature is void and it is the duty of the Justices to declare it void.

Since the Jeffersonians were unwilling to give Marbury his commission, they were in no position to attack the decision. Marshall had used the situation to establish the independence of the Judiciary and also to mold the attributes of Congress. Henceforth, Congress was to be subject to the Court's great restraining check.

This great decision was crucial in the history of Congress and of the United States. It marked the first time that the judiciary of any nation had gained the authority to set aside an act of the law-making power. It was a great new step in Anglo-American political science.

Giles, greatly disturbed, was determined to make one more attempt to bring the judiciary under legislative control. His opportunity arose, he thought, when the House of Representatives brought impeachment charges against an abusive Federalist Judge, Samuel Chase. By the time the Senate sat as a Court, Giles was a Senator and, therefore, one of the jurors. Soon a shocked John Quincy Adams discovered Giles by the fireside discussing the case with the prosecutor from the House of Representatives.

Now, Giles theorized, an impeachment should not be a criminal prosecution at all. It should be nothing more than an inquiry by the two Houses of Congress to determine whether the office of any public man might not be better filled by another. The Houses could then remove a man with "dangerous ideas." It was a drastic recommendation offering to give the legislature control over both of the other branches of Government. Adams must have been relieved that this time Giles did not seem to be making converts. Then it turned out that Randolph, who presented the prosecution's case against Judge Chase, was also unconvincing. The Republicans failed to muster the necessary approval of two-thirds of the Senators, and the impeachment proceedings failed.

The power struggle with the judiciary was lost. Giles' theory was forgotten. The judiciary retained the independence and power so brilliantly won by Marshall, and the future of Congress had thus been altered.

"*The Executive Is . . . Already Too Strong.*"

By now it was obvious that how Congress would use its powers and whose leadership it would accept were two questions that were inseparably entwined.

As long as Giles was in the House, the Representatives were doing the Executive's bidding. Giles acted as the President's chief spokesman and as their leader. In May of 1802, Jefferson noted with satisfaction, "The legislature . . . have carried into execution . . . almost all the propositions . . . in my message at the beginning of the session." Half a year later, this happy situation had changed.

In January, Federalist Senator Plumer wrote to a political friend, "The Democrat party want an acknowledged . . . leader in the House. Giles is sick. . . . Randolph has more . . . talents than any other member of the party, but . . ." It was not only Randolph's appearance that was against him. His high-pitched voice, his biting sarcasm, his bullying manner, and his aristocratic aloofness were all hard for other men to accept.

Randolph, nevertheless, had followers and had impressed some influential men with his genius. Speaker Macon made him Chairman of the Ways and Means Committee. Since this committee considered all matters relevant to revenues and expenditures, and to the public debt, Randolph was floor leader a good part of the time whether the other Congressmen all liked him or not. He took charge of presenting to the full House the bills and reports that came from his Committee. In addition, as the members doubtless knew, Macon believed that the Chairman of this foremost committee should be someone friendly to the administration, and the President had made the Virginian his confidant. That, for the immediate future, secured Randolph's position as majority leader.

At first this arrangement appeared to be succeeding. The House members seemed willing enough to respond to the guidance that flowed out of the relationship between their leader and the Executive and an atmosphere of harmony existed that was soon put to a critical test.

In order to accept Napoleon's offer to sell Louisiana, the administration had to win the approval of the House. The treaty could not be implemented without an appropriation. Randolph's devotion to a strict construction of the Constitution and to the rights of the States was well known. He nevertheless loyally supported the treaty. He realized that it called for eventually granting citizenship to the inhabitants of that area and that consequently new faces would appear in the halls of Congress, but the only change he demanded was an amendment to the provisions for the immediate government of the territory.

As a result, only Federalists attacked the constitutionality of the proposal. In the Senate, Uriah Tracy of Connecticut claimed that the phrase in the Constitution (Article IV, Section 3) that said, "New States may be admitted by the Congress into this Union" only referred to domestic States, or States formed from territory already agreed to be part of the nation. It did not refer to adding foreign territory like Louisiana.

Senator Pickering of Massachusetts likened the Union to a commercial house. You could not admit a new partner or partners without the consent of the original members of the firm. He could foresee the reduction of New England's influence when the population of these vast "foreign" lands to the southwest gained representation in Congress. Consumed by anxiety, Timothy Pickering—a veteran of the Revolution, a member of the Constitutional Convention, and a former Federalist cabinet minister—spread sentiments of secession.

Others were critical of the congressional plans for the temporary government of Louisiana; John Quincy Adams objected to any plan, since the people of Louisiana had no option but to submit. As yet Adams was a man without influence, but high-ranking Republicans also disliked the situation.

In November of 1803, the President resorted to a gentle tactic for propelling the course of events. He wrote to John Breckinridge of Kentucky, his trusted spokesman in the Senate, "I thought I perceived in you the other day a dread of the job of preparing a constitution for the new acquisition. With more boldness than wisdom I therefore determined to prepare [an] . . . outline, and send it to you. . . . In communicating it to you I must do it in confidence that you will never let any person know that I have put pen to paper on the subject . . . you will . . . copy it and return . . . the original . . ." Here was one method of guiding legislation without heading directly into the "bloody teeth and fangs" of both the Federalists and those who had previously been convinced that "the executive is the branch of our government which . . . is already too strong. . . ." It proved successful. In March of 1804, Congress passed an act to help the inhabitants of the area prepare for self-government.

On another occasion, Jefferson wrote privately to Randolph with suggestions for legislation which, the President casually explained, "I had thrown into the form of a bill." In spite of their minor differences Jefferson evidently expected to rely on Randolph's continuing support.

Three months later the chairman's shrill voice filled the House chamber with condemnations of the administration.

Bribed members of the Georgia State legislature had sold 35,000,000 acres of public lands to speculators for the disgracefully small sum of a cent and a half an acre. After Georgia citizens cried "Fraud!" and tried to void the binding contract, the problem and the Yazoo lands were ceded to the Federal Government. By then, the speculators had made resales to innocent purchasers. Commissioners appointed by Jefferson (from his own cabinet) recommended that Congress compromise its way out of the scandal by making appropriations available to settle with these claimants. Randolph was outraged, terming it ". . . the monstrous sacrifice of the best interests of the nation on the altar of corruption."

This was not the only time when Randolph's slashing attacks could make others fear the debate would end in a duel. He was not, however, alone in criticizing the compromise. Giles told John Quincy Adams that the proposal would be most unpopular in Virginia. Adams, among others, was appalled by the manner in which Postmaster General Granger boldly lobbied and made himself an agent for the claimants. Both he and they were unsuccessful. The Congress appropriated no money for settlements until years later when the Supreme Court denied Georgia's right to void the original contracts.

Perhaps because the Yazoo matter was so controversial, Jefferson was not prepared for Randolph's next attack. It happened that, while negotiating a border dispute with Spain, Jefferson needed money for a diplomatic purpose too delicate to be explained in the public journals. The President's message to Congress spoke of force, but to Randolph he spoke of buying our way. He wanted an appropriation of two million dollars to come out of the Ways and Means Committee.

Randolph refused even to propose the measure. Instead, he upbraided the President for double-dealing by saying one thing for the record while actually wanting another. Unquestionably, Randolph remembered that once before the President had obtained a huge sum without disclosing why he wanted it. Randolph refused to be a party to offering the House this kind of leadership.

Jefferson listened to Randolph's criticisms and then asked Massachusetts' Congressman Barnabas Bidwell to present his proposal. In return, Randolph publicly denounced the administration, which he said relied on "back stairs influences" and sending whispered messages to govern the House.

Jefferson, in a letter to Bidwell, pointed out that Randolph had not been averse to "back stairs influences" when he was a party to them. In spite of Randolph, in both the House and the Senate the "secret bill" asking for the two million was put to the test and was passed. John Quincy Adams then wrote: "The measure has been very reluctantly adopted by the President's friends, on his private wishes . . . His whole system of administration seems founded upon this principle of carrying through the legislature measures by his personal or official influence. There is a certain portion of the members in both Houses who on every occasion . . . have no other inquiry but what is the President's wish." Jefferson had defeated Randolph. Jefferson, not Randolph, was leading Congress.

"No Check on Expenditures"

It was not long before Randolph was energetically trying to make the legislature exert its authority over the Executive Department in another area. The incident started with a few remarks by D. R. Williams of South Carolina. "When I first came to Washington," Williams said, "I went to the Navy Yard [and] saw an elegant building going on. I inquired under what appropriation this was authorized, and was answered, 'Under . . . contingency expenses.' "

Williams felt that every gentleman should be able to tell his constituents how the public money was being spent. Obviously, the term "contingencies" told them nothing. Williams wanted it to be struck from the present naval appropriations bill and a list of separate items requiring fixed sums substituted for it.

Congressman Dana of Connecticut, of course, recognized what the gentleman from South Carolina had in mind. When the Jefferson administration had first begun, they had heard much noise about making specific appropriations as the policy recommended by the President. Recently, however, Dana recalled, Congress had appropriated two million dollars for the President without any specification of the object. He could only infer that this policy "could not be carried into effect."

Randolph did not try to defend his associates for allowing their authority to be diluted to please a popular President. Instead, he announced that he had written a note to the head of the Navy Department asking for other information and calling the sum for contingent expenses "unnecessarily large." In answer, the Secretary said he did not think the sum too large, but gave no explanation. Randolph was sure that Congress had no check on expenditures. If the expenditures of the Navy exceeded the sum Congress allowed, Randolph had no doubt that Congress would make up the deficiency, as if its power to appropriate were a mere matter of form.

Having thus mocked his associates he moved to strike a request for $3,500 to complete the Marine barracks in Washington. He commented that "though the building was finite, the appropriation for it appeared to be infinite." At the time, the House responded to his sarcasm and agreed to pass his motion by a large majority. That was on Wednesday.

On Saturday the Representatives put the money for the barracks back in the bill. It seemed that the Secretary had already obtained an advance on the amount from the private funds of one of the officers. The man had to be reimbursed. Furious, Randolph seized his first opportunity to tell his colleagues that their power over the public purse had become "less than a shadow."

Randolph was even more outraged when the House condoned the actions of architect Benjamin Henry Latrobe. Finding that he had already used up more than his annual appropriation without completing the south wing of the Capitol in which the Representatives were soon due to convene, Latrobe called together the chief mechanics, the foreman of carpenters, the cabinetmaker, stonecutter, mason and lumber merchant. By laying the facts before them, he persuaded them to work on at their own risk. Congress, he was confident, would not fail to remunerate them. Thus, by the time the House assembled, deficiencies of $51,000 had been incurred. According to Randolph, this was a figure greater than the expense of some State governments. And yet Representative Sanford of Kentucky had obtained the consent of the House to bring in a bill to provide for the deficit.

"If this bill is agreed to," Randolph warned, he "must consider all control over the expenditures of public money . . . abandoned."

Virginia's Congressman, Joseph Lewis, felt the Government's faith was pledged. The fact was that without the money the workmen would not be paid.

To Randolph this situation was worse than the matter of the barracks. There Congress had made up expenditures the Executive chose to incur, but Latrobe was only a private agent. "I will never consent," he announced.

Again he was defeated. The deficit was made up without his consent.

It must have given him some slight comfort when later it appeared that there were some practices Congress intended to control. Nicholson's investigation had revealed that money appropriated to build ships had been used to buy land on which the ships could be constructed. For a while, however, little was done with this information. Then, at the very end of Jefferson's second term, Congress passed and the President signed the famous Appropriations Act of 1809, providing that "sums appropriated by law . . . shall be solely applied to the objects for which they are . . . appropriated."

It said: "All warrants drawn by the Secretary of Treasury, or of War or of Navy . . . shall specify the particular appropriation . . . to which the same shall be charged . . ." Moreover, the War and the Navy Departments were to report to Congress every January 1 "a distinct account" of the money they had drawn up until September 30.

Congress had taken a major step toward exerting its authority over Executive action, but if Randolph's bullying remarks had influenced this move, it was only indirectly.

"An Unhinged State"

Ironically it was Randolph who would one day complain to his constituents that freedom of speech had been restricted in the House of Representatives. His own conduct contributed heavily toward this eventuality.

As Randolph's influence sank, his temper rose. While he mocked the inability of the House to control Executive spending, he ranted against the prevailing foreign policy. Again and again he focused on the import prohibitions. They were intended as a blow at the British, who were harassing American vessels and, while rounding up their own deserters, were impressing American seamen. To the Jeffersonians, these import laws were a peaceful alternative to a resort to arms. To Randolph, the restrictions were "incipient war measures."

England was at war with France and fighting for her life. The maritime trade that Congress sought to protect, he said, was "a mere fungus of that war."

If supplying French territory plunged the country into a fight with England, Randolph predicted, "you will come out without your Constitution . . . We shall be told that our Government is too free . . . weak and inefficient . . . That we must give the President power to call forth the resources." And if the United States helped to defeat Great Britain, where would this country be, he asked, but under the despotism of France and Bonaparte?

Suddenly, Randolph was attacking the President and Mr. Madison. His speeches were endless. He abused all who disagreed with him. His tirades were so vehement that it was impossible to keep a quorum in the Senate while he had the floor in the House.

The spectacle he produced motivated Sloan of New Jersey to devise a plan. As a preface to his suggestions, Sloan described Randolph delivering a harangue, wildly flinging his arms about and causing papers and even hats to fly in every direction.

"Are you prepared to permit that member to invade the Speaker's chair; [and] . . . pointing directly to another member . . . order him to sit down, . . . [and call] an aged member of this House . . . an old toothless driveller . . . ?" Sloan asked. He next recalled an occasion when the House was discussing "the British business." Randolph had pulled himself out of a sick bed to occupy the floor for almost the whole of the two first days of debate, denouncing the "evil designs" of the administration.

Worse than Randolph's words were his actions. With the typical dislike of military authority displayed by the original Republicans, he had deliberately delayed the appropriation bills for the Army and Navy, hiding the estimates in his desk drawer or in his pocket.

To prevent future chairmen from following that example, and to prevent members from being insulted by chairmen, Sloan offered his resolution: "Resolved, that, hereafter all standing committees of the House of Representatives shall be ap-

pointed by ballot and shall choose their own chairman." Had
Sloan's resolution been adopted and maintained, the history of
the next decade would have been very different.

As it was, except for a few instances, the Speaker's prerogatives to make appointments remained intact. So did Sloan's exasperation. At the same time the disorder in the House continued,
while the number of men who were growing impatient increased.

"A Suitable Opportunity to Debate the Question"

Times were difficult for the Congress partly because they were
difficult for the country. Both belligerents, France and England,
were molesting American shipping when Jefferson in 1807 proposed another economic substitute for war, the Embargo Act.
It passed, and ships were forbidden to set sail for either England
or the continent in the hope that the battling nations would
agree to respect American rights rather than be deprived of
American products.

As the Jefferson administration drew to a close, it was obvious
that the President's embargo had not intimidated the belligerents. Instead, it had disrupted the country's economy. Ships
rotted beside wharfs piled high with cotton that could not be
exported. Sailors and sailmakers were among the jobless and
often emigrated. Boston's Representative, Josiah Quincy, called
the situation absurd. The power to regulate commerce was not
the power to destroy it. As Boston papers talked openly of
ending the Union, Congress faced the issues of commercial ruin
and possible war.

The lawmakers differed so in their reactions to the crisis that
legislating would have been difficult even without those members who virtually paralyzed House action. At this point Randolph, who was no longer chairman of Ways and Means, was
not the only offender.

Jefferson is in rags, impoverished by his own embargo. Cartoons like this one helped to alienate the President's following in Congress

Barent Gardenier of Kingston, New York, it was said, could talk until midnight or until morning, not converting but inflaming his listeners. He announced that he was proud of the delays he had caused when the Embargo was under consideration. His verbal blows sounded to George W. Campbell of Tennessee like an echo of "the petty scribblers in the party newspapers . . . destitute of even the semblance of truth." While charging that the Embargo was meant to help France blockade England, Gardenier accused the majority of "forging chains to fasten us to the cart of the imperial conqueror [Napoleon]."

Shouting "Order!" Campbell jumped to his feet to find others also up in protest. But since Speaker Joseph Varnum had made Campbell Chairman of the Ways and Means Committee and hence a leader of the House, Campbell took the responsibility of defending the administration. The angry discussion ended in Gardenier's challenging Campbell to a duel, which Campbell accepted. John Eppes, Jefferson's son-in-law, agreed to be his second.

Though Campbell wounded Gardenier he did not change his behavior, and the Republicans could not stop Senator Pickering from spreading sentiments that were much like Gardenier's. Massachusetts' other Senator, John Quincy Adams, was a convert to the Republican cause but was in the Senate only until June of 1808. He resigned his seat after learning that his State legislature would not reelect him because of his defense of the Embargo. In the months ahead he would be one of the first to recognize "the termination of that individual personal influence which Mr. Jefferson had erected [over the Congress]."

Meanwhile, the wrangles over the embargo caused the matter of limiting debate to become an issue in the House. The question was brought up in 1809 when the Representatives, having passed a law enforcing the embargo, had gone on to discuss another topic: Did they need an extra session of Congress, to meet a few months thence? It was late in January when Josiah Quincy demanded to be heard. "All the proceedings concerning the enforcing embargo law . . . had been arranged somewhere else previous to their being brought into debate on this floor," he charged. He saw no other way of explaining the speed with which the act had passed the Committee of the Whole and the House in one sitting, and he complained that he had been denied his right to a suitable opportunity to debate the question.

Eppes pointedly asked the Speaker if it were in order to discuss a bill that had already passed while the House was considering a different question. When Varnum said it was, Eppes appealed to the Representatives, urging them to vote to overrule the Speaker, set a new precedent for limiting debate, and silence Quincy.

D.R. Williams was outraged by this treatment of Quincy. "If there be not talent enough in this House to refute his arguments in the name of God, let us stand convicted!" he thundered.

With that, Eppes withdrew his motion and debate continued virtually unlimited in the House, which now numbered over 140 members. It was inevitable that the House would soon again be asked to decide what they would call "orderly discussion" and what "disruptive tactic."

The next time the issue had to be faced, it was, as before, in connection with the troublesome topic of trade restrictions. After the election returns showed Federalist gains, the Representatives had heeded the voices of the people, deserted the President, and repealed the Embargo. When the unsuccessful Non-Intercourse Act (which Congress passed as a mild substitute for the Embargo) was about to expire, two measures were introduced, both named after ex-Speaker Macon, who was now Chairman of the Foreign Relations Committee. Macon 2, which finally passed, lifted all trade restrictions but with a pledge: Non-intercourse would be restored against either of the two fighting nations, France or England, if the other ceased violating American rights.

Soon there was sharp disagreement in Congress as to whether France actually had yielded to the pressure. Napoleon's government claimed that on the basis of the pledge in the bill, he was revoking his Berlin and Milan Decrees against United States shipping. Like many an American Congressman, Britain remained unconvinced. She therefore retained her Orders in Council. After the President issued a proclamation against Britain Congressman Eppes proposed a new law to ban British ships and products from United States ports.

February 27, 1811, found the Representatives at an evening session battling over what to do. The Federalist Congressmen did not trust France. Moreover, they kept in mind the flood of petitions against the Embargo.

Randolph, who also detested Eppes' proposal, twice moved to have it postponed. Both times he was unsuccessful. Others tried equally unsuccessfully to have the measure amended. Randolph then moved that the bill be recommitted for further revision. When this also failed Matthew Lyons moved that the bill be reread as it now stood.

It was one-thirty in the morning when the Speaker stated Lyons' motion. After hearing it, Gardenier stood up and began pouring out an endless number of loosely connected thoughts. To stop him from suffocating the measure under a blanket of everlasting debate, Thomas Gholson, Jr., of Brunswick, Virginia, interrupted and called for the previous question. Simply stated, Gholson was asking for an immediate vote on the motion to read the bill through. A motion for the previous question is not debatable. The Speaker therefore asked the members, "Shall the question now be put?"

They voted that it should.

Gardenier still went on talking, commenting now on having the bill read, and Gholson objected. Debate at this point, he argued, was out of order.

Speaker Varnum said he would like to uphold Gholson, but due to a previous ruling in the House he did not think he could cut off this debate. "It was in order."

Gholson appealed to the House to overrule the Speaker and outlaw any discussion after the previous question had been demanded. By now the weary House members felt that they had tolerated more than enough. Only a few months before, the new President had referred to their proceedings as being "in an unhinged state." In the wee hours of the morning of the 28th they voted Gardenier out of order, passed Eppes' measure, and decided for all time that a vote in favor of calling for the previous question ended debate in the House.

More than a new rule had been born. The House had put a bridle on its own proceedings. The episode indicated the readiness of an increasing number of Representatives to welcome a firm master to the Speaker's chair. Randolph would have been well advised to take note.

Meanwhile, a tall, lanky Kentuckian named Henry Clay had been readying himself for his role in history.

Part IV

The Henry Clay Generation Organizes

The Congressional Scene

The more men argue over how the Congress should be organized and what function it should fill, the more they refer to the Henry Clay period. Whenever critics complain that Congress should exercise more initiative and exert more authority, someone will think of Clay and his followers in the House of Representatives. They seized the initiative and for a short time conducted a congressionally dominated Government.

Critics of the seniority system like to remind everyone that Clay was elected Speaker of the House the day he took his oath as a member of that body. To guide the public business with "dispatch," he changed the Speaker's role from moderator to leader, enforced new rules limiting debate, and far from respecting seniority, put recent arrivals in charge of the committees. Because these eager young men were well organized and knew what they wanted, they swayed both Congress and the President.

While evaluating Executive-Legislative relationships in 1964, Senator Clark of Pennsylvania refused to let anyone forget that Clay's group pushed the country into the War of 1812. That catastrophe might have been avoided if President Madison had exerted more influence. Instead, Clay launched into his long career as a challenger of Presidents sparring continuously in domestic as well as foreign affairs and longing to bridle even the veto power.

Much of his jousting went on during a particularly disheartening

113

period of congressional history. Seeing the Federalists disappear after the War of 1812, President Monroe hoped there would be a long "era of good feeling," without political parties. Clay doubted it. His contemporaries watched in sorrow as petty factions and jealous cliques, each attached to a would-be presidential candidate, replaced the older, more philosophical groupings of political thinkers. When, in addition, the controversy over admitting Missouri hardened sectional animosities, the future looked bleak. It required a series of parliamentary innovations to cope with the challenges of the times.

It was also during this period that the standing committees began to multiply, allowing the novel problems faced by the growing nation to be studied intensively. Already the Louisiana purchase had created the necessity for the House committee on public lands. Then the disruption of the import trade caused by the embargo and the War of 1812 spawned home industries and hence gave birth to a separate committee on manufacture.

The Representatives, still searching for ways to control Executive spending and the use of the nation's funds, devised six committees on public expenditures. All this was part of a trend. The Congressmen were facing the fact that a committee of the whole could not possibly examine all the petitions, evaluate all the suggestions, and work out all the details in all the areas of possible legislation. Their solution was a system of standing committees, whose members became specialists in some phase of congressional activity. Consequently, before this era ended it became evident that the convictions of the Speaker, implemented by his choice of committee members, could direct the history of the nation.

"To Dispatch the Public Business"

Henry Clay had studied law in his native State, Virginia. He had entered politics in his adopted home, Kentucky. The year 1803 found him a member of the Kentucky State House of Representatives. December of 1806 found him riding his horse down Washington's Pennsylvania Avenue. Kentucky's Senator Adair had resigned and the State Legislature had sent Clay to be a replacement for the few months that remained of the Ninth Congress.

When he claimed his seat, this daring young man was violating the constitutional requirement that a Senator be at least thirty years of age. In later life it would embarrass him to have this fact remembered. Meanwhile, he had arrived in time to see the Senate thrown into a panic by the suspicious activities of the former Vice President, Aaron Burr.

Burr's career had seemingly come to an end two years before, when he killed Alexander Hamilton in a duel. Now there was talk of his plotting an unauthorized military expedition against Spanish territory, threatening the peace and endangering the Union. The President was trying to get more details. Evidence mixed with rumor indicated that what Burr wanted was to be President of an independent area and lead it into conquering Mexico. The Senators in their anxiety wanted to suspend the right of habeas corpus—the right of a person held under arrest to demand to be taken before a judge who might order his release. Clay calmly told a friend there was "no occasion for such a bill," but since he had once served as Burr's attorney, the Kentuckian said little during the discussion. Instead, he watched the senior statesmen in the Senate chamber.

Doubtless he was impressed when the House members refused to be panicked into curtailing the liberties of innocent people. Several of the Congressmen quoted the Constitution: "Habeas Corpus shall not be suspended, unless when in case of rebellion or invasion the public safety may require it." The Representatives decided that only an extreme emergency could justify such action. Habeas corpus was not suspended.

Clay found his next tour of duty in the Senate, starting in 1810, to be even less satisfying. He watched while Senator Samuel Smith of Maryland, in the shipping business, managed to defeat a trade restriction bill proposed by the administration. The bill, aimed at countering British and French aggression, seemed to Clay an excessively feeble defense; like a leaky boat, it was only better than no craft. When even it could not pass, he decided that America needed "a new race of heroes" to cut the nation's ties to Europe and preserve the independence won by its founding fathers. He was excited enough to want to invade Britain's North American stronghold, Canada.

"I prefer the troubled ocean of war . . . to . . . ignominious peace," he told his elders. If they did want to fight they must either try the administration's plan of economic coercion or lose all self-respect.

He had little hope of influencing Smith. The Marylander had defied the Madison administration before. Smith, Giles and Leib of Pennsylvania had gone so far as to let the President know they would not "consent" to Gallatin's being appointed Secretary of State, and reluctantly Madison did not appoint Gallatin. Not surprisingly, Smith's opinion and not the sentiments of the brash Kentuckian swayed the Senate on the trade bill. It was two months before the measure could be replaced by another.

By then Clay had made what he later conceded was a blunder, hurting his own fight for the national defense. It happened when a vote had to be taken on whether to renew the charter of the Bank of the United States. In the press and in the halls of Congress the old arguments against the bank were again raised. There was no phrase in the Constitution that granted Congress the power to charter a company. Giles clung to this view. It was the position he had shared with Madison against Hamilton. The President had since changed his position and now felt that the precedent established by the bank's existence settled the question, but Madison said very little. He let Gallatin and Senator William Crawford fight for the bank.

Clay listened and acknowledged that at times Congress must act on the basis of implied powers, but he thought the implication must be obviously necessary to carrying out the duties of Congress; otherwise Congress would usurp prerogatives that belonged to the States. Experience had not yet taught Clay how necessary a national bank could be to a country at war, with an empty treasury and an army to feed.

He did not yet know that private financiers would fail to lend the Government even half of what it required. He had not yet shared the disappointment of men who realized that the bank, had it existed, could have provided the necessary loans in anticipation of tax receipts. It could also have provided usable paper money to compete with local bank notes. When the already desperate United States Treasury accepted these, it often found they were not cashable for anything like their face value.

None of this could Clay foresee, and unfortunately this time the young Kentucky Senator's opinion was vital.

When the vote was counted, there were seventeen Senators voting to renew the charter, while seventeen other Senators, including Mr. Clay, voted "nay." The tie let Vice President Clinton cast his ballot to kill the bank.

In the fall of 1811, with the war spirit rising, Congress convened a month early. In November the President in his annual message to Congress reviewed once more the injuries inflicted by the belligerents on American commerce. The grievances were not new, but scores of new Congressmen were weighing the President's words. Among them were the "War Hawks." These men were convinced that their constituents at the polls had intended to pass sentence against the doctrine of submission. They were tired of ineffective substitutes for armed retaliation; they hoped to flex the nation's muscles and avenge the nation's honor; they blamed the British for the Indian raids, and they demanded a fight for "Free Trade and Sailors' Rights." Clay, who by now had left the Senate to be elected to the House, was one of these.

During this session he was able to spend more time with men who shared his views. He was staying in the same boarding house as South Carolina's Langdon Cheves and two of that State's freshmen Congressmen, John C. Calhoun and William Lowndes, and another newcomer, Felix Grundy of Tennessee. Because of their living in it, the building was soon nicknamed the "war mess." Lowndes wrote home describing his "comfortable room with a fire" and praising his new friends who shared his impatience with the slowness of political progress.

The ambitions of these young men from the "war mess" were threatened at least as much by the older Republicans, such as Randolph and Macon, as they were by the Federalists. Consequently, it was a tremendous victory for the newcomers when on opening day Henry Clay was elected Speaker. Now he could appoint the committee members. And he considered one qualification paramount: agreeing with the War Hawks.

From then on, the members of this small group were powerful men. Soon, Grundy was reporting their attitude in a letter to Andrew Jackson: "[W]e [will] have War or Honorable peace before we adjourn or certain great personages [will] have produced a state of things which will bring them down from their high places..." These sentiments evidently had been made clear to the President and Secretary of State Monroe.

Only shortly thereafter, in early December, Lowndes wrote his wife: "Mr. Monroe has given the strongest assurances that the President will cooperate zealously with Congress in declaring war, if our complaints are not redressed by May next."

If the Secretary of State's commitment was to be relied on, it was essential to arm the nation. The War Hawks devoted the whole session to this purpose, with Randolph indefatigably keeping up his resistance. When a bill to provide 25,000 extra troops came before both Houses, Randolph ridiculed it. George W. Campbell (who was a Senator this session) admitted, "You ... must act," but warned, "so large a regular force [will] drain your Treasury ... and paralyze the best ... measures of your Government." They were both ignored. The bill passed.

The War Hawks' next problem was how to pass a bill to enlarge the navy in spite of the traditional Republican abhorrence to naval forces. "Navies always were the tools of tyrants, employed in wars of ambition," according to the older Republicans. Even proposing the increase took courage, but courage was one thing the War Hawks, and particularly Clay, had in abundance.

On January 17, Cheves, as Chairman of the Committee on Naval Affairs, brought in a bill to build ten 38-gun frigates. He indicated he would later ask for funds for even larger ships.

Sitting in the Speaker's chair, Clay could not enter the debate, and yet he had no intention of remaining silent. It was therefore no accident but rather, as one of his friends put it, "half understood [by his followers] that all important affairs were to be discussed in Committee of the Whole in order that Clay's voice should not be lost." Speaker Clay would appoint the committee chairman who would occupy the Chair and preside over the proceedings in the Committee of the Whole. Then, after joining the other Representatives on the floor, Clay would ask to be recognized. Once recognized, he could dominate the debate with his already-famous gift of oratory.

This time he told the House that a navy was as essential to the survival of our commerce as the shepherd and his dog were to the safety of the grazing flock.

If his arguments seemed a bit farfetched to his audience, Clay had other ways of winning support. His very personality drew men to him, for time and again he made it a point to be generous in his opinions of his fellows and, moreover, to get to know them. Visiting from mess to mess and from party to party, he enthusiastically counteracted the chatter of his opponents over a glass of wine. Repeatedly he got what he wanted, but on January 27, 1812, he did not get a big navy. The Cheves plan was voted down.

The Congress settled for repairing old ships and permitting the arming of merchant vessels, and for building harbor defenses. It also committed itself to raising taxes if war came.

With this as preparation, on March 15 Clay wrote a memo to Secretary of State Monroe.

Sir:

Since I had the pleasure of conversing with you this morning, I have concluded . . . to ask the consideration of the following . . .

That the President recommend an embargo to last, say, thirty days, by a confidential message;

That a termination of the embargo be followed by war. . . .

The embargo period was to be used to get all American ships home and into port.

On March 31, Monroe met with the House Foreign Relations Committee, chaired by Peter Porter, a young-looking New Yorker with a round face and wispy hair that had trouble staying in place. Porter had already told the Congress, "Forbearance has ceased to be a virtue."

During the exchange of comments, South Carolina's freshman Congressman, John C. Calhoun, promised the Secretary that Congress was willing to finance the war. Monroe then agreed to have the President recommend the embargo but added, "The Executive will not take upon itself the responsibility of declaring that we are prepared for war." On the contrary, Monroe explained, the unprepared state of the country made it necessary to delay hostilities. In this Porter agreed with Monroe. More time was needed for preparations, but in spite of that John Calhoun was still impatient.

His feelings did not change when on April 1 the President, still stalling for time, sent a confidential message to the House asking for, not a thirty-day, but a sixty-day embargo. "He reluctantly gives up the system of peace," Calhoun complained.

The President was not alone in his reluctance. The Senate lengthened the sixty days to ninety, and in this form the President signed the bill which he described to Jefferson as "a step toward war."

Before the ink on the bill was dry, Federalist members of Congress, hoping to help their party in the coming local elections, had hired a messenger to race overland warning their constituents to send their ships sailing to escape the coming embargo. That done, they turned their attention to the election of State lawmakers.

In Massachusetts, Governor Elbridge Gerry and the legislature, in their desperation to get a preponderance of Republicans elected, redrew the voting districts, turning one district into a ridiculous shape resembling a salamander. A Boston paper called it a "Gerry-Mander" and published a cartoon which, in addition to the anti-embargo and anti-war sentiments, helped defeat Gerry's bid for reelection for governor. His reaction was to accept the invitation that came from the Congressional caucus to become a candidate for the Vice Presidency.

Evidently his reaching his 68th birthday had not dampened the fierce independence he had displayed as a member of the Continental Congress, as a signer of the Declaration of Independence, as a delegate to the Constitutional Convention, as a member of the United States Congress, and then as his country's diplomatic representative in France. It was this record that made his fellow Republicans offer him as a national candidate in the face of the righteous indignation of Massachusetts voters who later obtained the repeal of the gerrymander Act.

At the time, Grundy of Tennessee, who knew he too would soon have to face the voters, had developed a different device. Since his constituents were strongly anti-Federalist, he explained to Josiah Quincy, "I must abuse you or I shall never get reelected . . . you understand I mean to be friends notwithstanding . . ." Grundy was reelected and remained friends with Quincy. Meanwhile in a caucus meeting the Republicans again nominated Madison to be their presidential candidate. After that they rushed through a resolution directing Speaker Clay to require all absent members to return to the House. It was evident on Capitol Hill that something important was about to happen.

"The Question . . . Is Not Before the House."

As often happened, what was most important was not what seemed so. Randolph had correctly guessed that the President's war message was on the way and he made a desperate attempt to block the inevitable. The attempt resulted in a permanent change in the House rules. It was a change that may have influenced American history more than the war itself.

Rising in the House, he said he had a proposition to submit.

He knew war had not yet been declared, but if it were, he said, "this Government will stand branded to the latest posterity . . . as the panders of French despotism."

Calhoun rose to make a point of order and Randolph temporarily sat down. "The question of war is not before the country," Calhoun insisted, "it is not before the House." He wanted Randolph silenced.

At this point, Clay had vacated the Speaker's chair for a moment, and his substitute found the objection not valid. Randolph had announced that he was going to make a motion, and in the past it had been usual in such cases to permit a wide range of remarks.

Randolph, back on his feet, thanked the gentleman from South Carolina for the respite. He went on to point out that

"This war for commercial rights is to be waged against the express wishes . . . of the great commercial section of the United States."

The truth of his statement made it more aggravating. It was not the New England shipping interests but Southerners like Calhoun and Westerners like Clay who were demanding a fight for "Free Trade and Sailors' Rights."

Calhoun rose again. He asked that "the gentleman from Virginia" be required to submit the proposition he intended to make.

Clay by now had returned and he upheld this demand. "Unquestionably," he said, "the proposition might [even] be required to be submitted in writing." To defend this finding Clay pointed out that it was the duty of the Chair to keep the observations made on the floor relevant to the subject being debated. This duty certainly could not be performed, he argued, unless the Chair knew the nature of the subject.

Calhoun picked up his cue. "I then call upon the gentleman to submit his proposition," he said.

Randolph insinuated that they were afraid to hear him but Clay handled that by merely saying, "The gentleman will please to take his seat . . . his motion must be submitted before further debate."

Randolph did not sit down. He continued: "My proposition is, that it is not expedient at this time to resort to a war against Great Britain."

At that point the Speaker amazed everyone with his question: "Is the motion seconded?"

The recorder was not sure what happened next. He wrote, "Mr. Randolph or some other gentleman expressed surprise that a second . . . should be required [before the motion was explained]."

The Speaker said it was required. In addition, Clay objected that Randolph's motion was not in writing.

Randolph promptly appealed from the decision.

Congressman Charles Goldsborough of Maryland was shocked. His first impulse, he said, was always to support the Chair, but he could not concur in this decision. What was under consideration was a member's right to defend his motion with explanatory remarks. The Maryland Congressman had never known this right to be called into question before. On the contrary, he recollected instances where members had made long speeches of one, two, or three hours prefatory to a motion.

Goldsborough admitted that there were times when the motion was offered for no other reason than to afford an opportunity for a speech but, he said, the House had always acquiesced. The members' privilege was sanctioned by usage. Goldsborough considered the privilege to be essential. "What chance was there . . . of obtaining . . . a vote in favor of a naked proposition unsupported by any elucidation from the mover . . . ?" he objected.

Clay finally put the question: "Is the decision of the Speaker correct?"

The Constitution says that one fifth of those present can demand a roll-call vote forcing the journal to record who calls Yea and who Nay. Now that demand was made and carried out. And when the calls were counted, Clay was upheld 67 yeas to 42 nays.

By that time Randolph had written out his motion and reoffered it. Ceremoniously, Clay read it from the chair, but when Randolph tried to discuss it, he was again called to order. Congressman Nelson pointed out that the House had not agreed to take up his motion. The Speaker also upheld this objection.

Again Randolph appealed, saying: "Has it come to this, that members of this House shall grow grey in the service, and in proportion to their experience become ignorant of the rules of proceeding . . . ?

The Speaker requested the gentleman to confine his remarks to the question of his appeal. Custom, said the Speaker, "gives to the senior members of the House no right to which the juniors are not equally entitled."

At this point, Randolph's friend, former Speaker Macon, rose to explain that while the chair had been wrong and Randolph right on the first point of order, the Speaker was correct on this, and the House must now decide whether to pursue the subject. In deference to his old friend, Randolph withdrew his appeal. The House then voted 37 to 72 (again by roll call) not to consider Randolph's motion.

Clay told the editor of the *National Intelligencer* that two principles were settled by the episode. "The House," he said, "has a right to know . . . the specific motion which a member intends making, before he intends to argue it . . . and [the House] reserves to itself . . . the power of determining whether it shall consider . . . [his motion]"

As to Randolph's motion, Clay felt that the House had been considering his topic (war) all spring, "exciting both passion and alarm," until everyone was exhausted.

As Clay looked back over the session it seemed to him that Randolph had expressed himself more than any other member. At times, Clay admitted, Randolph had been brilliant. The moment had, nevertheless, finally arrived when his fellow lawmakers had made their decision.

As it happened, the members of Congress passed their declaration of war a day after Parliament yielded and repealed the Order in Council. Had the proceedings in Congress been allowed to drag on until the news arrived, the War of 1812 might not have taken place.

This the Congressmen had no way of knowing. They did know, however, that there were now in the chamber Representatives from eighteen States and delegates from five territories. (Along with the Senate they had enacted a bill granting statehood to Louisiana in spite of Quincy's threats that passing the measure would dissolve the Union.) Harrassed by Randolph, and conscious of the ever-increasing number of voices entitled to be heard in the chamber, the members submitted to Clay's increased regulation of their debates. In the years ahead the powers of Congress, as a body, would increase but never again would individual Congressmen enjoy an unlimited and unending opportunity to express their views in the House of Representatives. The House had so decided in its effort to rule itself.

The Seriousness of the Crisis and the Details of the Bill

The world of the War Hawks had much in common with an earlier political era. It was a gathering of anxious men who met in Philadelphia in 1787 and tried to design a Congress with enough vitality to promote the general welfare and provide for the common defense. A quarter of a century later it seemed as if they had only begun the great task.

Never did a majority in Congress have more cause for anxiety than the Republicans during the War of 1812. By the time the Thirteenth Congress met for a special session in May of 1813, they were seeing the war which they had so eagerly started crumble into a disaster. True, there had been a few naval victories, but the British had captured Detroit and defeated the Army at Niagara. The War Department wasn't recruiting anything like the number of volunteers Congress had authorized, and inside the congressional chambers the opposition to the conflict was vocal and growing.

Deprived of their customs receipts by their own embargo and by the enemy's successful blockade, Congress was forced to borrow money. But when George W. Campbell left the Senate early in 1814 to become Secretary of the Treasury, he discovered he could not place half the necessary loans. After that the Treasury lacked the means not only to finance the war but even to meet its day-to-day expenses.

That summer the lawmakers were about to reconvene in a desperate special session, when the British landed. After debarking in Maryland they marched on the capital and triumphantly set the public buildings on fire. Only a few weeks later the arriving Senators and Representatives rode into the nearly gutted city. Small buildings lay in charred ruins. The White House was uninhabitable. The roof on the Representatives' wing of the smoke-stained Capitol had collapsed.

Under the fallen roof of the Capitol, desks, chairs, and library books had been reduced to rubble; and an object of more significance than its size would indicate was also gone. Since the First Congress the Representatives had kept in their chamber the likeness of an eagle with outstretched wings. It perched on a globe which was attached to a pole made of thirteen tiny rods. This was the Mace, a solemn symbol of authority. On entering the chamber one glanced to see if it towered from its highest pedestal. If so, the House was in session. Should the Representatives be meeting more informally in a Committee of the Whole, the eagle would be set on a lower stand. On orders from the Speaker it could be snatched up by the Sergeant at Arms and "presented" before an unruly member to remind him where he was.

The loss of their library books and the destruction of their Mace did not escape the notice of the angry Representatives when they assembled in the overcrowded hall of the Patent Office Building, arguing bitterly whether to quit the city. Clay was away at Ghent, acting as one of the peace negotiators. The Speaker was Langdon Cheves. It was Cheves, wearing his thin-rimmed spectacles, who presided over the disgruntled members while private citizens set to work to build a temporary brick Capitol. It would be the end of 1815 before Congress could occupy this structure. By then Latrobe would be renovating the wrecked House and Senate chambers with sandstone, marble, brick and metal. When Latrobe resigned, architect Charles Bulfinch continued the work. There was so much to be done that it would be 1819 before the Congressmen were back in their own quarters. They had by then acquired Jefferson's library to replace their own.

In the interim the legislative process had to continue and the Congressmen did their best to conduct their business in what quarters they had, using a wooden replica of the Mace.

However, their familiar routine could not mask the threat of national bankruptcy. The empty treasury and the chaotic state of the currency remained. The young war hawks were eager to expand the legislative authority to cope with the nation's problems.

The crisis thus stimulated another episode in the evolution of Congress. Goaded by their young leaders and not knowing how else to ward off complete financial catastrophe, once-reluctant statesmen agreed to reconsider letting Congress charter a bank. Eppes and Clopton of Virginia still felt that the scheme was unconstitutional, but others were at last converted. Congress, they decided, was entitled to charter the bank because the bank seemed necessary to carry out the Government's functions. This was also the view taken in urgent pleas by the Secretary of the Treasury, Alexander Dallas. Moreover, Dallas' convictions had been known before he was confirmed by the Senate.

In October, 1814, the matter was before the House. At this point in the middle of a war, with the country's survival at stake, it became evident that having the majority agree to establish a bank and having the majority agree on the details of a bank bill were two altogether different matters.

Calhoun persisted in getting the Treasury bill so amended in the Committee of the Whole that it no longer resembled what Dallas wanted. With the friends of the bank thus divided, the bank bill was sent back to committee. The committee members then failed to agree among themselves.

That did not change the fact that forming the bank was the only visible way of continuing the war effort. Moreover, as Grosvenor had pointed out, it was not simply a question of arranging for loans with which to pay soldiers, but of devising a workable system. If the Government was to meet its obligations it would have to have a reliable currency and one that could easily be transported. Local bank notes were nearly useless wherever the bank that issued them was unknown, and it was impractical to drag gold long distances over the bad roads.

To other Representatives it was at least as essential that Congress end the humiliations heaped on the Government whenever it tried to pry money out of the nation's few rich men. Many of these financiers lived in New England, where even State Governors refused to support the war fully. Their local papers encouraged their opposition. Readers were subjected to repeated references to the words Jefferson and Madison had drafted from behind the scenes to go into the Virginia and Kentucky resolutions at the time of the Alien and Sedition Acts.

The Constitution, they said, is a "compact" between the separate States. Jefferson had Breckinridge tell the Kentuckians, "[E]ach party has an equal right to judge for itself [what are] infractions . . ."

Madison's friend John Taylor told the Virginians, "[I]n the case of a deliberate, palpable, and dangerous, exercise of . . . powers not granted. . . , the States . . . have the right . . . to interpose." Both Kentucky and Virginia had called on the other States to join them in declaring the Alien and Sedition Acts unconstitutional. Possibly because of Madison's restraining hand, what other "proper measures" could be taken were left indefinite. But sister States relied on the Supreme Court to void improper laws and rejected the compact of States' Rights theory. Nevertheless, there was little doubt in the minds of the Congressmen why now, a decade and a half later, the resolutions were again being quoted. Extremists in New England were fanning the flames of disunion.

In December delegates from five States, chosen in three instances by their legislatures, were meeting in secret session in the Hartford State House. Their grievances, their mutual defense, (which the federal Government seemed unable to provide) and their proposals for modifying the United States Constitution were all being aired.

The very existence of such a meeting, whose outcome was as yet unknown, added to the tensions inside the halls of Congress as the new year approached and still no generally accepted plan for the bank had been found.

Randolph was temporarily gone, having been beaten for reelection, but Calhoun soon found himself dealing with a massive advocate with a deep brow and a firm stance. He was a sophisticated Federalist from New Hampshire who had been in the House only a year and a half. His name was Daniel Webster. In the past, Webster had mocked the majority for being "moved by wires," like puppets on a stage. He was uncomfortably conscious of both their caucus meetings and the party discipline imposed by Clay's men. "No Saint in the calendar," Webster complained, "ever had a set of followers less at liberty, or less disposed to indulge in troublesome inquiry . . ." Decisions, he concluded, were thus made somewhere other than in the Representatives' chamber, and the legislative process had thereby become a "farce."

Now he took advantage of this contention's being, for the moment at least, anything but true: he plunged into the debate, conceding nothing to Calhoun or the administration except that a bank formed on proper principles would be good for the nation. He opposed the plan to allow the President to appoint five of the bank's directors, since to be useful the bank would have to be independent. He objected also to what he considered was the impossibly large sum the bank was expected to lend the Government.

Once again the debate reached a climax. When the question was put, 81 were for the bill, 80 were against it. This time the Speaker, Cheves, demanded his right to add his vote. He cast his ballot to tie the vote, and by so doing defeated the measure. Badly shaken, it was said, Calhoun crossed the floor and tearfully begged Webster to help him draft a new bill.

To this the younger man consented, but nevertheless the situation had become more desperate than before. The rules forbade any further consideration for the rest of the session of of a bill that had been defeated. There was one thing that could be done, and Hall of Georgia took the initiative. He moved to have the House reconsider its vote. When the question was again put: "Shall the bill pass?" Kentucky's Samuel McKee rose to the rescue He moved to recommit the bill. In the committee another attempt could be made to devise an acceptable measure. To this the Representatives agreed.

Shortly thereafter the House and Senate did agree on the details of a plan, but the President decided that they had made the bank's authorized grant to the Government too small. He vetoed the Act and the work had to begin again.

This was how matters stood on February 14, 1815, when a message arrived from New York carrying a proposal of peace from Ghent. Three days later, the Senate ratified the treaty ending the war, and with it the war-nurtured threat of disunion. The members of Congress were not only greatly relieved, they were numb with exhaustion. They wearily adjourned March 3.

As far as the leading War Hawks were concerned, their joy at the war's end was at least equalled by their determination. If they could help it, this nation would never again be so weak. Never again should Congress have to struggle in the middle of war to design and create its source of economic support.

Calhoun would one day be called the great nullifier and fanatic sectionalist, but at this moment he was so filled with nationalism that he would soon join with Clay in wanting a protective tariff. Home-made products need not be imported through a blockade in time of war. Domestic producers could help pay for defense. Still disturbed by the nation's military failures, Calhoun blamed them in part on the country's financial problems. With this weighing on his mind, he once again sponsored a bank bill.

This time he made concessions on the details of the bill. According to the new bill, the Government's creditors could use their notes to pay partially for their bank stock. The bank's capital had been reduced to $35,000,000. The President was still to appoint five of its directors, but the bank was freed from making the staggering loan originally contemplated. Instead, it was to pay the Government a $1,500,000 bonus in three installments, spread out over four years.

In this form the measure passed and became law in April of 1816. A little later, in 1819, under the leadership of Langdon Cheves, the bank would provide a safe, convenient currency and greatly benefit commerce, justifying all the struggles to agree on a bill. Nevertheless, before it even opened its doors, the bank was attacked as a symbol of that philosophy of government that advocated expanding the might and authority of Congress—this when Clay, who was now back in the Speakership, had plans that relied on stretching congressional might and authority as far as it would stretch. In fact, the voices of his Republican followers would have sounded strangely familiar to Alexander Hamilton. There were two big differences between their "nationalism" and his. First, they firmly intended to keep control of the Congress, the Government, and the budget in the hands of the members of Congress. Also, the new nationalists were led, not by an intellectual, such as Hamilton appeared to be, but by Clay, a warm, colorful, and ingratiating orator.

"Our Rightful Control Over the Public Purse"

There was one part of their program in which Clay's followers did not meet as much openly avowed Executive opposition as they might have expected.

Earlier, the Representatives had adopted a suggestion made by Eppes to control Executive spending more closely and at the same time relieve the overworked Ways and Means Committee. They had set up a Committee on Public Expenditures.

Now two years later in 1816 they set up six standing committees on expenditures. The members were to look into the account books and study the vouchers of whatever Government department was placed under their surveillance. The Departments of War, Navy, Treasury, and the Post Office, and the management of the public buildings, were each checked by a different committee.

"Not a cent of money ought to be applied but by our direction, and under our control," Calhoun told his colleagues. They found this easier to believe than to enforce. In 1817, it became evident that somehow a barracks and a military road had been financed without their consent. Congressman McKee of Kentucky went so far as to suggest that to try to correct this type of abuse of Executive discretion was hopeless.

Calhoun disagreed and had several recommendations to make. First, appropriation laws should be written in more detail. In addition, the records showing expenditures should cover the same calendar period. He regretted that appropriations were made from January to January and expense records from October to October, making it nearly impossible for Congressmen to compare the records. Most of all, he wanted to abolish the President's limited right to transfer funds from one branch of a department to another at times when Congress was not in session. In the warmth of his outrage he made the exaggerated claim that this amounted to the right to dispense with appropriations.

At first the Congressmen seemed too involved in other struggles to act in this area, but then later, after Calhoun had left the House to serve in the cabinet, an incident took place which aroused their interest in his point of view.

What happened was this: Congress had passed an act empowering the President to use the Navy to sweep the seas clear of vessels engaged in piracy or in the now illegal importation of slaves. However, it had not given the Commander-in-Chief an increased naval appropriation with which to do the job.

While discussing the situation in the House Samuel Smith of Maryland, Chairman of the Ways and Means Committee, had the clerk read a letter from the Secretary of the Navy. The Secretary made an allusion to "a warrant of transfer," which caught the attention of Henry Storrs of New York. The transferred money apparently had come from a very old appropriation, and the New Yorker was under the impression that any such unexpended balance in the Treasury was to go after two years to the surplus fund. Storrs asked the Chairman about this, and a very interesting practice came to light.

The War and Navy Departments consistently saw to it that there were no extra funds being held in their accounts.

To accomplish this, they withdrew their appropriations from the Treasury and, as the law permitted, deposited the sums with the Treasurer of the United States. The Treasurer then acted as if he were the private banker, or agent, for the departments. As such, he took the position that once a sum was drawn and in his hands it no longer had to be returned to surplus, even after its authorized purpose had been achieved. Here was money the Executive could spend without appropriation from Congress.

When Smith insisted that the practice was no secret, Clay took offense. He protested against Smith's conclusion that because Congressmen had been silent on the subject they had assented to the practice. "Perhaps not ten members of this whole body knew of it," he said, He hoped the proper committee would hasten to lay before the House a bill to prohibit the practice for the future and maintain "our rightful control over the public purse . . ."

In spite of Clay's indignation, there was one clue to what had been happening that might have alerted the House members. Storrs brought it to everyone's attention, "If gentlemen will examine," he said, "they will find that . . . for several years past . . . the surplus fund . . . has been scarcely an item." He then noted that the Representatives were unfortunately unaware of how much of each appropriation was left over, and therefore what might have gone into the surplus fund.

He reiterated the point Calhoun had made earlier: A new law was needed to make the expense accounts rendered to Congress cover the same period as did the appropriations passed by Congress, so that the figures could be compared more easily.

It was not insignificant that when Storrs spoke the country was in the grip of a terrible postwar depression. Congressmen wanted to spare the pocketbooks of their constituents. Being able to study the Executive's accounts was almost a prerequisite to being able to cut them.

Meanwhile, a more lasting restraint over the departments was enacted in 1820. Secretary of War Calhoun may have grimaced when he realized that the act's stringent intent was based on his own recommendations. Spurred on by Clay, the Congress enacted that:

> . . . [I]t shall be the duty of the Secretary of the Treasury, to cause to be carried to the account of the surplus fund any moneys appropriated for the Departments of War, or of the Navy, which may remain unexpended in the Treasury, or in the hands of the Treasurer, or agent . . . whenever . . . the object for which the appropriation was made has been effected . . .

The same instruction was then reworded to apply to leftover moneys held by the Secretaries of the two departments.

Financial statements from the departments were now made due on the first of February and were to cover all the previous year. Moreover, no money was to be deemed subject to transfer once it had been drawn from the Treasury and placed in the hands of the Treasurer. The practice of having the Treasurer act as a department's agent was outlawed in 1822. Evidently the Chief Executive conceded the wisdom of these rules, for President Monroe signed them into law.

Congress had once more tightened its hold on executive spending, and this was not the last time it would grasp the nation's purse strings with renewed firmness.

Act, or the Power Is Gone Forever

A power struggle between the Congress and the Chief Executive had started shortly after the war and revolved around the question of how much authority Congress possessed under the Constitution. To Clay and many of the others it was self-evident that both domestic commerce and military security necessitated a system of roads and canals. The war, they thought, had demonstrated the dangers of being without highways when food, munitions or reinforcements had to be rushed to a regiment's rescue.

As early as December of 1816, Calhoun had suggested that a committee be appointed to consider putting the annual bonus, which the law required the new national bank to pay the Government, into a fund to build roads and canals and to improve waterways. The Committee was appointed with Calhoun as its Chairman. In February, 1817, he introduced the Committee's bill, saying, "Let us then bind the Republic together with a perfect system of roads and canals. Let us conquer space."

The friends of the proposal had every reason to be confident. A succession of Presidents had admitted the need for internal improvements. Jefferson had spoken of using Federal funds for education and for roads. Of course, both he and Madison had suggested the need for a constitutional amendment to give Congress the authority to undertake such projects, but Calhoun brushed this aside. He said he was no advocate for refined arguments on the Constitution. "The instrument . . . ought to be construed with plain good sense."

Congress, he remembered, had the power to collect taxes and to provide for the common defense and the general welfare of the United States. Providing funds to build roads and canals was both a defense and a welfare measure, according to his reasoning.

As soon as Calhoun finished and sat down, Clay made a point of thanking him for his proposal. No subject was dearer to the Kentuckian's heart but, in spite of the Speaker's support, not everyone in the Chamber would accept Calhoun's broad interpretation of the Constitution.

To many the references, in the beginning of Article VIII of the Constitution, to "general welfare" and to "common defense" were merely an announcement of aims or goals. The powers that Congress might use to pursue these goals were carefully enumerated in the succeeding paragraphs. The right to build roads inside the sovereign States was not included. The most that Congress could do was to designate a particular existing road to be a post road.

Gold of New York was disgusted. "When shall we have any principle settled and at rest in this Government?" he asked. He went on to insist that "Improved roads may . . . enliven industry and mitigate the pressure of war."

It was obvious to him that they were proper subjects for Congressional action. It had been so decided years ago, he told the Speaker. Congress had been given full power over both defense and commerce among the States.

While he talked, others were remembering that while Jefferson was in the White House Congress had approved the route for the Cumberland Road. Reviewing old decisions had helped to dispel the constitutional scruples of anxious Representatives when the bank was the issue. Several Representatives tried that technique again. This time it did not work.

Not everyone conceded that the history of the Cumberland

Road was a relevant precedent. That road had been the result of a compact Congress made when Ohio was admitted into the Union. The money for the project came from land sales. Besides, there were men in Congress who said that the building of the road had been unconstitutional and they saw no reason to repeat the error.

Mr. Madison, in his last message to Congress, while asking for a comprehensive system of roads and canals, had admonished the lawmakers to resort "to the prescribed method" of enlarging their powers. Even moderately careful readers could have understood that the President still thought an amendment necessary. Yet Clay and Calhoun, perhaps because they were so accustomed to persuading Madison to adopt their recommendations, were utterly unprepared for what happened to their bill. "[N]ot even an earthquake," Clay said, "could have excited more surprise than when it was first communicated to this House."

One day before he was to leave office and the congressional session was to end, Mr. Madison reasserted the power of the Chief Executive by vetoing the bill. His message read as if he was being haunted by the delegates at the ratifying conventions. To accept Clay and Calhoun's view of the general welfare clause in the Constitution, he explained, would render nugatory the careful enumeration of the powers of Congress. It would give to Congress a general power of legislation, instead of the defined and limited one the ratifiers had understood. This Madison would not allow.

Clay made a desperate effort to pressure the House into overriding the veto. Not only did he vote on the question "Shall the bill be reenacted over the President's objection?" but he voted first, before any of the other Representative's names were called by the clerk. Sixty loyal members voted with the Speaker, but that was barely more than half of the men gathered in the chamber. Lacking a two-thirds majority of those attending the House, the revolt failed and the veto stood.

Clay was even more exasperated with the next President. Mr. Monroe did not wait for an act of Congress. He announced at the beginning of the Fifteenth Congress that he fully agreed with his predecessor, that Congress lacked the authority it was trying to assert.

Clay fumed. The usual procedure was for the President to wait until he saw a bill that had passed both Houses before he commented on it. The Speaker could not condone this tactic of anticipating legislation "and telling us what we may or may not do . . . I have no doubt but that the President was actuated by the purest motives . . . [However] the proceeding is irregular and unconstitutional," he told the House. "[M]oreover . . . the question is now a question between the Executive on the one side, and the Representatives of the people on the other."

The President's assertiveness was only a part of what engrossed Clay. From the Speaker's chair it looked as if an avalanche was descending to bury Congressional effectiveness. Even though Calhoun had written into last year's bill a clause requiring all the work on internal improvements done inside a State to have the assent of that State, there were those who considered the program an intrusion. Clay begged the Representatives "to examine this doctrine of State rights, and see to what abusive, if not dangerous consequences, it may lead." Even as he spoke, financiers in Maryland were contesting the right of Congress to charter the new United States Bank.

Clay conceded that by assuming unwarranted power, the legislature could menace the spirit of the Constitution. It had done so by passing the Alien and Sedition Acts. To this admission, he quickly added his warning that "the general Government may relapse into the debility which existed in the old confederation and finally dissolve . . ." To head off a repetition of the same old failures, Clay in March of 1818 had a campaign under way to uphold the powers of the legislative branch.

"If we do nothing this session but pass an abstract resolution on the subject, I shall consider it a triumph . . . we will assert, uphold and maintain, the authority of Congress," he told the House.

The abstract resolution Clay wanted was a declaration that Congress had the power under the Constitution to make appropriations for building roads and canals. What, he argued, was the Constitution intended to accomplish if not to strengthen the Union? "[U]nion and peace were the great objects of the framers . . ."

To strengthen the Union, Congress must claim its powers

immediately, before the sentiments uttered by three Presidents became irrevocable tradition. Act! Clay insisted, "or the power is gone—gone forever." In regard to the practicality of obtaining a constitutional amendment, Clay thought it out of the question. Undoubtedly he sensed that the States were in no mood to enlarge the powers of Congress again. If this was true, it would be disastrous to beg them for the authority to build roads and thus admit that Congress did not already possess the power. If the resolution now before the House asserting this authority should fail to pass, Clay admitted, "I confess, I utterly despair."

After long debate, Clay's followers carried their point. The House declared "that Congress have power, under Constitution, to appropriate money for the construction of post roads, military and other roads, and of canals, and for the improvement of water courses." The force of the declaration was doubtful, and it did not end the controversy, but it gave the Speaker's side an official pronouncement that they could quote to rebut the Executive's declarations.

The View from the Window
of the Department of State

While Clay continued to watch over Congressional activities from the Speaker's chair, former Senator John Quincy Adams scrutinized them equally keenly from his office as Secretary of State. Inevitably, from there the view was different. For example, Clay's dramatic campaign to maintain the rights and independence of Congress seemed to Adams like so much oratory to justify the Speaker's will to dominate.

"Clay's project," he said in his diary, "is that in which Randolph failed: to control . . . the Executive by swaying the House of Representatives."

Understandably, there were times when the Secretary found the Speaker's conduct exasperating. For instance, while Adams was in the process of trying to acquire Florida by negotiating with Spain, Clay was in the process of building support in Congress for recognizing the independence of Spain's rebelling South American provinces. In the House he drew verbal pictures of millions of people struggling "to burst their chains and be free." He wanted Congress to repeal the laws that kept the United States neutral. He claimed that "we should recognize any established government in Spanish America."

Hearing all this, Adams trembled for his negotiations.

Then, without a request from the Executive, Clay, in March of 1818, proposed that Congress appropriate $18,000 to pay the salary of a minister to one of the insurgent republics and in this way grant it recognition. Clay's own friend, John Forsyth of Georgia, told him that the proposal went too far in trying to "stimulate" the Executive.

For the time being, Clay was without sufficient support to win the appropriation, but Adams was too well aware of the Speaker's powers over other men to rest reassured. He conceded that Clay's influence was due in part to a "sort of generosity which attracts individuals," but he was equally conscious of less likeable attributes in the Speaker. Adams considered Clay ambitious, impatient, loose-moraled and half-educated. Futhermore, Adams resented Clay's deliberate drive to sabotage the relationships the Executive cultivated with other members of the legislature.

It happened that Adams had edited the remarks Representative Henry Middleton had used in explaining to the House the need for action to oust marauders from Amelia Island on the Florida coast. Middleton had requested the Secretary's assistance, and Adams saw nothing wrong with this combining of the executive and the legislative functions. He could recall when as a United States Senator, he had asked Albert Gallatin to look over a bill. Clay, however, was of quite a different frame of mind.

The Speaker dubbed Mr. Middleton an incapable chairman who, instead of submitting his own report, had delivered a message to the House that came directly from the same inkstand as the Executive's papers.

Adams' reaction to Clay's "rancor" was to insist to his diary that "this [type of consultation] had been a common practice between the chairmen of committees and heads of Departments ever since the existence of the Government."

In this the Secretary had the President's concurrence. Monroe had already instructed Adams to send for John Forsyth, Chairman of the Committee on Foreign Relations, and to communicate with him freely upon the posture of our foreign affairs.

From then on Adams noted that Clay goaded Forsyth, chiding him not to be a tool of the administration. Adams feared that the mild, amiable Georgian would not be able to withstand Clay's pressure. Therefore, when Forsyth hinted that he would soon propose a measure hostile to Spain, and this measure turned out to be a resolution to seize Florida, it seemed to Adams like a reckless move to manifest the Chairman's independence. Adams had to be grateful when Secretary of the Treasury, William H. Crawford, brought the news that Forsyth's committee was not going to support this aggressive policy to pressure the administration.

Normally Adams resented Crawford. It irked Adams to hear him boast that he drew up bills for committees, who presented them exactly as he drew them. Furthermore, Crawford was at least as ambitious as Clay. Both wanted to be President.

Adams recorded of Crawford, "I do not think him entirely unprincipled, but his ambition swallows up his principles." Then Adams blamed Crawford's behavior in part on the caucus system whereby members of Congress met to select a presidential candidate. As Adams analyzed the situation, the only possible way for a department head to obtain the Presidency "is by ingratiating himself personally with members of Congress." He had no doubt that this was what Crawford intended. What bothered Adams was that the members of Congress being wooed by the would-be candidates had "objects of their own to obtain." These included patronage jobs, either for themselves or for friends or supporters.

The temptation to form corrupt coalitions was immense. Adams, moreover, was convinced that both Clay and Crawford considered that their prospects depended on the failure of the current administration. It was with this conviction in mind that Secretary of State Adams evaluated the drive in Congress to censure General Jackson.

The General, acting on vague orders that permitted him to suppress Indian riots, had court-martialed and executed two British subjects for inciting the Indians and had captured two Spanish posts and a fortress.

Shock reverberated not only from the military committee reporting on the issue to the House, but also from the Seminole War Committee, which reported to the Senate.

Senator Lacock of Pennsylvania called the General's actions as unconstitutional as they were impolitic. In the House, Chairman Thomas M. Nelson insisted that the military had no jurisdiction to try the British civilians. He offered a resolution that the House disapprove the proceedings. Simultaneously, he explained that his committee had withheld comment on the bombardment and capture of the Spanish posts because negotiations with Spain were in progress. Nevertheless, there were many who felt his committee had not gone far enough. The Constitution gave to Congress the sole power to declare war. Jackson had usurped that power.

For two reasons—in order to let the Speaker participate in the debate, and in order to permit the broadest possible discussion of the issues—the House referred the report of its military committee to a Committee of the Whole on the state of the Union.

Clay quickly took advantage of his right to the floor. Caesar and Napoleon, he warned, had both overturned the people's liberties. He did not accuse Jackson of similar ambition, but he thought a precedent was at issue. If Jackson were to be praised and not censured, as some gentlemen had proposed, it would be a triumph of the military over the civil authority—a triumph over the powers of the House.

While Clay's words filled the air, Adams was trying to convince the Spanish diplomats that Jackson's campaign was justified as a "defensive" measure. It was, he charged, necessitated by Spain's failure to carry out her treaty obligations to police the savages.

At this point Forsyth, who earlier had helped the administration in the House, was now in the Senate. He had been told that he would be nominated by the President as minister to Spain. Adams, consequently, marveled at the imprudence with which the Georgian supported the attacks on Jackson against the interests of the Executive. A formal resolution of censure did not pass, in spite of Clay, but that was not owing to any effort by Senator Forsyth. When Adams finally obtained a treaty ceding Florida to the United States in 1819, he felt that he had achieved it in the face of formidable and avoidable obstacles. For these obstacles he blamed both Clay and Crawford.

Clay's opposition to the administration was less obnoxious than Crawford's, simply because the Speaker was not a part of the Executive's cabinet. There were even times when Adams reluctantly conceded that the Speaker's program of stimulating the Executive had brought results.

"Mr. Clay," he noted in his diary, "having attempted to raise an opposition party . . . favorable to the South Americans, and having insinuated that Mr. Monroe's administration was partial against the South Americans, the President has thought it necessary to counteract this party maneuvering . . . by professions of favor to them . . ."

As a result, in February of 1821, the House passed a resolution giving support to the President if he should decide to recognize the new Latin America States: and in 1822, Clay's view point finally prevailed. The President, with congressional support, sent diplomatic missions to Latin America.

Apart from all this, there was the matter of internal improvements. In this area also, Clay's persistence was having an effect. It was true that Monroe vetoed a bill to repair the Cumberland Road. The President objected particularly to the toll gates called for in the measure. Congress could not, as the President saw it, enforce the collection of tolls without encroaching on the police power of the States. At the same time, he publicly conceded that Congress had "an unlimited power to raise money" and to appropriate it for purposes of national (not local) benefit.

Here was a major concession to the friends of a more effective Congress. It was another victory for Congress as well as for Clay.

At times, then, Clay did succeed in bringing the influence of the House to bear on the Executive. His power, however, was never absolute and never free from competition, including the competition from heads of departments who were willing to help write legislation.

In Court

Meanwhile the advocates of a more effective Congress realized a great victory that was not decided in either the Senate or House chamber.

In March of 1819, Daniel Webster won a gigantic lawsuit before the Supreme Court: *McCulloch v. Maryland.* The attempts of Maryland officials to tax the United States Bank, combined with their claim that Congress had never had the power to incorporate the monster institution in the first place, finally came before the Justices. Relying heavily on Webster's brief, the Court ruled that Congress could use any legal means it wished to carry out its stated powers. "The power of creating a corporation," said Chief Justice Marshall, "is not . . . a great . . . independent power . . . but a means by which other objects are accomplished." Thus Congress had every right to incorporate the U.S. Bank.

Marshall then went further. In defense of Maryland's bank tax, the State's attorney general had referred to the theory that the Constitution was a compact between the States. The Court simultaneously rejected both the compact theory and the State's claimed right to tax Federal property.

First, the Court said, the power to tax involves the power to destroy. The States could not thus regulate or destroy the acts of Congress. On the contrary; "The nation, on those subjects on which it can act, must necessarily bind its component parts."

Furthermore, the Government of the Union was most emphatically not a compact between states but a government of the people. The Constitution said, "We the People . . . establish this Constitution . . ." The States had merely consented to call and abide by the ratifying conventions. In those conventions the representatives of the people had adopted the document and decided that "This Constitution and the laws of the United States which shall be made in pursuance thereof . . . shall be the supreme law of the land."

In short, it was the prerogative of Congress to pass laws in the name of "we the people" which the States as fractions of the Union could not counteract.

Here then was the Court's pronouncement of the powers of Congress over the nation and the relationship of the States to the Union. This mighty judicial pronouncement with its ring of finality might have ended the compact theory had it not been for another shattering development. A course of events that was to change the future of Congress had begun before the Court ruled.

"Missouri Compromise"

On a quiet Friday in December, the Speaker presented a memorial from the Legislative Council and House of Representatives of the Territory of Missouri . . . "praying that they may be permitted to form a Constitution . . . and be admitted into the Union on equal footing with the original States." At the time, the matter was referred to an appropriate committee without apprehension.

Two months later, in February of 1819, an enabling act to admit Missouri was before the House. On the 13th, Congressman James Tallmadge of New York rose to offer his famous amendment. He wanted to forbid the importation of slaves into the new State and to provide that all children born in Missouri after its admission be free at age twenty-five. In spite of Clay, who argued vehemently against "conditional admission," the Tallmadge amendment passed the House. The Senate promptly removed it from the act. When the session ended, neither chamber had made any concessions to the other. Missouri had not been admitted, and the Congress had changed.

Both Congress and the nation were rent by violent sectional differences. Memorials flowed in from State legislatures and town meetings. The Northerners claimed that Congress had the authority to block the extension of slavery into a new State and Southerners loudly contested the proposition. One elderly politician referred to this battle as "the new state of parties" in Congress.

The House, he noted, had a preponderance of antislave men, but the Senators represented eleven slave and eleven free States. Any new admission could tip the balance either way. Faced with these facts the Sixteenth Congress braced itself for a bitter controversy.

Watching, Secretary Adams bemoaned the fact that in both Houses the talented speakers, with the lone exception of old Rufus King, came from the South. King himself wrote home to New York, "The North wants force. . . ." Incessant predictions of an end to the Union did not frighten King. He saw no more reason to make concessions to the South than to be distracted by the throngs of zealous lady visitors who came into the chamber and even onto the floor in such numbers that every available seat and sofa disappeared under a mass of full skirts.

In the House Randolph shook his finger and in his high pitched voice screeched that the women were "out of place." He was in a foul mood and admitted that he considered it the greatest misfortune to be born the master of slaves, but he loudly insisted he would tolerate no interference with the practice on the part of the Federal Government.

His rigid stance was reinforced by Howell Cobb of Georgia. Perhaps the climax in the controversy came for Clay during an awful night session that he vividly recalled in later years. The Representatives were working under difficult conditions. The scarlet curtains that hung behind the marble pillars merely muffled the annoying echoes heard during debate. It was no wonder the air was stale. Candles were placed all around the crowded chamber as well as in the chandelier, and in addition, fires burned in four hearths. A man fainted, and Clay, who had rushed to investigate, was returning to the Chair when he was stopped in the aisle by Randolph. "Mr. Speaker," Randolph said, "I wish you would leave Congress. . . . I will follow you."

The remark emphasized what Clay already knew. There had been talk among the Southern members of quitting Congress and leaving it in the possession of the North. It was almost impossible to reason with Randolph. Before the long "Misery debate" ended, Clay was exhausted both in mind and body, and still all the rest of the session's business lay ahead. It was not beside the point that the House at that time adopted another change in its procedures.

Formerly matters had always been considered in the order in which they had been entered on the docket, or calendar. Now, following a motion from the floor, some scheduled proceedings were to be postponed to make way for others. Smith had pointed out that certain appropriations were now pressing matters. The order of business had to be rearranged to meet the emergency. When the Sixteenth Congress agreed, it was fashioning a powerful new legislative weapon. Later political leaders would decide when, if ever, certain specific matters were to be considered. So armed, they could and would change the course of events.

Meanwhile, a compromise measure came from the Senate. Missouri was to be admitted as a slave State, but slavery was to be forbidden in the rest of the Louisiana territory. This part of the proposal had been designed by Senator J. B. Thomas of Illinois. Also tied to the bill was the admission of Maine. Maine was to be a free State, but escaping slaves caught within its borders were to be returned to their masters. King called the bill "the fruit of Northern cowardice." Benton of Missouri called it "an immense concession to the non-slave-holding States." Both sides felt they had capitulated.

Clay wrote to a friend: "I gave my consent . . . and employed my best exertions to produce this settlement. . . ." Congress had changed and Clay had changed. Clay, the war hawk, had become Clay the compromiser.

On hearing the proposal, a number of Representatives loudly objected to the "omnibus" technique of lumping the admissions of Maine and Missouri in the same bill. To deal with all the objections and to break the deadlock between Senators and Representatives, a joint conference committee was appointed. It recommended that the Senate proposal be divided in two and passed. The exhausted House so acted.

If any of the members sighed with relief and thought they had at last heard the end of the Missouri matter, they were to be sadly disappointed. There was more to the problem, as they would learn in their next session.

The Second Session

The Missouri Compromise was finally passed in March, and it was mid-May before Congress finished the rest of its business and adjourned. Before the next session began, Clay decided to remain a Representative but resign his Speakership. After writing his resignation, he delayed his return to the Capitol.

The Clerk called the second session of the Sixteenth Congress to order, and the divided House faced the task of electing a new Speaker. John W. Taylor of New York was an eager candidate, but he had been prominent in the fight to restrict slavery. Needless to say, the Southerners did not want him. Running against him, in addition to Smith of Maryland, was Lowndes of South Carolina. Lowndes was a slaveholder, but he was also an acknowledged leader whose quiet manner had inspired the affectionate confidence of the entire House.

It took two days and twenty-two ballots to decide the contest. Taylor did at last carry the House, but the long-drawn-out contest demonstrated how truthfully Adams had called the Missouri issue "a flaming sword . . . that cuts in every direction."

The flames from this sword were still crackling when the House and Senate met to open ballots and declare Monroe the reelected President.

There was an uproar when Congressman Livermore of New Hampshire challenged the counting of Missouri's electoral vote. Since Congress had not yet approved her constitution, he claimed, Missouri's admission to the Union was not complete.

As Monroe's victory was almost unanimous, the hubbub was nothing more than a maneuver in the Missouri controversy.

The North was outraged because Missouri's constitution excluded free blacks from the State. King called the clause a violation of the United States Constitution. Certainly, citizens from any State were entitled to their citizenship privileges in all the other States. Listening Southerners felt that they were being attacked, and the whole Congress seemed about to explode.

Nothing had narrowed the breach when Clay urged the formation of a special joint Senate-House Committee. Joint committees had been used before to plan ceremonies and to formulate mutual rules. This time the joint committee was formed to solve a problem, and moreover, it was to put the weight of its prestige behind getting its recommendation accepted.

Clay himself drew up the list of names of members he wanted appointed. He then called on the committee members and used his influence to instill in them a spirit of conciliation. King was disgusted, but the strategy worked. The joint committee recommended, and Congress decided, that Missouri should be admitted if she would agree not to pass legislation designed to enforce the offensive clause denying citizens from other States their proper rights.

Thus ended a struggle that had convulsed the Congress for three sessions. It was over, but so was the good feeling that had followed the war of 1812. The North had won time to build strength, but the evolution of Congress had suffered a terrible setback. In the Congresses to come, men would look at even the bank question with a changed viewpoint. If Congress had implied powers to do anything that might be called a "means" to carrying out its stated powers, it could now claim that an act of emancipation was only a "means" to some great goal. So thought some men who had once been nationalists. Henceforth they would be more concerned with their States' rights.

The Men of Congress and the
Next Campaign

The hectic stirrings of the next Presidential contest had started in Congress as soon as the members announced the election of James Monroe. From then on, for almost four years, the candidates' rivalry shaped the course of Congressional events. For one thing, Taylor of New York was replaced as Speaker by Philip Barbour of Virginia. The Crawford forces hailed this as a victory. Two years later, they were less happily agitated when Clay, who was also a presidential candidate, won back the chair.

Looking out over the chamber, Clay could see that two former members, Webster and Forsyth, had returned to the House. Besides these senior statesmen there was a comparative newcomer from Lancaster, Pennsylvania. James Buchanan.

After being elected as a Federalist, Buchanan had arrived to take his seat in December of 1821. Not yet thirty and very eager, he had commanded the floor three times before the middle of January. His views were his own, but his autobiography reveals that he was awed and possibly guided by Lowndes of South Carolina. Thus Buchanan was alert when Lowndes' old friend Calhoun needed a spokesman in Congress.

Calhoun's War Department budget had been mercilessly slashed the year before. His funds were now virtually exhausted and the Secretary had written a desperate letter to Samuel Smith of Maryland, Chairman of the Ways and Means Committee. Smith was having trouble inducing the House members even to so much as consider the emergency.

By that time it was obvious that Lowndes was too debilitated from rheumatic fever to fight for Calhoun. Lowndes had not taken his seat until the end of December, and his tall frame was so stooped and feeble that Buchanan guessed his death was not far off. Thus it happened that Buchanan took the floor to fight for a deficiency appropriation that would allow Secretary Calhoun to pay the overdue bills of the Indian Bureau.

Buchanan was well aware, but had no intention of saying, that these attacks on the Secretary were partly inspired by the coming presidential race. While bad times had caused a falling off of revenue and a spirit of economy in Congress, it was also true that Calhoun was a possible presidential candidate. Instead of dwelling on that, Buchanan gave voice to a maxim of his own to guide the members in their efforts to control Executive spending. As a lawyer, he felt compelled to insist that "an officer of your Government, high in the confidence of the people, shall be presumed to have done his duty until the reverse of the proposition is proved."

If Congressman Buchanan thought this point should have been self-evident to legislators who claimed to be implementing the Constitution, he was too tactful to say so. Modestly he asked them if they were not being rash in asking the Indian Bureau suddenly to cut its expenses in half. To do this, he said, the Secretary would have to assume the functions of Congress. He would have to decree which of the Bureau's legal obligations were to be performed. Congressmen were thus forcing the Executive to alter the law. They were, in fact, destroying their own prerogative to define Executive spending.

Whether or not their action was part of the effort to eliminate Calhoun as a presidential candidate in the next campaign, the result of it had broader implications. Buchanan's argument is valid today against the "meat axe" approach to budget cutting.

The members were also inviting a possible Indian massacre by not financing the gifts, rations and services they had led the Indians to expect. However, McDuffie of South Carolina had already suggested this point. Buchanan, therefore, ended his pleading and waited. After more discussion, an appropriation to meet the deficiency was put to a vote and passed.

Grateful supporters of Mr. Calhoun must have wondered if their new-found champion might not be persuaded to support the Secretary of War for President. Buchanan, however, had told the House that he was no partisan of Mr. Calhoun's. He merely had meant to do him justice. Now he busied himself with other matters and with taking care of his district. He had his own problems to face in his next campaign.

Carefully he wrote two separate resolutions. Both of them beginning "Resolved: That the Committee on the Post Office and Post Roads be instructed to inquire into the expediency of establishing a post road . . ." Both resolutions succeeded, thus authorizing a new Post Road through his district. The resolutions were reported in Buchanan's home paper, the *Lancaster Journal.* It was also of interest to his constituency that Mr. Buchanan proposed and chaired a committee that won his State a little extra revenue. The United States ceded to Pennsylvania all rights to the uncollected fines due "for nonperformance of militia duty" during the War of 1812. For this effort, also, the Congressman won a paragraph of recognition in the *Lancaster Journal.*

Buchanan needed all this favorable publicity, since the Federalist Party was seeing its last days. He would have to scurry to build a broader following that could secure him a political future. Eventually his activities compelled him to choose between the presidential candidates and he became a Jackson man.

While Buchanan was making up his mind, Missouri's new Senator, Thomas Hart Benton, was carefully recording the developments of the campaign; and nobody was more deeply involved in its progress than the junior Senator from New York, Martin Van Buren. Both of these men had entered the Senate in 1821 as Buchanan entered the House. Large, bold, and fiercely independent, Benton had no use for caucuses or party discipline, but this rugged individual would one day lead the Senate Democrats.

As if to provide a contrast to Benton, Van Buren wrote with pride that he did not think any State in the Union had better party discipline than New York.

The New Yorker had good reason to appreciate his State's political background. He was serving as William Crawford's campaign manager, and he could not match Clay's talent for oratory or Calhoun's gift for logic. Moreover, he had not enjoyed the equivalent of Calhoun's formal Yale education. Instead, Van Buren had taught himself American history.

While reading the record, he decided that he knew why others had been markedly more influential than Alexander Hamilton at the Constitutional Convention. Hamilton, having failed to first consult with key delegates, had destroyed his own influence by suggesting that the President hold office for life. Obviously "He was without skill in reading the characters of men or the signs of the times."

Those qualities that Hamilton had lacked, plus a sense of humor and an ingratiating manner, were traits that Van Buren cultivated. With them he had already built an organization so completely dedicated to his interests that it was called the "Albany Regency." Its members were frequently referred to as Van Burenites. To keep them in the ascendancy he rewarded supporters with public appointments, and did so more ruthlessly than any political leader before him. Utilizing the spoils system on the Federal level was very much a part of his plans.

Van Buren also was equipped to profit intellectually from his political scars. His followers had tumbled Governor Dewitt Clinton from office in 1822. Then, still unsatisfied, they removed Clinton in 1824 from his rightful place as a Commissioner of the Erie Canal. The canal project owed its existence to Clinton. Subsequently the sympathy of the voters was aroused, and Clinton came back to the Governor's chair in 1825.

Listening to this bad news from the polls while picking unenthusiastically at his breakfast in his New York residence, Van Buren eyed his informant, a politico who had been instrumental in the harsh treatment that Clinton had received. "I hope, Judge," the Senator scolded, "you are now satisfied that there is such a thing in politics as *killing a man too dead!*" This was a lesson that Calhoun was yet to learn—and learn in relation to Van Buren.

Meanwhile, the vehemence of the contesting factions in the coming presidential campaign increased, making their contemporaries wonder how anybody could have believed in a continuing "Era of good feeling." Even after Calhoun withdrew to run for Vice President, there were still four battling Presidential candidates: John Quincy Adams, Henry Clay, William Crawford, and Andrew Jackson, all of them still calling themselves

Republicans. Only one of them, though, had been nominated by a Congressional caucus. That was Crawford, and he was Van Buren's man.

Normally, Van Buren would have had every reason to be optimistic. However, the newspapers were attacking the nominating caucuses and warning the public that "our Presidents [actually] . . . receive their appointment at the hands of the members of Congress. . . ." Here, they said, was "a conspiracy against the liberties of the people," operating to evade the whole system of checks, "and to throw the executive into the arms of the legislature." Even if not binding on the nation, the caucus nomination was invariably effective. "System and combination," the Philadelphia *Aurora* said, will always defeat superior numbers. "They are the regular forces . . . opposed to the raw, undisciplined militia."

Loudly echoing these sentiments, Crawford's rivals—who, according to Benton, anticipated his victory—united in boycotting the caucus meeting. It was useless for New Jersey's Senator Dickerson to argue that members went to these caucuses only in their private capacities. In answer, South Carolina's Senator Hayne needed only to describe the scene. "[T]he Hall of legislation is appropriated for their use; the officers of the House are stationed at the door . . . [and the caucus chairman sits in the Speaker's seat]. All this, when it was known that members . . . are prohibited from being electors."

The boycotters so depleted attendance that no one would ever again dare to call a congressional nominating caucus. Thus in the heat of campaign rivalry the Congress voluntarily destroyed one of its own restraints on the Executive. Whether this was a good idea or not, it was the result of the factional rivalry that was characteristic of those times.

As for Crawford himself, he was soon to suffer a stroke and be defeated by his own poor health, but not before the Representatives had again become deeply entangled in his campaign. The next episode culminated in a congressional investigation.

The Investigation

The note that started the probe had been penned by Ninian Edwards, a former Senator from Illinois. Addressed to Clay, it charged Crawford with mismanagement.

Edwards was already heading for the border in a surprising hurry to start his appointment as Ambassador to Mexico when the House Sergeant-at-Arms overtook him and haled him back to testify. In his note to Clay he had included ten newspaper articles filled with his accusations and mysteriously signed "A. B." These he avowed to have authored himself. What impressed Benton was the newspaper in which the "A. B. papers" were published. It was the *Washington Republican*, whose editorial interests favored Mr. Calhoun.

Ever since the First Congress, the Representatives had been exercising their right to conduct investigations. No committee could serve as a court, but so long as the members limited their inquiries to areas where they might conceivably want Congress to legislate or appropriate, the full House felt no hesitation in empowering them to send for papers or persons. Particularly of late, Congress had been perfectly happy to allow such inquiries into the behavior of Executive officers. This time it was different. The demand for an investigation put Speaker Clay, who was still a candidate, in a delicate position. Every member of the House was a friend of either the accused or one of his rivals.

Of the committee Clay did appoint Martin Van Buren said, "It was composed of seven of the most respectable members of the House, viz., . . . Mr. Floyd and Mr. Randolph of Virginia and Mr. Owen of Alabama, who were friends of Crawford's; Daniel Webster and John W. Taylor, who were supporters of Adams; Edward Livingston, who was in favor of General Jackson; and McArthur of Ohio, a friend of Clay."

Both Benton and Van Buren noted with satisfaction that when the committee satisfied itself of the utter falsity of the charges, Edwards resigned his office. The smear had been successfully handled by the congressional process.

The presidential campaign of 1824 went on.

Clay's rivals were forced to praise his committee, which must have added to his prestige, but as a presidential candidate he still made a losing showing. No other candidate won so few electoral votes. It was Jackson who was ahead. Much to the interest of those ambitious junior statesmen who were busily gauging the shifts in the political wind, the General had not only the largest electoral vote but also the largest popular following. This was significant, since now eighteen of the twenty-four States allowed all the voters, and not merely the State legislators, to cast ballots for electors.

Nevertheless, because of the four-way split, nobody had captured the necessary majority of electoral votes. Hence, according to the Twelfth Amendment, the election had to be decided in the House among the top three contenders. There, as everyone knew, Clay was in a position to lead his supporters in behalf of his own choice. It was also a known fact that the Kentucky legislature wanted its sons to vote for Jackson.

Even before the House assembled, the *Columbia Observer* carried rumors of a corrupt bargain between Clay and Adams. The author of the article, who had first intended to remain anonymous, was Congressman Kremer of Pennsylvania. Perhaps Kremer was not among those who remembered Clay's earlier disapproval of Jackson and might have expected him to prefer Adams to a "military chieftain."

To defend himself against the scandal, Clay took the same course that had been followed earlier by Crawford's friends. On February 3, 1825, he drew the attention of his fellow Representatives to the *Observer* and had the Annals of Congress record him as saying "He anxiously hoped . . . that the House would be pleased to direct an investigation into the truth of the charges. . . ."

This time the committee was elected. It included Webster; two former Speakers, Taylor and Barbour; and also Forsyth. On February 9, Congressman Kremer refused to appear before them to defend his remarks, and the investigation ended there.

The issue did not. To many, Kremer seemed vindicated when Adams won in the House and promptly named Clay Secretary of State.

Benton, in his memoirs, recorded for posterity that he knew the tale of "bargain and sale" between Clay and Adams was untrue. At the same time he had another complaint.

"Jackson was the choice of the people . . . and . . . undoubtedly the second choice of several States whose votes had been given to Crawford . . . ." Representatives who gave their votes to Adams, the Senator charged, "had assumed a guardianship over the people, and implied the necessity . . . to guide them for their own good." They were, in short, acting against the will of their constituents. Benton was delighted later, when the voters turned the Adams men out of the House at the next election.

After watching the proceedings, Senator Van Buren in his autobiography also conceded that "Adams was an honest man . . . incorruptible . . . [and] an enemy of venality." Nevertheless, Van Buren reported, "That there would ultimately be a union between the Crawford, Jackson and Calhoun parties to resist the . . . views . . . and to overthrow the new administration was . . . certain at the moment when that administration was ushered into existence. . . ." The fact was that Adams had been made President against the known wishes of the majority of the people, making the ambitious young Senators stand aloof.

Some of the same thoughts were occurring to Vice President Calhoun. Clay had acted against the wishes of his constituents. Calhoun wrote an admirer, "I will not be on that side, I am with the people. . . ."

"The people," as he was astute enough to calculate, were being admitted to the polls in ever-increasing numbers as property qualifications became a thing of the past.

To many of these new voters, the victory of John Quincy Adams was a victory for the leadership of the old privileged classes. A crowd gathered in the snow in Washington to burn the new President in effigy. The bank, the internal improvements, and especially the tariff, which Clay championed as "the American system," seemed to such men to be special benefits for the few.

All this was clear when Clay's name came before the Senate as the President's choice for Secretary of State. As Van Buren analyzed the situation, if the statesmen from the other political factions were not strong enough to defeat the appointment, they could still lend credence to the charge of "bargain and sale" by voting against Clay.

Van Buren noticed that Senators who were eager to vote "nay" included some imposing names. The friends of Crawford who opposed confirmation were led by ex-Speaker Macon, now a Senator and more revered than ever before. Calhoun, who sat silent and erect in the Vice President's chair, also had friends ready to register their disapproval of Clay. They were headed by Calhoun's fellow South Carolinian, Robert Y. Hayne. Van Buren did not join either of these groups.

Van Buren considered that Kremer's charges had never been justified and he did not want to use his vote to lend credence to a tale that no investigation had established. He was therefore not displeased with his fellow Senators when they confirmed Clay. The investigational process had thus worked to limit the force of unfounded smear. Nothing, however, gave Adams and Clay the popularity and prestige that only the will of the people could give.

"The Dignity and Privileges of the Senate Were to be Preserved"

President Adams' message urged the building of public roads and canals and the establishment of a public university. Here was exactly what the advocates of a powerful Congress had been demanding. Perhaps more than anyone else, Vice President Calhoun realized that the plea came too late. The magic hour for such pleas had passed.

Others in the chamber were recalling Randolph's words: "If Congress possesses the power [to do all this] they may not only enact a Sedition law . . . but they may emancipate every slave in the United States . . . and where will they find the power? They may . . . hook the power upon the first loop they find in the Constitution; they may take the preamble [or] perhaps the warmaking power [or] all of them."

In 1824 Randolph had carried his loathing of implied powers to the Senate. It surprised no one to see him here near his old friend Macon—the latter dressed in a dark blue suit cut in the style of the Revolutionary period. Far from appearing to be obsolete relics, many of their views on States' Rights and a strict construction of the Constitution coincided with the philosophy of the emerging leadership of the future. Adams' administration was already doomed, but as yet the President did not know it.

While Vice President Calhoun was appointing committees, almost half of which were to be unfriendly to the administration, the President was going ahead with his plans, still oblivious of the hopelessness of his situation.

Back in his White House office, Adams conversed with John Taylor. Together they weighed the prospects for Taylor's reelection as Speaker of the House and then talked over the composition of the committees Taylor would appoint if he won the Chair. Adams was characteristically maintaining his old attitude, favoring close executive-legislative relations. In keeping with this, he arranged to have Clay ask a friend to dissuade Webster from running against Taylor.

As Adams remarked, Taylor had already been encouraged to expect 109 votes. "but from encouraging expectations in such cases large deductions must always be made . . . there are numbers [of members] who excite hopes in all the candidates with a view to have credit with the successful one for having contributed to his victory."

Evidently, this time Clay was able to fulfill the President's request. Webster did not run, and Taylor was elected. Moreover, Webster, who had campaigned in the House to make Adams President, was not offended. On the contrary, he advised the administration on the timing of measures that it wished to put before the House.

Here was gratifying cooperation, and Adams permitted himself to be lulled into a false sense of security, as a steady stream of members of Congress respectfully came to call.

When Forsyth came, he mentioned that Adams in his annual message had announced that he was sending ministers to a conference of South American States meeting in Panama. The Georgian wondered if this was not a change of policy.

It is easy to imagine the President's reaction. As Secretary of State he had written the Monroe doctrine, making it clear to the Holy Alliance that the new world was no longer open for fresh colonization. Now he coldly drew himself up and stiffened his small frame in response to Forsyth's insinuation that he had changed his earlier determination not to become involved with the liberators.

Adams thought Forsyth was witnessing not a change in policy but "a change in circumstances." The South American leaders who would soon assemble at Panama, expecting to form a federation for their mutual defense, were representing heads of State. The United States was still neutral toward Spain and her remaining colonies.

There were more signs of trouble when Macon, who was Chairman of the Committee on Foreign Relations in the Senate, made his call. The President mentioned his eagerness to send ministers to Panama, and Macon said he had "no charge from the committee to speak of that." He intimated that he would be against it.

Shortly thereafter Adams suddenly learned that the Senators were considering a resolution charging him with usurpation of power for asserting, without first obtaining the concurrence of the Senate, that ministers would be sent to Panama.

At first Adams was shocked. "They constitute themselves accusers, triers and judges," he complained.

In this mood he read the words in a report from Macon's committee, written by Senator Tazewell: "[I]t is not expedient, at this time, for the United States to send any minister to the Congress of American Nations assembled at Panama. . . ."

It was true there were Senators who feared the conference would entangle the nation in a highly precarious military alliance. It was a fact that others feared the United States would be joining a forum on liberating slaves. But what depressed Adams the most was that these arguments were only a piece of the picture. As the President at last realized, here was a coalition of the followers of the defeated candidates making their hostility felt on a matter of foreign policy and claiming the privileges of the Senate for the purpose.

Adams reacted. He answered an inquiry from Van Buren with pointed tactlessness. He avowed that he did not understand the motives of the Senators. After that the atmosphere grew even more unpleasant as Randolph became stimulated by the discord. He took the Senate floor to harangue against the administration, calling Adams and Clay a combination of Puritan and Blackleg; and he implied that the invitation to the Panama conference had been forged by Clay.

When Clay challenged him to a duel, Randolph (according to Benton) claimed his Senatorial immunity to being held responsible for any words spoken in debate, including words incriminating any minister of the Executive. Then he accepted the challenge and deliberately fired away from Clay.

Unlike the fighting cock of Kentucky, Adams, the staid New Englander, did not demand a gun fight. Instead, someone writing under the pen name of "Patrick Henry" scolded Calhoun for not keeping order in the Senate. To this the Vice-President objected that he was not a member of the Senate but merely its presiding officer. Unless a Senator asked for a ruling he felt he had no right to interfere with debate. Much of this fencing between the President's advocate and the Vice-President went on in the public press, with Calhoun also using a pseudonym. Calhoun then repeated his definition of the Vice-President's position to the Senate.

There were others who agreed with Calhoun, and they had their own way of dealing with Randolph. They deserted the room and left him without a quorum. These men felt that only Senators should call for order and the Vice-President could rule only on a complaint. There was no sense in letting a member of the executive gag legislative debate.

This was the way the matter stood for a time. The Senate, however, can change its rules as it sees fit, and it has done so.

As of this writing the Vice-President can call a Senator to order for casting aspersions on another Senator or a State, but he cannot limit a Senator's right to criticize the Executive. In effect, Senators have decided that the presiding officer can stop transgressions of the rules they have made for themselves.

As the Adams administration continued, the relationship between the Legislature and the Executive did not mend. With encouragement from the President's friends in the House, ministers were at last confirmed by the Senate and dispatched to the Panama conference, but they arrived too late to participate. In addition, Congress also passed a Rivers and Harbors bill, but other than that most of the "President's dreams" were ignored.

The first Congressional election deprived Adams of his majority in the House. The next Presidential election turned him out of office. After that, the election of Andrew Jackson brought more than a "military chieftain" into the White House; it brought into power a national hero and strict constructionist who was supported by the hordes of new voters. Most important of all, it brought an end to the era of congressionally dominated Government.

From then on, Clay fought a losing battle from the Senate floor to limit the might of the Chief Executive. He failed partly because Jackson had as powerful a personality as his own; but a much more significant reason for his failure was the simple fact that times had changed. The new President and his followers represented the wishes of the oncoming generation of new voters.

Part V

The Jacksonians and Their Rivals

The Congressional Scene

From the very beginning, a member of Congress had been expected to express the views of his constituents and to fight for their interests. And yet, as millions saw it, a glorious new era had begun when President Jackson thwarted his opposition in Congress. His popularity permitted his lavish use of the veto. Since he was idolized by the multitudes, and since the multitudes could now vote, he was able to initiate a trend in Executive assertiveness, making willful Congressmen struggle with him and later with his successors.

Moreover, since the Jacksonians went further and did more than their predecessors to organize the electorate, this fortified their claim that they were the rightful representatives of the people. They and their President spoke the popular will. If the others in Congress wanted to survive, they had better adjust.

At the time, the giants in Congress did as much as the President to cope with the catastrophic problems that faced the nation. When they were unwilling to bow to his control, they claimed that they represented what was best for the citizens. They reminded the Democrats in Congress that Jefferson never used the veto: he inspired his followers by his liberal views and political judgment. They could have added that Clay's men had put the leadership of Congress and the nation into Congressional hands, and those hands were not going to release it easily.

Who would control Congress, and how it would be controlled, could then not be separated from the old problem of executive-congressional relations. At the same time it remained as it had been, a contest between the leaders of the factions. But now, as the local requirements for suffrage shrank and the country grew, and as industry expanded to compete politically with agriculture, more factions emerged. More leaders came to Congress to look around for friends with whom they could form a coalition, hoping to be part of the controlling majority.

To these men the old bank issue and the tariff squabble painfully reemphasized the conflicting demands of the agrarian South and the commercial North, and of the hordes of newly enfranchised workers and their industrial employers. The same could be said of the controversy over internal improvements and the question of how to handle the public lands. None of them could be discussed without weighing a man's responsibility to his constituents.

None of the issues could be argued, moreover, without defining the powers of Congress and judging which responsibilities should be left to the States. And even the casual onlooker in the gallery, who had pushed his way to his seat to hear the great orations, felt that the speakers, while listening to different groups from the outside and thus developing different concepts of government, were fired by conviction. As this visitor might have guessed, their zeal produced new tactics, causing battles within battles to agree on new rules and standards of conduct.

"For Home Consumption"

For some time the hum of the approaching chorus of less affluent voters had been growing more audible. For their benefit, in 1824, Congress had passed an act abolishing imprisonment for debt. Simultaneously, as the number of voters grew, their representatives spent more time helping them.

This was true of both the Jackson men and their elders. After ex-President Adams became a Congressman, he also attended to requests from his home district. There was an error in a veteran's pension record, and Representative Adams secured the needed correction. A few of his neighbors hoped to become agents for the Post Office, and he called on the Department to suggest their names. Local merchants had problems with the State Department, and Adams interceded for them also.

At least one Representative was exasperated by some other types of attention the members were giving their constituents. On a Wednesday in the March of 1828, William Haile of Mississippi rose to suggest a change in the rules. He had been told that at the last session of Congress a single gentleman had introduced into the House no less than one hundred and thirty-five resolutions of inquiry. Another gentleman had introduced thirty-six. And all these subjects had been examined and reported on by committees. "Perfectly needlessly!" Haile said. "Two thirds of them [the inquiries] were intended for home consumption." The reports were printed at public expense and sent home so that the constituents of whoever had moved the inquiry would be impressed.

Haile then broached his main point. "The most finished orations of Demosthenes . . . could be read in forty minutes . . ." he said, but, Congressional orators required two to three days to discuss a subject. This verbosity, Haile insisted, resulted in the members' subsequent imprudent rush to finish the public business at the end of the session. Representatives voted away millions in ten minutes or half an hour in the midst of so much hurry and confusion that Haile doubted that two thirds of the members knew what had been done or not done.

The House not only disagreed; it found Haile's bluntness offensive. House members coughed throughout his speech and for the time being took no action to refer his complaint to a rules committee. Eventually the struggles that lay ahead would force the House to limit debate, but Haile did not live to see it.

Meanwhile, each orator was convinced that he was helping to inform and guide the public. It was, after all, Vice President Calhoun's ability to elucidate a complex question, making it seem clear and simple, which had helped so much to win his position of political leadership. He was not a jovial good fellow like Clay, and up to now he had not been a man who catered to the voters. Yet Calhoun held the loyalty of his constituents by his ability to put forth his positions, presenting each issue distinctly but as part of a political creed that must be maintained.

The value of such orations impressed Calhoun's contemporaries, especially as members now faced serious problems in handling the conflicting demands of their various constituents. The members felt they had to expound on the nation's problems.

There were also times when the warring demands of the various voters led their representatives to devise means in addition to their arguments to shape the course of events. The tariff question was one example.

More and more the Southerners' constituents were objecting to the protective tariff. As planters they felt they were being mercilessly fleeced to fatten Northern manufacturers. Arguing in their behalf, Senator Hayne of South Carolina called the principle of protection unconstitutional.

Representative George McDuffie, from the same State, came close to saying as much to the House: The tariff, he contended, was an enormously unjust tax on the many for the benefit of a few wealthy capitalists, and this without even the pretense of any motive connected with defense. To perpetrate this injustice under the guise of regulating commerce was "a gross and fraudulent abuse of constitutional power."

New York's legislature disagreed and accordingly had instructed Van Buren to support the policy of protective duties. Up to 1827 he had obediently spoken and voted accordingly. But, he wrote in his autobiography, "the more I became acquainted with its character . . . the more my repugnance to it became strengthened." The policy of protection, Van Buren decided, was "unwise and illiberal," and "kept on foot by politicans to secure the support of a class of men whose selfish appetite increased with indulgence."

At least some of Van Buren's followers felt burdened by the price increases that a protective duty imposed, and he began to plan its overthrow. His strategy took into account the fact that the tariff had a hold upon the minds of more active voters in his State than he could afford to offend. With this in mind, he appeared in Albany at a pro-tariff convention called to support the "woolens bill" and spoke for nearly two hours.

Later Van Buren heard that a wool buyer had commented to a friend, "That was a very able speech."

"Yes, very able," Van Buren's friend agreed. Then, after a considerable pause, the buyer inquired, "On what side of the tariff question was it?"

To deepen the mystery, Van Buren absented himself from the Senate when the proposed tariff on woolens was put to a vote. No one knew better than he did that the question posed a threat to his rival, Vice President Calhoun. If Calhoun was ever to win the Presidency he would need to carry the manufacturing States. But meanwhile, his present supporters in South Carolina, who resented these levies, were growing increasingly vocal. When the New Yorker did not answer the roll, the vote on the tariff was a tie. Calhoun was forced to cast the deciding ballot and he voted to kill the measure.

A year later, when the so called "Tariff of Abominations" was devised, Jackson's men spiced it with high duties on raw materials used in the North. Ralph Ingersoll of Connecticut reported that the Southern gentlemen distinctly admitted that they had loaded molasses with a doubly heavy duty for the purpose of rendering the tariff brew too odious for the New Englanders to choke down.

In this they were disappointed. New England Representatives refused to be manuevered into taking the blame from their constituents for destroying protection. They carried the bill to enactment, making both sides realize that the passing of this unfortunate act was only a preliminary skirmish, and that the conflicting interests in Congress were traveling toward future more ominous clashes. And these clashes also were the result of each Congressman's efforts to serve his followers back home.

The Details All Fitted Together

To Jacksonians like Benton and Van Buren all the integral parts of the program devised by Clay's National Republicans were obnoxious and they all fitted together. The tariff provided the money for internal improvements. The improvements were a means by which Congressmen plundered the Treasury for the benefit of their constituents, and the bank was the nursing mother of the entire system. It provided the milk of currency and credit for commercial schemes that relied on the tariff for protection.

Jackson's loyal follower James K. Polk of Tennessee told the House that, as part of this "American System," New Englanders wanted to restrict the sale of western lands and thus retain a population of paupers in the East, ". . . driven into manufactories, to labor at low wages for their daily bread."

Polk, like the others, objected to the system as a whole. He called internal improvements a sponge to suck up excess revenue.

He meant no offense to his colleagues in the chamber, he insisted, and added: "[F]ew districts . . . will resist the lure of . . . a road or a canal, if you will hold it out to them . . . For a time the people [in my district] seemed to be carried away. . . . We were to have a main route." But Polk told the House that when the people reflected that the money was collected in taxes paid in part by themselves, their better judgment took over and they rejected the project. He was positive that the people living in other districts would soon reach the same conclusion. One person who did not agree was the Senator from his own State, Hugh White.

White found the road issue most disturbing. When a dirt road was offered to his area, he wrote, "I am against the *power* to make the road, but I would infinitely rather vote for a decent one . . . If we are really to sell our principles for pay, . . . Why not give us a macadamized turnpike . . . ? Give us as good as is given to others."

White spoke as many felt. The Federal Government should not be in a position to lure and patronize the citizens of the States with promises of roads, but if these benefits were to be available, a Congressman must get his electorate their fair share.

As to the rest of the "American System," White responded with approval when the President in his first annual message to Congress warned the stockholders of the United States Bank and their mentors in the Capitol. He, Jackson, challenged both the expediency and the constitutionality of their institution.

Benton was also jubilant. He remembered that when times were hard the bank was suing the poor debtors. The Missourian feared the bank "with its colossal money power—its arms in every State . . . its power over the State banks—its power over the business community [and]—over public men who should become its debtors or retainers . . ."

He could have named Daniel Webster. As the bank's spokesman in Court and Congress, Webster did receive a retainer from it. There was also the well-known incident of the New York editor who after receiving a loan switched his editorial policy from pro-Jackson to pro-bank.

Benton feared corruption would endanger free government. Above all he was delighted with Jackson's position because he was sure that the theory which authorized the bank's existence was a menace, letting Congress "do what it pleased under the plea of 'necessity.' "

Like Polk, Benton was convinced that the people back home in all the States were electrified by the President's message, but knowing that the opposition would fight for its system he predicted that "a great contest was coming."

Meanwhile, in the South, the "tariff of abominations" had fanned a spirit of rebellion. Vice President Calhoun resorted to his old technique of presenting his wishes in the form of a political creed. To lead the South Carolina radicals toward what he called a constitutional solution of their problem and thus avoid worse mischief, Calhoun furtively wrote nullification propoganda. His "Exposition and Protest" enlarged on the Virginia and Kentucky resolutions and held that a State convention could properly nullify an act of Congress. Thus geographic minorities could protect their interests. It was the type of States' Rights doctrine Webster loathed.

He made an opportunity to say so on a December morning in 1829, after Senator Foote of Connecticut presented a resolution to limit the sale of public lands. It happened that Foote had taken the floor immediately following a discussion in which the Senate decided to continue the practice of attaching a short preamble to each bill, explaining its purpose.

Hayne had then pointedly mentioned that if the real purpose of the tariff of 1828 had been prefixed to it, he could have gone to the judiciary and challenged the act as discriminatory against the South.

Hayne's remark was enough to irritate Webster, but Benton's next speech was a worse insult. He charged that the Foote resolution was proposed for the sole benefit of Eastern employers, supporters of the "American System."

Webster had to spring to the defense of the East. What was equally important, since he championed the concept of a strong national government responsive to the will of the national majority, he had to make sure that New England was part of the majority. Only a coalition with the West could guarantee that. Webster thus preferred to cross verbal swords with Hayne, not with Benton.

Before long, a packed gallery and a spellbound Senate were hearing Webster warmly intone the friendly feelings of the East toward the West. Webster next contrasted this friendship with the hostility Southerners felt toward the internal improvements needed to develop the West.

Both orators slipped from subject to subject. On January 25, Hayne denounced the public debt and defended slavery, favoring it over the wretched condition of free Negroes in the Northern cities. Then again he attacked the tariff. Easterners were treating the other States like colonies, making them pay dearly for manufactured goods. The West would do well to stand with the South against the East. Before Hayne finished he had alluded to New England's conduct during the War of 1812.

Webster seized this as the time to bring up the doctrine of nullification, which he understood was maintained by the gentleman from South Carolina. "I cannot conceive that there can be a middle course, between submission to the laws . . . and . . . rebellion," he charged.

Hayne rose and interrupted Webster in order to refer him to the Virginia and Kentucky resolutions. By then Hayne had already claimed that the Federal Government could not be allowed to judge the constitutionality of its own acts.

At this point it was already the twenty-seventh of January, and Webster was in the middle of his second reply to Hayne. The occasion was to be commemorated in an oil painting by G.

P. A. Healey which now hangs in Boston's Faneuil Hall. In the picture, Webster stands erect, his brass buttons catching the light, and his clenched fist is poised on his wooden desk as he labors to make the details of the conflicting philosophies of American government clear to his contemporaries.

We can almost hear him hotly deny his opponent's premise, as he insists that the Constitution belongs to the people, not to the States. The people did not authorize the States to interpret the instrument for them, much less to arrest the course of their Federal Government. Instead, they reposed their trust in frequent elections and in the establishment of an independent judiciary. South Carolina's doctrines, he said, led "directly to disunion . . ."

To this, Webster added his famous warning against "those words of delusion and folly 'Liberty first and Union afterwards.'" He was well aware of what was already being said at the political meetings of Southern extremists. He concluded with "that other sentiment dear to every true American heart —Liberty *and* Union, now and forever, one and inseparable!"

The visitors in the packed gallery had heard the problems and rivalries of the day so forcefully and eloquently explained that the speech still deserves its reputation as one of the greatest congressional orations. They and the reading public had, perhaps, absorbed a little constitutional law; at the very least they had been inspired in favor of the Union, and were more aware of the doctrines that threatened its survival.

And as for the problem of the public lands, it was not entirely forgotten in the scuffle. It would be brought up again later as a variation of Clay's "American System."

"The Senate Do Not . . . Consent"

Benton had predicted a great contest between the President's friends and his opponents in Congress. The extent of that contest became evident when President Jackson began sending the names of his would-be appointees to the Senate. Again and again the vote was close. Twice the statesmen were tied. Each time Vice President Calhoun voted to uphold the President's choice. Then, when the Senators did refuse to confirm a nominee, Jackson was decidedly unwilling to take no for an answer.

In the notable case of Mr. Samuel Gwin, Senators Poindexter of Mississippi and Bibb of Kentucky offered the Senate a number of resolutions. Bibb's statement reviewed the facts.

While the Senate was not in session, Gwin had been given a "recess appointment" as register of the land office in Mt. Salus, Mississippi, but the President had to submit the appointee's name to the Senate when that body reconvened. (It appeared that Gwin was not from Mississippi, and Poindexter may have objected to having this patronage job given to a man from outside the State.) In any case, the Senate did not consent to the appointment of Samuel Gwin, and on December 22 the Secretary of the Senate carried the news of the rejection to the President.

Jackson waited a respectful amount of time and then renominated Gwin, requesting the Senate to reconsider. On the tenth of July the Senators voted to let the nomination lie on the table.

Jackson's reaction to this was to give Gwin another, interim appointment as soon as the Senate adjourned. Bibb called this "an unwarranted exercise of power by the President . . . which if suffered to pass in silence . . . would tend to deprive the Senate of the control over Executive appointments intended by the Constitution."

Poindexter called the action "a palpable violation of the Constitution." As he saw it, Jackson's right to give a man an interim appointment expired after the nominee had been rejected. The Senator wanted an explanation from the Executive department. Jackson obliged.

The nomination of Samuel Gwin had been laid on the table, the President recalled. Therefore, said Jackson, "a vacancy in the office was found existing in the recess, which the public service required to be filled, and which was filled by . . . Samuel Gwin. I therefore nominate the said Gwin to the same office."

On another occasion the Senate had passed a resolution that

"It is inexpedient to appoint a citizen of one State to an office which may be created or become vacant in any other State without some evident necessity therefor."

The President's reaction was to attack the resolution as an unconstitutional attempt to restrain his authority, and to announce that when the Senate applied it against him he would refrain from any further attempt to fill the vacancy. In later years he explained to a friend what he intended to accomplish by this move. In effect his argument was that if they, the Senators, left an office not filled, and hence the service to the public neglected, the vengeance of the people would fall upon them.

Underlying all this controversy was the belief of the Jacksonians that the duties of public office could be kept simple and thus that any intelligent man would have sufficient talent to fill any post. They also contended that their "spoils system" was a way of rotating men in office in order to spread opportunity and to prevent the development of a governing class.

Clay, who in 1831 returned to the Senate, called the Spoils System detestable. He saw the honors and dignities of public office being put up for a scramble which he predicted would follow every presidential election.

His attitude provoked Senator Marcy of New York into defending his fellow Jacksonians. "When they are contending for victory, they avow their intention of enjoying the fruits of it . . . They see nothing wrong in the rule that to the victor belong the spoils of the enemy."

Marcy did not stop there. Clay, he insisted, applied the same rule when he had a chance.

Moreover, when Clay condemned Jackson, he was forgetting the circumstances under which the General's administration came to power. Marcy undertook to remind him of this. "He came in, Sir, upon a political revolution . . . Criminations and recriminations were made. Slander . . . flooded the land. When the present Chief Magistrate took upon himself the administration of the Government, he found almost all the offices, from the highest to the lowest, filled with political enemies."

Jackson, it was clear, believed that his nominees were good men who were being rejected because of their political affiliation with him. He would have none of it. Like Poindexter, he was thinking of the constituents back home. But home in Jackson's mind encompassed all the twenty-four States in the Union.

The Senate thus was given an indication of the effectiveness of the weapons in the President's political arsenal. Webster admitted to a friend, "Were it not for the fear of the . . . popularity of General Jackson, the Senate would have negated more than half his nominations."

Webster was, nevertheless, optimistic. He seems to have been thinking in terms of offsetting Jackson's popularity with the masses by gathering the support of Senators elected by their State legislatures. What Clay wanted, however, was to see the public become disenchanted with Jackson. And early in the administration an episode occurred that made the wish become father of the belief. The episode involved Van Buren.

Dazzle and Seduce

For the longest time Van Buren, who was now Secretary of State, had been anxious to put reins on the numerous attempts to commit the Government to the construction of internal improvements. As he expressed it later, "the wits of Congressmen were severely taxed in devising and causing to be surveyed and brought forward [proposals for projects] . . . they designed to dazzle and seduce their constituents." Worse, the prospect of seeing Government money poured into an area caused the wild spirit of speculation that characterized the times to become wilder yet.

As Van Buren reports the episode, it was understood between the President and himself that he would watch for a bill that would offer the Chief Executive a good opportunity to expound on the constitutionality of these public works.

The bill authorizing the Government to subscribe to the stock of the Maysville-Lexington turnpike appeared to present the looked-for occasion. The bill, which had passed the House and

In this very well known cartoon, Jackson, endowed with the veto power, which he holds in his left hand, is managing to reign like a king over Congress and the nation.

King Andrew the First   *Library of Congress*

was likely to pass the Senate, provided for a road which started and ended in the same State, Kentucky. Van Buren was ready to condemn the project as local and not national, and, therefore, not within the province of Congress. He was, hence, most anxious that the Senators not discover his plans in time to change the bill a little and make the road more national in character.

His disappointment must have been profound when Colonal Richard M. Johnson of Kentucky called at the White House asking to see the President "on a delicate matter." Johnson was disturbed. He had heard rumors of the coming veto. It would not have ruffled Jackson in the least had Clay come to plead for the project. He thought Clay was pressing for the measure, but Representative Johnson, an ex-soldier and an ex-Senator, was a Jackson Democrat. Moreover, he was a popular man. His name had headed the list of those who fought to abolish imprisonment for debt.

"You will crush your friends in Kentucky if you veto that bill," Johnson told the President. As Van Buren remembered, the President got out of his chair, and the rapid conversation that followed included this exchange:

The President: Sir, have you looked at the condition of the Treasury . . . at the appropriations already made . . . ?

Colonel Johnson: No, General, I have not, but there has always been money enough . . .

The President: I stand committed before the country to pay off the national debt . . . are you willing . . . to lay [extra] taxes to pay for internal improvements?

Johnson: No, that would be worse than a veto.

As the Colonel was about to edge his way out, Van Buren sprang to the rescue of his own plan. He quickly remarked that Johnson had evidently made up his mind that the President was going to veto the bill, but in fact the President's earnestness was in response to Johnson's own strong speech. Jackson took the hint and quickly assured his visitor that he would not make up his mind without giving the matter a thorough investigation.

Johnson was not fooled. He returned to the House and told his friends that nothing less than a voice from heaven would prevent the old man from vetoing the project. Actually, the administration's viewpoint was not without support in the House. Consequently, Robert Letcher of Kentucky, who often worked with Clay, claimed the road was justified, since it served as a link, helping the traveler to reach a river or highways that did cross State lines. He was answered by a Georgia Congressman, who thought that description applied to any road in the country. Nevertheless, the bill passed and, as expected, Jackson vetoed it.

Clay acted as if the veto was a voice from heaven. In May of 1830, he wrote from Ashland, Kentucky, to Daniel Webster: "The veto of the Maysville bill has produced uncommon excitement in Kentucky . . . Jackson supporters have openly renounced their faith.

"We shall attack the veto by promising an amendment of the Constitution . . ." Clay was obviously hearing from constituents who agreed with him and told him what he wanted to hear. Thus flattered and encouraged, Clay himself became a victim of the bedazzlement which Van Buren had attributed to the voters. He returned to the Capital in 1831, eager to continue the contest with Jackson.

"Kill Him Dead"

Calhoun was as eager as Clay or Webster to provide for the needs of his followers by merging their interests with those of others to form a winning coalition. Hence, for a while, he and Van Buren, though bitter rivals, were both key members of the Jackson administration. Consequently it proved most significant that Calhoun and his immediate followers had been pushed out of that coalition before the administration faced its next big test in the Senate. There were a number of reasons for his fall from favor.

The President had learned—from Van Buren's friend Crawford—that Calhoun had advised President Monroe to discipline Jackson when Jackson on his own initiative had seized Spanish forts and hanged British civilians as part of his campaign against the Seminoles in Florida. Besides that, Calhoun and Mrs. Calhoun had refused to accept socially one Peggy Eaton, a tavern-keeper's daughter who was married to Jackson's Secretary of War. Most important, Jackson in no uncertain terms had expressed to Calhoun's face his disapproval of the doctrine of nullification. Hayne's sentiments had been attributed to Calhoun even before the Vice President's authorship of "Exposition and Protest" was known. Calhoun could therefore no longer hope to be Jackson's heir apparent to the Presidency. He had it seemed, been replaced by Van Buren, who was then enjoying an interim appointment as Ambassador to the Court of St. James.

This was the situation when Van Buren's name came before the Senate for confirmation. After the nominating message was received, it was referred to the Committee on Foreign Relations. After it was reported out, it was tabled. Eventually, following a motion made by Marcy of New York, the Senators agreed to consider it.

The debate was conducted according to the rules in secret session, mostly on January 24 and 25 of 1832 and then, after the vote, the secrecy was lifted, revealing the following facts:

Clay resented Van Buren's willingness to make concessions to the British while negotiating trade treaties. The Kentuckian did not fail to attack the spoils system, which he attributed to Van Buren and to the party that Van Buren led in New York. Others had referred to the Eaton affair and to the campaign of attacks that Van Buren had allegedly made against Calhoun.

Without disagreeing with them, Clay summed up the feeling of many in the chamber when he wrote, "I regret that I find myself utterly unable to reconcile with the duty I owe to my country, a vote in favor of this nomination. I regret it, because, in all the past strife of party, the relations of ordinary civility and courtesy were never interrupted between the gentleman whose name is before us, and myself." It was hard to dislike Van Buren. What Clay objected to as much as anything else was Jackson's sending the "little Magician" to England first and asking that he be confirmed later. The Chief Executive was again stretching his powers to the fullest.

Finally the vote was taken, and it was a tie. Benton claimed the tie was contrived to put the Vice-President in the position of deciding the contest with his vote. He claimed he heard Calhoun whisper to a friend, "It will kill him, sir, kill him dead."

If so, Calhoun had been led into making a fantastically stupid mistake. Benton credits himself with having predicted to Moore of Alabama, "You have broken a minister and [thus] elected a Vice President." It was the Clinton situation all over again. The public could be counted on to see the vote as partisan vengeance.

Handling the Bank Issue

Benton hoped that the public would also see the bank controversy as another partisan maneuver. Clay wanted to make it an election issue and persuaded the bank's president, Nicholas Biddle, to cooperate.

The bank issue had been part of the background music accompanying all the clashes of Jackson's first administration. As the election approached, both sides felt that their opponents were exploiting as well as airing the issue. In seeking support for his stand in the Senate, Jackson could rely on Benton's broad shoulders. He could count on Polk in the House. One person he could not rely on was George McDuffie of South Carolina, chairman of the Ways and Means Committee, which studied the bank passage in the President's message.

The Speaker, Andrew Stevenson, who had picked McDuffie, was a Jackson man described by John Quincy Adams as biased, partisan, and willing to make such bargains as promising committee assignments to men who would support him for the Speakership. However, since Stevenson had been a director of a branch bank, it was conceivable that when he first made the appointment he was not averse to McDuffie's views. Later, of course, the Speaker went along with the President.

Unlike the President, McDuffie was not convinced that the bank had alarming powers. He saw that little was novel in what its managers were authorized to do. On the contrary: "It is the right of every individual of the Union to give credit to whom he chooses, and to obtain credit where he can get it," he argued.

He disagreed with the Chief Magistrate. The bank had gone a long way to improve the currency. The bank had steadied smaller banks. "The committee," he reported, "have no hesitation in saying, it has been productive of the most signal benefits to the community."

With these sentiments Adams agreed. He was so decidedly in favor of the bank that while traveling through Philadelphia he had divested himself of all his personal interest in it so he could fight for it with clean hands. From an official lobbyist for the institution who came calling, he had since learned that McDuffie had done the same. This was gratifying, particularly as the two men had not always been able to agree on the proper way to handle a controversial issue. Adams wanted all tariff measures entrusted to the Committee of Manufactures, which he chaired. He and his committee had done considerable work on the problem of making concessions to the South. Nevertheless, on two occasions. McDuffie reported his own recommendations from the Ways and Means Committee, encroaching upon the functions of the Adams group. When thus offended, Adams could be caustic, but this time his good will was recaptured by McDuffie's attitude on the bank.

Adams was pleased when McDuffie introduced the measure to recharter the bank—this despite the fact that its charter still had four years to run. In the Senate George M. Dallas introduced the same recharter resolution, admitting that he was apprehensive lest the institution might be drawn into some real or imaginary conflict with a higher favorite of the American people.

Benton's reaction was that Clay and his faction had evidently dominated their own party caucus. When they forced this measure through they must have expected that the President would veto it. Jackson had expressed his reservations on the bank question. At the very least he would want the charter greatly modified, but even this had been largely ignored. This, then, was a political maneuver, and Benton decided he was also capable of maneuvering.

The Missouri Senator carefully listed every conceivable charge against the bank and gave the list to Representative Clayton of Georgia to "smuggle it into the House." On February 3, 1832, Clayton took the floor and read the charges from a narrow slip of paper, which he then rolled nervously around his finger while he explained that he wanted an investigation.

According to the rules, since the proposition was a request for information from the Executive, it had to lie over for a day before it could be voted upon. In our own time it would wait a week. At that juncture the House knew that it wanted the probe. The question in everyone's mind was, should McDuffie's committee consider the fifteen charges against the bank? The committee was friendly to the bank, and McDuffie, as its chairman, had already defended the bank against the charges.

The custom was not to refer a resolution to a committee that was already hostile to its content. If Stevenson should appoint the committee, however, it would surely be anti-bank. Adams was only one of a large group who did not want that. There was another possibility: The committee could be elected.

With McDuffie's consent, the debate soon revolved around whether to elect or let the Speaker select the investigators. After the vote ended in a tie, Adams looked around, noted which of his associates were absent, and bitterly remarked that carelessness had won.

What happened next was expected. Speaker Andrew Stevenson of Virginia appointed a largely anti-bank committee. McDuffie was on it, and so was Adams, but they were outnumbered. The members traveled by coach to Philadelphia to question Nicholas Biddle about loans that had been made to newspaper editors and to a member of Congress, and to inquire into other matters of bank management. The majority report did not impress the House or stop the recharter bill from passing but did develop material for the President to use in his veto message.

Jackson referred to both Clayton's attack and the "incomplete" work of the committee. He said, "Suspicions are entertained, and charges are made of gross abuse . . . An investigation . . . so restricted in time as to make it incomplete and unsatisfactory, discloses enough to excite suspicion and alarm . . ." In the light of these suspicions by members of the House of Representatives, and since the charter had four years to run, Jackson thought the bank should have withdrawn its renewal application.

Moreover, Jackson would not be bound by the Supreme Court decision that the bank was constitutional. The Congress, the Executive and the Court must each be guided by its own opinion of the Constitution, he claimed. Besides, the Court had said that Congress could charter a bank. The Court did not judge all the details of the bank bill but left that up to Congress.

Characteristically, Webster slipped away from the main point while discussing the message.

"According to the doctrine set forth by the President," he said, "although the Supreme Court may have pronounced it [the bank charter] constitutional, yet it is, nevertheless, no law . . . if he in his good pleasure sees fit to deny its effect." Here, Webster claimed, was "pure despotism."

Webster had another basis for attacking the President. Throughout his message Jackson had treated the bank as a special convenience run solely for the rich. Jackson was injecting class rivalry into the next election. Webster was disgusted.

Benton, equally disgusted as he listened to Clay, Webster, and others, decided that the only reason for their speeches was to cry usurpation, predict economic distress and frighten the people on their way to the polls. They knew that they could not muster two-thirds of both Houses to override the President's veto. They had little more than a bare majority. Thus naturally the veto stood as the citizens turned out to vote. When Jackson was reelected, the work done by the men who made up the majority of the bank committee had played a part in the size of his victory. As Adams indicated, they had been selected for that purpose. The bank issue had thus been exploited as much by the Jacksonians as by the men who moved to recharter the institution. The committee had functioned to develop material for the President's veto, and in this way the members had been able to exert their influence at a time when they were not the majority in Congress.

Clay Counts Noses

Members who attended the second session of the Twenty-second Congress faced such a serious development that temporarily everything else including the bank issue was eclipsed.

South Carolina nullifiers had triumphed in their November elections. They called a State convention and voided the tariff for South Carolina, with a resounding threat to break from the Union if the Federal Government tried to use force to execute the law. Their next move was to invite other States to join them at a multistate convention.

Jackson threatened to hang the rebels as he had hanged troublemakers in Florida. He wanted a reduction in the tariff, but he also wanted a "Force bill" to enforce the law in South Carolina with Federal troops.

When Calhoun, who had resigned from the Vice Presidency, returned to the Capitol in January, 1833, as a newly elected Senator and chief spokesman for the nullifiers, it was hard not to admire his courage. He was literally risking his life against Jackson's threats. Calhoun's first move was to try to head off the Force Bill and thus without yielding protect his proud constituents from the wrath of their soldier-President. When the Force Bill came from the Senate Judiciary Committee, Calhoun introduced a series of futile resolutions embodying his theory of State Sovereignty. Had they been adopted, no Force Bill would have been in order.

By this time both the friends and the foes of nullification had written to James Madison evoking a denial that the Virginia Resolutions were ever intended to justify a single State in claiming the right to break a Federal law. The resolutions, said Madison, merely declared that the Alien and Sedition Acts were unconstitutional and did not in themselves sanction resistance to the Acts. Madison also rejected Calhoun's contention that a number of States should be able to meet and veto a Federal measure binding on the majority.

Propelled by ambition and encouraged by his friends, Calhoun mounts the staircase from nullification to anarchy to despotism. Meanwhile the Constitution lies stabbed on the ground next to E Pluribus Unum.

Despotism

Far from believing, as Calhoun did, that nullification was the only faith by which the Union could be saved, Madison thought that such a doctrine could destroy the Union. Speaker Stevenson and Daniel Webster had both heard from him. Webster, whose constituents wanted the tariff, had called a rally in Boston's Fanueil Hall to condemn the nullifiers and support President Jackson.

Returning to Washington, Van Buren decided it would have been hard to imagine a worse situation. The passing of Jackson's Force Bill could mean civil war, as Calhoun had been careful to make clear. But a week before the end of the session no other solution was in sight.

For eight weeks a compromise measure introduced by Congressman Verplanck of New York had been before the quarreling Representatives. Benton said it was supported only by the close friends of the administration.

Van Buren said that only Clay, whom he described as the "Father of the American System," could resolve the crisis and only by giving up some of his System. As Van Buren saw it, Clay had caused the emergency by his insistence on a higher tariff. Others blamed the lobbyists who hung around the Committee on Manufacture issuing their pleas against concessions to the South. But in fact Adams' committee had made concessions that were part of the disputed tariff measure then in effect.

After Calhoun called on him, Clay, in order to save the Union, undertook to write a new compromise less drastic than the Verplanck proposal but still deleting much of the protection his followers demanded. Calhoun proved receptive, because it was easier for him to bow to Clay than to bow to Jackson. Calhoun felt that the President, with his immense power and patronage, might have insisted earlier on a lower tariff and avoided the crisis instead of threatening force.

To Webster the compromise was not only a blow to New England's economy but also a violation of his own deepest convictions. He seemed nervous and apprehensive and went so far as to intimate that the others were reacting to panic. So Van Buren recorded.

The fact was, Van Buren decided, that Clay had "counted

noses" and knew that he had the formula that could settle the disturbances and reassure the frightened nation. Nothing Webster could say could stop him. Only the self-control that Clay had developed with advancing years moderated his remarks to his old colleague from Massachusetts. He was wily enough to bear in mind that he would soon need Webster's help with the bank issue.

The next hurdle confronting Clay's plan was not easily surmounted. Clay was now a Senator, and revenue measures originate in the House. Here was a prerogative, spelled out in the Constitution, that the Senators could not ask the Representatives to relinquish.

As a result, the House went on with its own angry argument until late on Monday, February 25, less than a week before the session would end. When Robert P. Letcher, a friend of Clay's from Kentucky, finally obtained the floor, Davis of Massachusetts noticed that some members were already putting on their coats to go home. Then he heard Letcher move to recommit the Verplanck bill to the Committee of the Whole with instructions to report in its stead Clay's measure, which could not properly start its legislative life in the Senate. The motion passed.

The House went into the Committee of the Whole. Letcher then moved that the Committee obey its instructions by adopting the bill he presented. This was done, and the Committee then rose and reported to the House.

At least some members were astounded and shaken by the audacity of the maneuver. They asked for time to consider, but the well-disciplined majority refused to grant it. The bill swept through like a hurricane.

When the House adjourned at eight o'clock, nothing remained but for Clay's bill to be engrossed so that the next day it could receive its third and final reading and pass.

When the House met the next day, copies of the Clay bill were already on the tables. In answer to fresh complaints and demands for delay in order to study the document, Congressman Edward Everett retorted that they had all had ample opportunity to see the Senate bill days before. Then, after cries of "the question," the House passed the compromise. But rather than defy the President, the Congress also passed the "Force Bill."

It was reminiscent of the days when the House had abandoned its Ways and Means Committee, preferring to listen to Alexander Hamilton, or the days when the War Hawks in the House had led the President and the Senate in foreign policy. At any given moment leadership might come from that branch of the Government that housed the leader. Clay had led the House. He had planned a measure Congressmen would accept and then canvassed to be sure he had enough votes to get it passed before he asked anyone to present the bill. Once he had enough support, he had his followers push the bill through. As long as he could do that, he was in command. He was still the leader of the House, even though he led it from the Senate.

Appeals to and from the People

The National Republicans had defied Jackson on the bank issue and their candidate Henry Clay had been beaten at the polls. Clay looked around for fresh ways of winning support.

Jackson started his second term with a request that the bank be further investigated as to its fitness to keep the public money. When the pro-bank Congressmen would not condemn the institution, the President had his subordinates make their own investigation.

They listed the large sums the bank had spent printing and circulating public speeches to promote its cause against Jackson. When subsequently the bank postponed the payment of a financial obligation owed the Government, Jackson seized the opportunity to withdraw the Government deposits.

What followed inside the halls of Congress was called the "panic session," of 1834. Hoping that the clamor of enough citizens would force the President to replace the deposits, friends of the bank mounted a lobbying campaign. Petitions poured into the capitol. Papers of protest with as many as six thousand signatures were presented to Congress.

Time and again one of these "distress memorials" would be presented by a Senator and Vice-President Van Buren and the attending members would sit through descriptions of the misery that had taken the place of the nation's earlier prosperity. Because the deposits had been withdrawn, the bank was left without sufficient funds to support the currency or accommodate men in business. Day after day was consumed in debating the validity of the protestors' claims.

When the Jacksonians still did not change their decision and return the deposits, distress committees flooded into the galleries of both Houses and called on the President. Webster, with his flair for the dramatic, ushered into the Senate chamber a committee of thirty of these petitioners, whom he stationed around the seats while he read their memorial.

As a result, people who agreed with the administration also began to petition, and at this point a novel problem presented itself.

A memorial addressed to the Vice-President for presentation to the Senate included language so indecent that it was unfit to be in the files. The signers also charged that some members of Congress who supported the institution had accepted loans and accommodations from the bank.

As the paper came from Pennsylvania, Van Buren handed it to one of the Pennsylvania Senators, William Wilkins, and suggested that he draw a line through the offending words before presenting it.

Wilkins, according to custom, stated the nature of the petition and then asked: "Shall it be read?" And the Senate voted "Aye."

The content was so inflammatory that Poindexter decided to examine the paper, and thus discovered that it had been defaced. He and Senator Preston of South Carolina objected. "What was read was not what we received," Preston said. Van Buren then admitted from the Chair that he had suggested the change and asked the Senators if they wanted to make a ruling on the question.

Clay thought they should establish a precedent.

The Senate voted not to receive the offensive petition. That meant that it would not be sent to a committee and no action would be taken on any request it contained. Today, once a message is read, it has to appear in the journal, but a Senator no longer reads a petition. He can hand it to the legislative clerk to be printed in the record, or he can indicate that he wants it referred to a committee. Then the parliamentarian, acting on behalf of the presiding officer, will make the referral.

At that time, in 1834, the counter-campaign was growing and many other petitions from Jackson supporters were arriving. Senators presented these and added their fiery speeches. Even without them, Jackson had no intention of bowing to public pressure on the bank matter after having won an election that had included the issue. If the President were to be pressured it would have to be by some other method.

At this point Clay, relying on his ability to lead the other lawmakers, offered the Senate a resolution censuring the President for snatching the funds from the bank while its charter was still in force.

The censure proposal also fitted in with Clay's other plans. He was starting a new political party. Its members called themselves Whigs, reminding the patriot of American resistance to George III and rallying men to join the resistance against "King Andrew Jackson." Westerners who wanted internal improvements, nullifiers who felt they had been harshly treated, and all friends of the bank were good prospects.

While Van Buren watched these developments, he also watched to see if there was any improvement in Clay's relationship with Webster. "Diversities in opinion and feeling" were something that he believed even Madison had utilized to control events.

Webster satisfied the Vice-President's curiosity by telling the Senate that while he did not wish to offend Clay, it was still regrettable that the question of removing the deposits had not been referred to the Finance Committee, which Webster chaired. Obviously, these former political allies had not yet overcome the mutual hostility they had experienced when Clay had pacified the South Carolinia nullifiers by sacrificing New England's tariff protection. Instead of being confidants, Webster and Clay were now rivals. Their new "Whig" coalition was going to have to work to hold together.

With so much at stake, it bothered Van Buren that the administration's rebuttal to their censure was not being properly presented. Under the rules, he himself could not enter into the debate, so he looked around for someone to speak for him.

In his autobiography Van Buren reports that he called on his friend Silas Wright from New York. "The President, as well as myself," he said, "feels that his real views have not, thus far, been sufficiently developed on the floor of either House."

Van Buren then proceeded to try to pressure Wright into doing more talking, but he found the Senator resistant. He claimed that others in the Senate were more competent. Before giving up, Van Buren wrote a speech, which Wright gave. But Webster recognized it as the Executive's point of view, in spite of Wright, who lamely claimed it was his own.

Since Wright was unsuccessful, Benton tried to destroy the censure resolution. He too was ineffective. The administration forces were feeling the loss of Calhoun's support. Clay won the passage of a resolution of censure which was so strongly worded that it eventually defeated its own purpose.

After much haggling, the Senators on March 28, 1834, did resolve "that the President in the late proceedings [involving the removal of the deposits] has assumed upon himself authority and power not conferred by the Constitution and laws, but in derogation of both." In short, the Senate accused the President of breaking the law.

That was a precarious victory, as it spurred Benton on to hunt for counteracting measures. In April, he gave notice that he was undertaking a campaign to get the criticism expunged from the record. The Senate, he claimed, was exercising none of its powers when it condemned the President. Instead it was making a judicial judgment without a trial.

At first his associates paid little attention to his campaign, but that did not stop Benton. Since Senators were still elected by State Legislatures, the Missourian looked to those bodies for help in instructing his colleagues.

By the next session the Senators were taking Benton seriously. Most of them, however, were also objecting to expunging anything from their journal. Such deletions would de-

SYMPTOMS OF A LOCKED JAW

"CLAY
"Might stop a hole, to keep the wind away."

In 1834 Clay led the Senate into censuring Jackson and then kept the President's answering protest out of the record. The confrontation between the two inspired this gloriously simple print, which has long been a favorite.

Symptoms of a Locked Jaw   *Library of Congress* stroy it as a record. They cited the Constitution, which required them to keep a journal, and obviously it should be accurate.

Perhaps Benton would never have succeeded in his campaign, but before it ended Buchanan was in the Senate helping the cause with clear, tactful logic. The Senators had condemned the President for firing his Secretary of the Treasury when that official would not remove the deposits. The Executive had enjoyed the right to remove any of his appointees since the First Congress of 1789. As to removing the deposits, the bill chartering the bank justified that too.

What bothered Buchanan most was the atmosphere in the Senate when the censure was passed. The trial of the President had continued for three months not by due process but by reading memorials. The resolution implied impeachable conduct, and Buchanan considered that the consequences would be dreadful if the Senate had the right to condemn an official for any such offense by merely passing a resolution.

Finally, on Saturday the 14th of January, the Democratic Senators held a caucus and decided to call up the motion to expunge the record the following Monday. They knew their opponents were going to try to talk the proposal to death, dragging out debate until the session was over. To prevent this the Democrats first agreed among themselves on the details of their motion and then vowed to sit out the night and refuse to adjourn until a vote had been called. To aid them in their tedious work a caucus member arranged to have hams, cold turkey and coffee ready in a committee room near the Senate chamber. When night came the Senators deserted the floor only a few at a time to raid the food supply . Then, refreshed, they returned to the hall to keep the session going.

Word of the maneuver had spread across the city, attracting an excited crowd who looked down from the Senate galleries, milled around the lobbies and pushed onto the Senate floor. There they stayed until the Missourian's careful plans succeeded and the opposition collapsed.

They saw the journal of March 28, 1834, being brought to the Secretary of the Senate, who drew broad black lines around that portion holding Clay's censure resolution. The Secretary then wrote firmly across the encircled area the words "Expunged by order of the Senate this 16th day of January, 1837."

The victory was not only Benton's. It was also a victory for future legislative-executive relations. Jackson may have used bad judgment in removing the deposits. Being prejudiced against the bank because of its connection with his political enemies, he had acted with rancor, but he had not violated the Constitution.

The Senate had committed an injustice by issuing a vague resolution that condemned the President for acts for which no impeachment proceeding could have been sustained. Benton's successful campaign had restrained the Congress from turning itself into a tribunal without rules.

"It Ought Not to Become Law"

There was more to Jackson's legacy to Congress. There were, among other things, a string of vetoes not based on constitutional questions. Jackson would veto a measure for any reason he thought justified. Thus, by broadly interpreting his power, he increased his control over legislation. That policy did more than any of his other activities to direct the future of Congress.

Clay was not powerful enough to whip Congress into overriding the President, but as far back as June of 1832 he had invented an ingenious alternative for the vetoed internal improvement bills. He would distribute to the States the proceeds from the sale of public lands, with the understanding that the money be used for improvements and educational projects.

From the very beginning, the Kentucky Senator had experienced nothing but trouble with the scheme. The matter of disposing of the public land came up at a time when he was about to run for President. He believed the land was "national property," but there were many against him who wanted the new States to have sovereign rights over all the lands within their own borders. If, instead, the money was distributed by population, the newer, sparsely settled States would get the least help, though they had the greatest need.

The Senate had a standing Committee on Public Lands, but the majority nevertheless wanted the question put to Clay's Committee on Manufactures. The Committee was embarrassed and so was Clay. If the Committee should be liberal toward the new States, the old States might complain. If it should favor the old States, the new ones would be dissatisfied. Impartial justice, Clay feared, would satisfy no one, and this was an election year.

As to the Senators who voted to refer the responsibility to him, Clay said, "The decorum proper in this hall obliges me to consider their motives to have been pure and patriotic." Having spoken, he presented his plan, which gave the newer States a little extra, and from then on he fought savagely for its passage.

In spite of his efforts, in mid-1832 his bill had passed only the Senate and not the House. At the next session, it took until the day preceding adjournment before a measure embodying Clay's formula was put before the President, and then the members of Congress packed their belongings and left the Capitol for nine months.

On Thursday, December 6, 1833, three days after the Senate reconvened, the President's private secretary, Mr. Donelson, carried the measure, still unsigned, back to the Senate. To begin with, Jackson complained that the bill had been given to him on March 2, the last day of the session; he therefore had had insufficient time to make up his mind. In short, Clay's plan had been pocket-vetoed.

The shocked Kentucky Senator insisted that the President's action was ". . . unprecedented and alarming." He declared that "unless the people of this country [are] lost to all sense of what [is] due to the legislative branch of the Government [and] to themselves. . . . they would not tolerate [it]." Here again was Clay's old hope that everyone would soon be disillusioned with the Jacksonians.

As usual, his indignation was not without some justification. The bill had been before the country for a whole year before it passed both Houses. Lack of time could not be an excuse for the Executive's actions.

Moreover, Clay was not impressed when Benton argued that 142 bills had been put on the books that session, and 90 of them had been signed on March 2, making it almost impossible for the President to deal with such a mass.

According to the constant practice of Congress, the President had been sent a copy of the bill when it was first introduced. At that time the measure had attracted great public attention, and Clay was sure the President had looked at it.

What the President had done, Clay charged, was to deprive Congress of the opportunity of passing the bill over his veto. Had he wished, Clay could have pointed to five words in the message that made this charge seem probable. The President's final judgment of the bill read, "[I]t ought not to become a law." Jackson felt that the bill violated contracts made with the older States to use the land to promote only the common good, and not mere local purposes.

His veto sparked a drive to reduce the veto power. The leader was Congressman Joseph Kent of Maryland. Madison, he recalled, had used the veto sparingly, Jefferson never.

Kent failed for the same reason Clay failed. Neither of them ever could command the support of a full two-thirds of the members attending Congress. Without that two-thirds, they could neither override a Presidential veto nor send a proposed amendment to the States.

Jackson still ruled Congress because he still ruled the voters. Considering himself the voice of the people, he was not intimidated by Clay, Kent or anyone else.

Shortly after reading Kent's formal proposal to limit the veto power, Jackson vetoed another bill. This measure authorized a compromise of payments owed by the King of the Two Sicilies to American merchants. The issue, said the President, was an Executive matter and did not concern Congress.

He next vetoed a bill establishing an adjournment date that would bind future Congresses. Finally, he vetoed an alteration of his rules requiring that debts owed to the Government be paid in specie. His ground this time was that the bill was too "liable to diversity of interpretation"—implying, therefore, that he had the right to negate an act simply because it was not clearly stated.

No wonder men like Clay and Webster considered Jackson a tyrant. He had permanently reduced the powers of Congress by this wide interpretation of the veto power. He had turned the veto into a greatly reinforced weapon which all future Presidents could use or threaten to use to intimidate the lawmakers. Congress would never be completely free from this check. Always, while planning legislation, it would have to consider what the President would accept.

The Rest of the Legacy

When Jackson's second term expired, the land question was still unsettled and the slavery issue was intensified by the emergence of the Texas problem. Jackson also left Congress with its control over the country's war-making powers still intact. As a General he had been critized for warlike acts when Congress had not declared war. But while he was President, Congress, in spite of his popularity, refused to let him risk embroiling the country in a war.

In view of what happened a decade later, it is interesting to observe that in the area of foreign affairs Congress restrained President Jackson on two occasions. Late in December, 1834, he asked congressional permission to make reprisals against the French Government for not paying long-overdue debts. However, the Senate passed a Resolution on January 5 stating that it was "inexpedient, at this time, to pass any law vesting in the President authority for making reprisals upon French property . . ."

After hearing John Quincy Adams urge executive-legislative cooperation, the House would have softened the blow by giving the President an extra defense appropriation, but the Senate disliked even that idea.

On March 3, 1835, with Congress due to expire at midnight,

the House and Senate held a joint conference on the matter, and it was after midnight when they agreed on a compromise. When the new proposal was carried to the House, many of the members had already left. Finding that he could not summon a quorum, Speaker Bell declared the Twenty-third Congress adjourned. That left the President without his extra defence appropriation to impress the French. The matter of the French debt had to be settled peacefully later with the help of British mediation.

Then, in 1836, the Texas question arose.

Led by Jackson's friend Sam Houston, North Americans who had settled in Texas successfully rebelled and separated Texas from Mexico. They then proclaimed a constitution recognizing slavery as legal. Jackson, while delaying recognition, nevertheless wanted to press claims against Mexico for "outrages" inflicted on the property and person of United States citizens. In December of 1836, he asked Congress for authority to send a naval squadron into Mexican waters. This time Congress again refused. For the second time its disapproval had been sufficiently aroused to make its members reassert their proper authority.

However, the President was not alone in his sympathies for the Texans. In February of 1837, House members managed to attach a rider to a civil appropriation bill providing a salary for a diplomatic representative to Texas, thus recognizing its independence. The money was to be used when the President thought the right time had come. He thought it had already come and secured Senate approval for his nominee before he left office.

That was the beginning of the next drama in the evolution of Congress. Already the term "Texas" was as inflammatory as those words with which it was irreparably connected: slavery, abolition, and war.

Sensing the tension in the air, Jackson, before he left office, asked Congress to pass legislation prohibiting circulation through the mail of publications intended to encourage insurrection among the slaves. He encouraged Calhoun, who wanted Congress to refuse to accept petitions for the abolition of slavery in the District of Columbia. It took a prolonged campaign to salvage the rights of Americans to petition their Congress on any subject. The campaign began before Jackson left the White House; it continued long after he was gone.

Part VI

John Quincy Adams and the Congress

The Congressional Scene

In Congress, as elsewhere, there are many types of leadership. Clay and Van Buren influenced their world by their ability to attract and organize adherents. Van Buren and Benton capitalized on their closeness to the President, and so did Polk. These men prided themselves on being Jacksonian Democrats, mouthpieces of the new age and its great leader in the White House.

In the midst of this, it was not a Jacksonian, but rather a Whig and a former Federalist—one who had never been willing to subjugate himself to party discipline—who bestowed the most valuable contribution of his age on an unwilling Congress.

In this period famous for the political enthronment of the humble man, it was a lofty ex-President, John Quincy Adams, who charged to the rescue of every man's right to communicate to his Congress.

When anxious slave-owners and their friends passed a "gag" rule against abolitionist memorials, the role of Congress as a free forum for the views of all the people was endangered. Realizing this, the ex-President made his great contribution to future Congressmen and their constituents. And in addition, before he left the scene, he struck a blow for the rights of Congressmen in their relations with the Executive.

Speak Seldom

John Quincy Adams was already sixty-three when he reentered Congress in 1831, an uncomfortable and anxious man. He had not been a popular President and he had no idea how the other Representatives would treat him. When at the outset they were courteous, Adams wrote, "Thank God" in his diary, and added a command to himself: "Speak Seldom." By his silence, he hoped to retain their good will. It was a trying resolution; for everything concerning the House and its functions fascinated the ageing statesman.

The pages of his diary quickly filled with descriptions of people, events, and procedures. He noticed that when ordinary bills were reported from committees, it had become the practice of the House to read only their titles and then declare them read. They were referred to the Committee of the Whole and made the order of the day for "tomorrow." But, he soon noticed that for a multitude of bills this tomorrow never came. Except when a motion to suspend the rules was granted, the bills for the day had to be taken up in the order that they were referred and many proposals were never reached.

One suggestion Adams did not make slipped instead into his diary. He regretted the time consumed examining private claims against the Government. There were a number of pleas for pensions for ex-soldiers or their survivors. The heirs of one citizen prayed for compensation for his horse, which had been requisitioned during the war. To Adams' disgust the House voted them an award.

"A deliberative assembly is the worst of all tribunals for the administration of justice," he wrote. "There is no common rule of justice for [deciding] any two of these cases." He was convinced that such claims should be taken to court.

While the Congressmen never did cede their prerogative of passing a private bill to right an injustice or otherwise help a "worthy individual," they did, three quarters of a century later, establish the Court of Claims to hear cases much like those Adams described. Meanwhile, while Adams was still in Congress, they set up a separate calendar for these private measures, so that they should be considered only at certain times and not interrupt other business.

Adams next discovered that there had been a caucus meeting of Jackson's opponents. All the anticipated measures of legislation had been reviewed and an opposition course agreed upon. Here was one activity Adams did not support. He was not starting the session precommitted to oppose the President's proposals.

The session had started as usual in early December. By mid-March, Adams was gaining confidence and proudly recorded it in his diary: "This was the second instance of effect produced by my share in a debate . . ."

Although not a Democrat, he was appointed chairman of one of the twelve standing committees, and after consulting with the Secretary of the Treasury, he drafted a tariff bill for the committee members to consider. The bill, later reported to the House and then enacted, showed that the committee had been guided by his suggestions.

He was less fortunate when the reapportionment question was raised. Each time the census was taken, Congress had to decide what formula to use to distribute representation among the States. Once the population was divided by the chosen figure, some States would be left with a quotient that included a fraction. In an effort to keep down the number of its members, Congress decided to ignore the fraction, and New England lost representation.

When the measure passed, Adams was riled and hurt, but when he made his views known, he showed little of the eloquence he later displayed. He complained to his diary that he had left out much of what he wanted to say.

Inevitably his sensitive mind found other causes that taxed his will to remain silent. Congress had a confused mode of constructing appropriation acts. Additions were made to these acts in order to get projects financed without first letting the members study their merits. Seeing this, Adams started what he anticipated would be a difficult campaign.

He wanted to keep new projects from receiving any funds until Congress had authorized the activity in question. To his surprise, he made progress, but in his diary he cautioned himself, "the success of the . . . movement is encouraging, but the evil usage will be constantly returning . . ." It would have helped his ego could he have known that the rule that he fathered, making it necessary for any proposal to be authorized by Congress before the members voted it any appropriation, was still in effect in the 1970s (although there are exceptions to the rule).

If all these things bothered Adams, there was one procedure that did inspire him. To Adams, the call for petitions on each Monday morning in the House was a most gratifying event. Back in his room at night, he described how the States were called by the Clerk to present their petitions. "It was, he thought, . . . a very striking exemplification of the grandeur of this nation and of the sublime principles upon which our Government is founded." Once again he could hear a colleague briefly describe one of these pleas and then suggest the committee to which it should be referred. Once again, with the eyes of his imagination, he could follow the messenger boy bearing the memorial from the members to the chair, leading Adams' attention to the colossal emblem of the Union above the Speaker's head.

Then one day he was forced to wonder whether petitions would ever again have the same significance. He had to ask himself if they would soon cease to be the truly free expressions of a free people sent to their Representatives. Probably he saw the storm coming before the challenge reached the House, for the campaign to gag the abolitionists started in the Senate. The issue was to arouse Adams to the point of shattering his resolution to speak seldom. He was to become so absorbed in his crusade to preserve the full meaning of the First Amendment that at an age when most men are ready to retire Adams suddenly blossomed.

He forgot his earlier self-consciousness and earned himself the title of "Old Man Eloquent," a description his contemporaries took from a sonnet by John Milton.

The Right of Petition and the Gag Rule

The plan not to receive petitions asking for the abolition of slavery in the District of Columbia began with Calhoun.

Abolishing slavery in the District would erect a refuge for runaway slaves and insurgents between two slaveholding States, Maryland and Virginia. Buchanan well understood Calhoun's objections to these petitions and himself moved that the recommendation of the memorialists be rejected. It was Calhoun's motion to refuse to receive the petitions at all that disturbed Buchanan.

"The Southerners," Buchanan said, "were fond of pointing out that Congress had no power to interfere with slavery in the States." He argued that they had no more right to touch the power of petition. "A representative republic, established by the people, without the people having the right to make their wants and their wishes known to their servants, would be the most palpable absurdity."

He cautioned the Southern gentlemen, "Let it be once understood that the sacred right of petition and the cause of the abolitionists must rise and fall together and the consequence may be fatal."

For one brief period, it appeared as if his wisdom would prevail. The Senate voted to let Buchanan read the abolitionist petitions he had received from Pennsylvania.

The rights of the citizens again prevailed when the Senate finished evaluating a bill implementing the President's recommendation to outlaw abolitionist literature from Southern mails. The measure would have made it illegal for "any deputy postmaster . . . knowingly to deliver . . . any pamphlet, newspaper, handbill, or other printed paper . . . touching the subject of slavery . . . in any State . . . where . . . their circulation is prohibited."

As the bill read, the deputy postmasters, who were to pass judgment on the mail, might one day even exclude the Constitution of the United States as touching on slavery. When Webster pointed this out he was answered by a Southern spokesman: "You have no right to diffuse publications through . . . the post office, for the purpose of exciting a servile war."

Davis of Massachusetts was disgusted to again hear this old cry of danger, always used against the freedom of the press as an excuse to establish a censorship over it. He would put up with the danger rather than let the deputy postmaster decide what should and should not be distributed. Clay agreed.

Anyone listening would have thought that petitioners had nothing to fear, and that their rights were in good hands. The listener would have been quite wrong.

The campaign to limit the right of petition had spread into the House, where Jarvis of Maine moved that all petitions to abolish slavery in the District of Columbia be laid on the table without being printed or referred to a committee. Henry A. Wise of Virginia moved to add a declaration that Congress had no power to abolish slavery in the District, any more than in the States.

South Carolina's Congressman Henry Pinckney moved that the Jarvis proposal be sent to a select committee and the committee be instructed to report that Congress had no power over slavery in the States and *ought not to* interfere with it in the District. There was so much to Pinckney's resolution that others demanded that it be divided into parts.

Wise found it infuriating, but the parts all passed. When Pinckney reported for the committee, Wise refused to vote, on grounds that the action would imply that Congress had discretion over slavery in the District. His attitude was expected, but nobody was prepared for the conduct of the gentleman from Massachusetts, John Quincy Adams.

When Pinckney repeated the oft-made statement that Congress possessed no authority to interfere in any way with the institution of slavery in any of the States. Adams was on his feet, demanding five minutes to prove that resolution false.

He was shouted down with cries of "Order" and the resolution was passed. Ordinarily, that might have ended it, but Adams had started a new phase of his career. He obtained the floor later in the day supposedly to support a move to dispense

Federal aid to victims of Indian raids. Congress, he said, was entitled to give relief in this area under its war-making powers. These were the same powers that might one day permit Congress to interfere with slavery in the States. His words were a prophetic warning but they were not the main thrust of his campaign.

It was Pinckney's third resolution that aroused Adams the most. "Resolved," it said, "that all petitions, memorials, resolutions, propositions, or papers, relating in any way, or to any extent whatever, to the subject of slavery, or the abolition of slavery, shall, without being either printed or referred, be laid upon the table, and that no further action whatever shall be had thereon."

When the Clerk called the roll on this proposition, Adams shouted over the calls for order, "I hold the resolution to be a direct violation of the Constitution . . . the rules of this House, and the rights of my constituents."

Nobody in the room could have expected that for the next eight years Adams would begin each new session of Congress with a strenuous attack on the gag rule.

Adams with his alert mind was well aware of the lessons taught by the biographies of both Clay and Van Buren. Well-organized forces can usually triumph, even when outnumbered. Adams had few supporters and no organization, but he was determined to demonstrate to this age, which had grown increasingly impressed with the powers of concerted action and party discipline, that conviction, will power, and persistence could still rescue freedom and the rights of the individual.

After the gag rule passed, Adams announced that he would continue to present all the memorials sent to him, and he received a flood of mail. The record shows that he presented abolitionist petitions from New Hampshire, New York, Michigan, and Virginia, as well as from Massachusetts.

In December, 1836, Speaker Polk decided that the rule had expired when the previous session ended, but in mid-January the rule was reenacted. Adams then began to ridicule as well as evade the gag. His favorite tactic was to ask for a ruling.

In this guise, he presented one abolitionist petition as unfinished business, claiming that he had been trying to present it before the restriction went into effect. He drew the House's attention to another by appealing from the ruling of the Chair that it fell within the ban. It did not, he insisted, use the word "slavery," but asked that Congress grant all the inhabitants of the area their rights under the Declaration of Independence.

The petition was subsequently laid on the table without being referred; but the crafty old gentleman had already made its contents known, not only on the floor of the House, but also to readers of the House journal.

Adams next caused a sensation by politely asking Polk whether he could offer the House a petition which he explained was signed by twenty-two slaves, and which he carefully held in his hand. If it had been up to him he would have presented it, he said, "but from the respect he paid the rules of the House, he had first asked the decision of the Chair."

Polk turned the matter over to the members. It was some time before Congressman Jenifer, of Maryland, had a chance to point out that Adams had never before paid so much regard to the decisions of the Speaker. On the contrary, on almost every petition day since the gag rule started, Adams, working to transgress the rules, "had come into collision with the Speaker."

Jenifer, being from a slaveholding State, was determined "to resist at the threshold . . . every effort to throw firebrands among the slave population." He did not like adding to the excitement, but should Adams present such a petition he would be willing to vote for his expulsion.

To cope with the threats and abuse aroused by his request, Adams had his arguments ready: First, he had not presented the petition. He had held it in his hand and asked for a ruling. Furthermore, it so happened that this petition was not a call for the abolition of slavery, but it was a petition against abolition.

Infuriated, Thompson of South Carolina immediately offered these resolutions.

"1. Resolved: That the honorable John Quincy Adams, by an effort to present a petition from slaves, has committed a gross contempt of this House.

"2. Resolved: That the . . . above named, by creating the

impression . . . that said petition was for the abolition of slavery, when he knew it was not, has trifled with the House."

A resolution of censure is a privileged matter and even today is taken up quickly in order to give the accused a chance to clear himself. In Adams' day, all other business was postponed.

At the time, Virginia's Mr. Dromgoole was too angry to debate. He rose only to ask Thompson to accept a modification of his wording, which Dromgoole sent to the Clerk's table. It changed the Thompson resolution to make it clear that Adams should be censured because "he had given color to the idea that slaves have the right to petition . . ."

Then came the reaction of another Virginian. On Tuesday, February 7, 1837, James Robertson frankly told the House that the Southern gentlemen had been called upon to unite and sustain the censure resolutions. Regretfully he admitted, "I cannot obey . . . without . . . violating . . . that liberty of speech guaranteed to every member in this hall."

Robertson then explained to the Speaker why he had not previously entered into the stormy debate. "I was, Sir, . . . unwilling to trust . . . [my] emotions." He added that he agreed with those who thought Adams had trifled with the patience of the House, to the great delay of its business, and had wantonly tortured the feelings of other members. This was exactly why Robertson wanted the House to act cautiously. It is in moments of high . . . exasperation such as we have just witnessed, that the most fatal precedents are established," he said, "and that, too, often under high and honorable motives."

He urged his friends to pause before they set a precedent that could recoil upon themselves and destroy the Constitution of the United States. By now it was well established that the House could refuse to receive petitions that were indecorous or insulting in their language. Why not, men argued, extend the rule to any petition that was undeserving? And why not censure anyone who disregarded the feelings of the House?

But, with Robertson's help, others saw the danger, and the first crisis in Adams' long battle was over. He had escaped being discredited and silenced or expelled for his persistence and his courage, and he was still free to go on with his crusade to rescue the rights of citizens to petition. He still had a lot of fighting to do. In all fairness, some of the credit for his victory goes to the other men in the chamber. Many of them were furious at Adams and prejudiced against his cause, but they still had enough respect for the Constitution not to disgrace the Congress by punishing a man for stating an idea.

The Difficulty of Obtaining Allies

When Thompson's recommendation of censure was beaten, he remarked bitterly, "It is not the first time that, in the moment of conflict, I have found myself abandoned by those who urged me into it."

He was lucky that Adams could not take advantage of another one of his remarks. He had warned the North against those new voters the laboring men, who would rob the Northern property owners either by lawless insurrection or by the ballot box. "Let gentlemen look to it; they are in quite as much danger . . . as we are," he cautioned the delegations from the nonslaveholding States.

In the chamber at the time was a Representative from New York named Ely Moore. Moore had been elected first president of the newly formed federation of craft unions of New York. He was the editor of a labor newspaper and the founder of a national federation of trade unions. Tammany, the powerful Democratic society of New York, had sponsored him for Congress.

The next time Moore took the floor, he digressed from the topic at hand to tell the House that Thompson wanted only the wealthy to vote, which Moore called a strike at the very root of free government.

Adams, who considered Moore "the prince of working men," watched with interest. What he saw was a handsome man six feet tall with a good command of language who might prove to be a natural ally. In the decades ahead, no group would have a greater need for the right to petition than Moore's followers and successors in the labor union movement.

But the longer Adams listened, the surer he became that Moore was a tool of the Executive. "He takes little part in debate and votes with the standing majority," Adams wrote regretfully. Moore, in short, was concerned with only one cause, the workers' rights. To that end Moore cultivated the Jacksonians, not Whigs like Adams. When the resolution to censure Adams was beaten, it was not because Moore helped him.

Meanwhile, Wise was still disgusted that the House had not denied having any jurisdiction whatever, anywhere, over slavery. While lamenting this fact, he let slip the information that the gag rule was the result of a compact, which the South had at last obtained from the Northern part of the Democratic party. That explained why Adams was having so much difficulty winning adherents. It would have been enough to discourage most politicians, but the old man fought on.

The Slow Road to Victory— ## *and the Road Blocks*

By mid-1838 Adams was also fighting against the annexation of Texas. The right of petition became embroiled in that struggle as attempts to lay on the table all petitions against annexation aroused the old man's wrath. Among the memorials which the Committee on Foreign Affairs did not want to bother considering were carefully written papers from State legislatures. The fact was that those who objected to annexation not only were haunted by the spectacle of more slave States but feared a war with Mexico. According to Adams, the neglect of their petitions was a betrayal of the committee's duties.

Adams agreed with the petitioners, and he preached and filibustered against annexation for three long weeks, until the second session of the Twenty-fifth Congress came to an end.

When annexation was delayed, Henry Wise and others counted it another grievance committed against them by the abolitionists and their friends like Adams. It was not insignificant that by now Adams knew that Wise could be ruthless. Wise had acted as a second in a duel fought with rifles, which had been motivated by remarks made by Congressman Jonathan Cilley of Maine on the floor of the House. Representative William Graves had been the challenger, but when Cilley was killed Adams blamed Wise for not persuading the duelers to quit.

The House did not have the power to try Graves for murder or any other crime. What the members did was to have a committee investigate whether the events leading to the death of Mr. Cilley constituted a "breach of the privileges of the House"; in other words, whether the incident jeopardized the safety of House members or the integrity of their proceedings.

As a result of the inquiry, the Congress put an antidueling law on the books, making dueling in the District of Columbia a felony and every person carrying or delivering a challenge subject to ten years at hard labor. That action in no way dampened the high spirits Wise had always displayed. (Before his career ended, he would be Governor of Virginia and would sign the death warrant for John Brown after the raid on Harper's Ferry.) He was a formidable adversary for Adams to confront in debate.

Fortunately, before Adams and Wise were again in collision, the older man had improved his standing in the House. This was partly the result of an episode involving the organization of the House at the beginning of the Twenty-sixth Congress, in December, 1839.

As was the custom before a new Speaker was elected, the Clerk presided. He soon interrupted himself to explain that five of the six New Jersey seats were being contested. At that moment the Whigs and the Democrats were so evenly divided that control of the House depended upon which of the New Jerseyites were to be allowed to vote. The Clerk refused to decide between them, saying that it was not up to him. Various suggestions were made, but each time the Clerk refused "to put the question" that would have let the House vote on what had been proposed.

After four days of wild confusion, Adams rose and advised the members to organize themselves and instruct the Clerk whom to include in the roll call. He himself offered to put the question and was chosen temporary chairman of the House. Finally, the election for Speaker was held, and by order of the House, neither group of New Jerseyites was allowed to participate.

This time Polk was not running. He had left the Congressional scene hoping to become Governor of Tennessee. Doubtless he had had enough of trying to control Adams, Wise and Bell.

Bell claimed that those who controlled the House, led by the Chair, managed to drop matters they did not like. Wise claimed that it was impossible to investigate the Executive departments because of the disinterest shown by those Polk picked to man his committees. In this, Adams agreed with Wise. He felt that Polk had arranged the committees so that they would carry out the will of the leaders of the Jacksonian majority. Led by the Whigs, the House let Polk's term expire without giving him the customary vote of thanks.

At first it appeared that Polk would be succeeded by Francis Pickens, of South Carolina. A large majority of the Democrats wanted Pickens, but he was late reaching Congress. By the time he arrived, other groups had campaigns under way for friends of their own and his opportunity was gone forever.

After eleven ballots, Robert W. T. Hunter, a Virginia Democrat with Whig friends, was declared the winner and next Speaker and was escorted to the Chair. He took the oath and swore in the members. Thanks to Adams, who had delivered the House from chaos, the work of the session could begin.

After the election incident, Adams slowly gained supporters in his fight to abolish the gag rule. But in spite of his new friends, the rule was made more stringent in 1841. Nevertheless, he went right on presenting all the abolitionists' petitions he received, as he felt obligated to do, and they included petitions declaring that Adams was a lunatic and should lose his committee assignment.

In January of 1842, forty-six citizens of Massachusetts sent Adams a petition praying that the Congress dissolve the Union, and he presented it. He moved that it be sent to a select committee, with instructions to report why the prayer should not be granted.

In the hubbub that followed it was hard for the reporter to hear all that went on, but Wise again wanted Adams censured. Adams again seized the opportunity to defend his views to the House. When a House member cried, "Treason," Adams had the Clerk read the Declaration of Independence, to prove that the people had the right to change their Government.

In February, Adams was still in the midst of the fiery ordeal, but once more he survived the assault. Once more his eloquence restrained the actions of the House, and once more he looked ahead to fight on against the destruction of the rights of his constitutents, be they abolitionists or not.

After March, he received some unexpected encouragement. Joshua Giddings of Ohio denounced a demand for the return of escaped slaves and was censured. He therefore resigned and was immediately reelected to fill the vacancy caused by his own resignation.

Earlier, Adams had warned the Representatives that if, in their hunger to remain at peace with the slaveholders, they ignored the right of petition, they would hear from their constituents. When—added to the flood of memorials which kept arriving despite the ban—Giddings was returned to the House in the face of the House censure vote, it was at last apparent that there was more than rhetoric to the ex-President's prediction, and after that his opposition began decreasing rapidly. As the Van Buren Democrats and the Southern Democrats grew further apart, the Northerners were less willing to sustain the gag rule. All this helped, but none of it won the battle.

What Adams had to do was use his knowledge of parliamentary procedure and his ingenuity to find ways to keep the issue alive, to prevent the gag rule from becoming an accepted precedent, until finally all the factors added up to giving him the support he needed.

In December, 1843, *Niles' National Register* reported that help was coming. The Van Buren Democrats had decided at last to favor the repeal of the gag rule. The rule, said the periodical, had kept the House in a state of turmoil and had given ten times more weight to political abolitionists than they would have acquired without this error. Finally, here was the support of a major faction.

In January, 1844, Adams, with the help of Van Buren's supporters, came within one vote of abolishing the gag.

Victory came at last in the Twenty-eighth Congress. In December of 1844, Adams presented his usual motion that Rule 21, the gag rule, be rescinded, and this time he had the votes. By a vote of 108 to 80, the ban against receiving abolitionist petitions went down to defeat. Having started virtually alone, Adams had finally overcome the once powerful and well-organized opposition.

His victory is not diminished by the fact that over the years the procedure for handling petitions has changed. At first, they had been read aloud into the record. In the early days of the gag rule, a member seeking to present a petition could make a brief statement of its content, but more and more often the members had been merely handing them to the Clerk, indicating the committee to which they were to be referred.

As of this writing, a Congressman can, if he sees fit, place a petition from his constituents in the hopper, the box at the side of the chamber into which proposed bills are placed. A petition so handled will be listed in the Congressional Record. Letters sent to a committee are frequently printed in the record of its hearings.

With the pressure to get more and more subjects out of the way, and to free floor time for other serious matters, it was inevitable that the leisurely methods of an earlier day should be so replaced. What has not been replaced is the attitude in the minds of the members of Congress and of their constituents, that the citizens have the right to petition their representatives and to have their memorials considered. That was all John Quincy Adams wanted, but it took Adams to get it.

Impacts of the Election

In the years after Jackson, the election returns decided much more than who would hold office. Men changed their attitudes, altered their plans, and adjusted the roles they intended to play on the political stage. What they thought the returns meant, how well they liked the outcome, and what hopes they nurtured, all guided their actions.

For example, in the fall of 1837, Richard M. Johnson was serving as Vice President, having been elected by the Senators when the voters failed to give any vice-presidential candidate a majority. Because of Johnson's election, the Senators gave the office more than its usual significance. For Johnson, the Senators rescinded a ruling made during the bank crisis.

At that time, on the basis of a partisan vote, they had deprived their presiding officer of the power to appoint standing committees. They gave that power to Johnson and later, after Johnson left office, they would again take back the privilege. At the same time, Calhoun, who was back in the Senate, was perfecting a change in his political maneuverings. After opposing Jackson, he did an about-face when Jackson's political heir, Martin Van Buren, took office in 1837. As the campaign of 1840 approached, Calhoun, in letters to his South Carolina followers, was supporting Van Buren for reelection.

This political marriage was somewhat surprising because Van Buren's enemies classed him with a New York labor faction, the Locofocos. And Calhoun had once written that the North had more to fear from its needy workers than the South from its slaves. The fact was that peace between these two (as Adams had discovered) rested on Calhoun's being able to count on the cooperation of Van Buren's friends on tariff issues and in avoiding the slavery question. When Van Buren failed to be reelected, Calhoun's concern was to keep the minority in Congress as large and well organized as possible.

So thinking, he fought his way through a Washington snowstorm to attend the "Little Magician's" last New Year's Day levee in the White House. He was there to keep the good will of the Van Buren Democrats and keep them looking toward the South for protection against the new Executive's party. In return, he expected them to keep faith with what he considered were their obligations to his partisans. This was what the election returns meant to Calhoun.

To the Whigs they meant something else. They had bypassed

A SELECT COMMITTEE OF ENQUIRY HARD AT WORK.

Committee of Inquiry   *Library of Congress*

Here are two views of a congressional investigation of Van Buren's activities. Thievery by a political appointee who held his office because of the spoils system prompted the probe. Above, left, the Congressman in the high chair is promising to reward everyone who coats the President with enough virtue. In the picture below, the President is strapped to the scrutiny chair. Even his ears are being pierced to see why he did not hear the complaints against his officer. But there is no trace of the smell of gold on his hands.

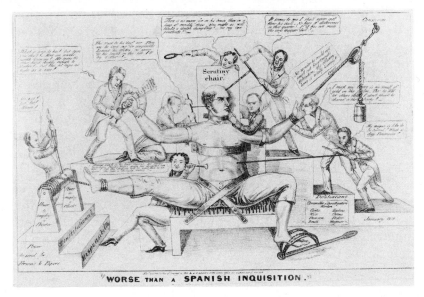

"WORSE THAN A SPANISH INQUISITION."

Worse than a Spanish Inquisition   *Library of Congress*

Henry Clay in an effort to win the Presidency for their party, and had offered the voters General William Henry Harrison. With him they had run a Virginian named John Tyler who had been the only Senator to vote against the Force Bill. Tyler had also resigned from the Senate when he could not abide the orders he received from his State legislature, showing that he was a strong believer in States' rights but at the same time highly independent. However, on the Whig ticket he was blithely referred to as "Tyler too."

When the Whig efforts were crowned with victory, Clay expected to be the administration's leader in the Senate, and on a Saturday evening, in February of 1841, a caucus of Whig Senators was held in the Senate chamber, where the policies to be recommended to General Harrison were fully discussed.

Webster, who was soon to be in the President's cabinet, was there; so were Senators Prentiss of Vermont, Crittenden of Kentucky, and of course, Clay. They decided to call an extra session of Congress to deal with the country's financial plight. The Treasury was empty and the Government was running a deficit. They wanted to pass Clay's land bill, reestablish the bank, raise duties, and devise measures for retrenching Government expenditures.

All this they confidently expected to do, when on April 4, only a month after his inauguration, President Harrison passed from the scene. As a result, the former Virginia Senator, whom the Whigs had called "Tyler too," took office.

At first Clay and his friends went right ahead with their plans. The special session of Congress, which President Harrison had summoned at their request, met in May. Clay wanted to hurry the work, but before he could even offer his bank bill, he had to obtain the repeal of the subtreasury measure passed for Van Buren, which replaced the use of Jackson's "pet banks" and let the Government retain and manage its own funds without resort to banks. To speed debate, Clay moved to skip some of the morning periods which the Senators devoted to miscellaneous inquiries and resolutions. Clay urged instead that they concentrate on the main discussion. He was overwhelmed by the objections.

The Democrats, particularly, felt that they would be denied a hearing on matters they wished to criticize, and Clay apologized, saying, "I do not like to be a dictator . . ."

To which Buchanan replied, "You do it so well, you ought to like it." Finally, however, Clay did get the sub-treasury system repealed. In July, he saw his bank bill pass the Senate at last.

It was accepted by the Representatives and went to the White House. By then there were rumors that the President would not sign it.

At this point, Adams, Clay, and their friends were confronted with the fact that they had put another man of Jackson's views and spirit into the White House. They feared that instead of letting Congress take back its pre-Jackson control of the nation's affairs, Tyler would more firmly establish a tradition of Executive supervision. So it proved.

Clay was furious. He had gone so far as to make concessions in the bank bill to please the new Chief Executive.

The President's friends had urged that the consent of a State should be needed before the bank could open a branch office in that State. Clay had compromised. A branch could be established anywhere unless the State legislature objected.

When Tyler still vetoed his bill, Clay felt betrayed. Soon he was again clamoring for a change in the veto power. The President's intimates in Congress seemed to him to be trying to break the victorious Whig Party. He ridiculed them as being less numerous than a "corporal's guard," and the nickname stuck.

Meanwhile, the argument centered around what the last election had meant. Clay said the people had demanded his bank and that the President should obey the public mandate or resign.

Tyler felt he could answer that. "It will suffice for me to say that my own opinion had been uniformly proclaimed . . . during a period of twenty-five years. . . . With a full knowledge of the opinion. . . . I was elected by the people Vice-President of the United States."

In the House, Representative Thomas Gilmer, from Tyler's own State, saw the election in still a different light. The public wanted economy in Government, he said, and in a verbal bow to Adams, who was still fighting the gag rule, he added that it had been echoed from one end of the continent to the other that the voters wanted "no proscription for opinion's sake."

To Adams, it was also obvious that the country had elected a Whig President and that Tyler occupied the White House only by accident. For all his political life, Adams had urged executive-legislative cooperation, but he felt forced to reverse that stand in the months ahead. Tyler's actions went beyond what he could accept, and he did not believe that they represented the will of the people. He, too, like the other principals in the political arena, had drawn his own conclusions from the election returns and, like the others, his findings helped to determine his conduct.

"Struck With Apoplexy by the Executive Hand"

The series of events causing Adams to reevaluate the attitudes that had always guided his political life started with Tyler's veto of a second attempt to pass a bank bill.

This time the Whigs held a caucus and voted their President out of the party. A few days later, the *New York Herald* announced that most of the cabinet had resigned and that they were sure it was under orders from Clay. Webster, however, remained as Secretary of State.

Calhoun was in the best position he had enjoyed in years. He wrote home that he would oppose, or support, measures offered by the Whigs, or by the administration, as they accorded with his policies. He felt the administration would be so weak that it would be compelled to take shelter either with his followers or with the Whigs, and would probably prefer his friends. He was right.

Tyler felt closer to the States Rights Democrats than to the Whigs and continued to veto Whig measures after the party members had fought them through Congress. This was particularly galling when the question of the tariff and the use of the proceeds from the sale of the public lands were involved. Managing the debates in the House on these measures had proved so difficult that the Representatives had again been driven into changing their rules.

What happened in the House was this: With Tyler openly hostile to internal improvements, the only apparent way the Whigs could get such works Federally financed was to distribute to the States the proceeds from the sale of public lands. Inevitably the question of phrasing bills for this purpose became a partisan matter, particularly as it involved raising tariffs to replace the distributed funds.

Thus the first session of the 27th Congress in 1841 found the Representatives floundering endlessly in their attempts to agree on a land bill. As Clifford of Maine told the Committee of the Whole, the arguments for and against the propositions had been urged so often that it was difficult to present them in any new light. If it were not for the duty he owed to his constituents, he would keep silent. That was in June.

In July the debate was still in progress. And in the informal Committee of the Whole the call for the previous question is not in order. On July 6 the exasperated Speaker, John White (a Kentucky Whig), gave the Rules Committee leave to interrupt. They had been instructed to report on all necessary revisions in the House procedures, but they were not doing that. They were reporting only one item. They proposed to reduce from two-thirds to a bare majority the number of ayes needed to discharge the Committee of the Whole, forcing it to end debate, take a vote, and report to the House.

When John McKeon, a New York Democrat, objected to the admission of such a fragment of a report, the Speaker overruled the objection. McKeon appealed to the members, but they sustained the Speaker and then voted to adopt the rule. This, as the future would reveal, was one of the more useful acts of the session. The House had allowed a Rules Committee to submit a rule which governed the immediate occasion. Here was a way of working which would one day become their accepted procedure.

As soon as the rule was adopted, Mr. Stanly, a North Carolina Whig, moved that the debate in the Committee of the Whole to appropriate the proceeds of the sale of public lands should cease at seven o'clock. Under the new rule, all he needed was a majority, and he got it.

At ten minutes to seven, Congressman Rhett, a fire-eating extremist from South Carolina, had the floor. A century thence, his bioragher, Laura A. White, would title him the "Father of Secession." He personified the element that had pressured the transformation of Calhoun from a nationalist into a nullifier.

It was Rhett who, after the first gag rule had lapsed, rose to a point of order to ask if the gentleman from Vermont [Slade] had a right to discuss the question of slavery in Virginia. He thought not, and he invited the whole delegation from all the slaveholding States to meet forthwith in the District Committee room. They went in such large numbers that it was necessary for the Speaker to adjourn the House for the day. Now, having fought with all his powers to keep the gag on abolitionist petitions, he faced a limitation on his own speech.

"I rise," he said, "under the extraordinary law passed this day: a law in my opinion next to the Alien and Sedition Law. The Alien and Sedition Law suppressed the liberty of the press, and this law which you have passed today suppresses the liberty of debate." He then observed that this tyrannical act violated the rights not only of the minority but of their constituents back home. He had hardly begun to give his views of the bill when the minute hand on the clock arrived at that point where all debate was to terminate. How Adams must have smiled.

A loud whisper was then heard from the hall: "Time is up. Time is up. Why does the Chair not announce it?"

Minutes later, several members were shouting, "Mr. Chairman! The time is up. It is seven o'clock." And reluctantly, the Chair silenced the voice that was urging further free discussion.

Finally, then, in spite of the close division in the Congress, the Whig forces passed their distribution bill. Emboldened by the willingness of the exhausted House members to accept reform, a Whig Congressman from Georgia, Lott Warren, moved that no member be allowed to speak for more than one hour to any question under debate, and the House passed this also, 111 to 75.

In September, the public land bill became law. It was a great victory, but the next year the old compromise tariff of 1833 expired, and the Whigs tried to pass a bill that would permit both an increase in the tariff and a simultaneous distribution of the proceeds from land sales. This bill Tyler vetoed. When, after the veto, Congress passed a second tariff bill that the President disliked as much as the first, he suggested that they not combine a temporary tariff and a permanent land policy in the same law, and he vetoed this bill also. As a result, on August 4, 1842, a headline in a Whig newspaper screamed VETO THE FOURTH. Never, said the paper, had a document been received with greater indignation. Having captured the Presidency at the polls, the Whigs still could not make their program law.

At this point, Adams, who in any controversy always had leaned toward supporting the President, found himself, instead, in sympathy with his fellow Whigs. He felt compelled to explain his change of position, and on August 10, 1842, he took the floor to express regret that any hope of harmony between the Executive and the Legislative branches was now blasted. Instead, the Congress and the President were, he said, "in a state of civil war."

Before making any suggestions as to what should be done, he itemized his grievances against Tyler. The second bank bill, he claimed, had been framed to meet Tyler's views to the very letter of his recommendations and nevertheless had been vetoed.

He went on to discuss that provocative matter, retrenchment. In the two Houses of Congress, he admitted, the spirit of economy had perhaps been overactive. Many thought so. Others counseled that the financial distress of the country called for some sacrifices on the part of its Representatives. The House had cut down on the stationery purchased for its members, reduced the number of page boys, and cut the doorkeepers' salary. But, Adams insisted, if there was to be any real saving, it must come out of the Army and Navy budget. In spite of Congressional proposals to the contrary, Tyler had asked for an increase for both services. Where was the spirit of retrenchment on the part of the Executive which Congress had the right to expect? Adams asked, thundering that Tyler offered Congress in this regard "words, words, and nothing else but words."

Adams made a brief reference to Gilmer's special committee set up to seek new economies in the Executive departments.

The committee had found that money was being spent for purposes not named in any appropriation. And it complained that other responsibilities made it impossible for the members to examine all the Executive departments in a satisfactory manner. Congress was nowhere near ready to set up a Bureau of the Budget, but the members foreshadowed this far-off event. They felt that some more thorough system of investigating expenses would be desirable.

After making a polite reference to the efforts of Gilmer's group, Adams came at last to the vetoes of the land and tariff bills. He succeeded in leading the House into breaking all precedents by establishing a special committee under his chairmanship to consider the veto.

The Committee's report concluded: "The power of the present Congress to enact laws essential to the welfare of the people has been struck with apoplexy by the Executive hand."

Wise challenged the House to try to get Tyler impeached, which the members admitted was impracticable. Instead they voted to accept the committee's report, thus putting their sentiments on record. They still intended to keep some reins on the rising tide of Executive aggressiveness, and eventually they did so.

At last, in 1845, Congress did overrule one of Tyler's vetoes. It reenacted a bill prohibiting the Executive from building revenue ships. After that, the Senate refused to pass a treaty annexing Texas, which Tyler wanted and Adams did not. That victory, however, was short-lived.

In fact, before Adams died in the Capitol in February, 1848, the Texas question had formed the basis for a shift in power from the Congress to the Executive beyond anything Jackson had ever dreamed was possible. Despite what Adams had said in his younger days, he had every reason to feel justified in wanting the House to watch the Executive henceforth with a more critical eye. His plea for cooperation had been a contribution when he made it. When his position was no longer applicable he had changed it, and this, too, was a trait the men of the future could well afford to imitate.

Meanwhile, the Texas drama and its impact on the evolution of Congress had begun, and it constituted the beginning of the next period in the history of both the country and the Congress.

Part VII

War and the Congress

The Congressional Scene

The Constitution gives only Congress the power to declare war. Only Congress can raise and support armies. Only Congress can provide appropriations for the supplies and maintenance of the fighting force. Moreover, the Constitution commands Congress to limit its military authorizations to two years. Even if they so desire, the Congressmen are not at liberty to provide the Executive with a permanent fund for financing a standing army.

In a closely related area, the founding fathers at Philadelphia made it impossible for the Executive to conclude treaties without submitting them to the Senate; and unless two thirds of those present concur in the proposed agreement it can not take effect. Theoretically, then, Congress had all the power it needed to guide the President through the Texas issue and avoid the unpopular war with Mexico. Both contemporary historians and the statesmen of that day have pondered over why the checks and balances so painstakingly placed in the Constitution failed to avert the tragedy of 1846.

However, even if Texas and all the territories acquired from Mexico had been obtained peacefully, the Civil War might still have followed. The Congress could not organize these vast lands without aggravating the frictions between North and South. Together the two conflicts precipitated another trend. The enlarged authority the Presidents had inherited from the Jacksonians was further increased when first Polk and then Lincoln served as Commander in Chief and held the office in wartime. Years back, Randolph had predicted that war—and the President's use of his war powers—could destroy the Constitution. There were some indications of this during the Mexican War. For a time the anti-war protesters in Congress were slow and cautious. Only when it became clear that the war and the moral issue of slavery had become inseparable did Representatives speak out to criticize the Executive.

During the Civil War, the danger to constitutional government was more apparent. Winning the war seemed more important than overseeing and checking the Executive, although Congress did build into its emergency legislation a few barricades to the complete destruction of civil rights. It did express opposition to the Executive's future plans. But mostly, Congress acted as a great committee to carry on the war, and Congressmen waited for a more appropriate time to reassert their prerogatives.

In short, Congress in wartime was, and is, much subdued.

To Prevent War

Back in 1838, Adams had fought against the annexation of Texas and warned that it would start a war with Mexico. Later, Van Buren and Clay also saw that danger. Benton, who hoped to prevent the war, analyzed the problem as having started in 1819, when Florida was purchased from Spain. Adams was then Secretary of State and Tyler was a member of the House of Representatives. The boundaries they and others agreed to accept treated Texas as being part of Spain's Mexican property when Texas should have been claimed as ours under the Louisiana Purchase. Benton had not given up hope of reacquiring Texas honorably. But now in 1844, he cautioned that the Southern extremists, as well as Secretary of State Calhoun and President Tyler, were all contributing toward a crisis with Mexico by their "fury to get it back."

President Tyler had ignored Mexican sentiment and ignored Congress when he secretly negotiated a treaty of annexation with the Texans. The Senators were then faced with the completed treaty and put in the position of either accepting that new slave territory or, by its rejection, providing the basis for the secession of the Southern States.

If the treaty could not pass the Senate, Southern radicals had declared, they wanted Texas brought into the Union on the basis of a joint resolution to be passed by a mere majority of both Houses. To get that majority, they were ready to go to Congress and threaten the dissolution of the Union.

They were also ready to pressure the Southern members, asking that a Southern convention should be called to demand an extra session of Congress. That session should decide whether to admit Texas or to take measures to end the Union. The movement was spread by the *Charleston Mercury* (a Rhett newspaper run by his relative), the *Columbia Carolinian*, the *Mobile Tribune*, and the *Richmond Enquirer*—all exciting their readers to a fiery pitch.

On the Senate floor, Benton said that the treaty, though loosely written, incorporated into the Union the left bank of the Rio Grande. Formerly, Texas had never approached the Rio Grande except near its mouth. What the United States was endeavoring to acquire by treaty with Texas was in part territory taken from Mexico. The Texans claimed it only on the basis of an agreement made with Mexico's ex-President Santa Anna at a time when he was their captive.

Further aggravating the situation, Tyler announced that while the Senate deliberated he would protect Texas from invasion. "Let Great Britain send an army *to lie in wait* upon our frontiers. . .and then see what a cry of war would be raised," Benton warned his colleagues, "Unless the Senate (or Congress) saves the country. . .We are at war. . ."

It was Calhoun, he claimed, who was in a rush to effect this annexation, because Britain had proposed to Mexico that she make emancipation a condition for the recognition of Texan independence. But the only means Britain would use to further abolition was advice. Benton did not share the anxiety of Senator Walker of Mississippi that Britain would dominate Texas if the United States failed to annex the area.

To the end of his days Benton would maintain that, had

Calhoun delayed negotiating a treaty of annexation, and delayed assurance of military protection, Texas and Mexico would have made their own peace eventually and annexation could have followed later without involving a war with Mexico.

Tyler, however, saw no need to wait. Mexico, he insisted, should now give up all claim to Texas. It had been almost nine years since the Mexicans had first tried to subdue the unhappy Texans. There comes a time when such struggles should cease.

Before the session ended, Benton was delighted to think that his advice would prevail. The Senate did not ratify the treaty, and *Niles' National Register* reported with relief that the Southern Congressmen left Washington without calling a secessionist convention. Since the friends of annexation carried through the nomination of James K. Polk for President at the Democratic convention, the editor felt that this explained the unwillingness of the Southerners to jeopardize their careers by calling a Southern convention. Instead, the friends of annexation took the stump for Polk.

Polk was running against Clay, who, overeager to get votes, damaged his own cause by making an ambiguous statement on the issue. He was, moreover, the older candidate and the more conservative. Polk symbolized the feeling of the next generation, which believed that the nation's manifest destiny was to push back its borders and extend its frontier.

When Polk won the election, Tyler took it to mean that the people wanted Texas. Benton was confronted with the fact that the House passed a resolution that said, "Congress doth consent that the territory properly included within, and rightfully belonging to the Republic of Texas, may be erected into a new State . . . in order that the same may be admitted as one of the States of this Union." The conditions attached to this offer permitted carving other States out of Texas territory.

Benton next suggested that the Senate should insist that Mexico's consent to the proposal be obtained. But that was hopeless. In spite of all his efforts, the offer to annex Texas became a joint resolution, and President Tyler ordered a messenger to carry it to Texas. Thus, when Polk took office, a long stretch of the highway to war was already paved.

The new President gently questioned Congressmen who came calling to determine how much support he might expect. He not only wanted to acquire Texas but was equally interested in the Oregon Territory.

When Calhoun (who was back in the Senate) called, he needed no prodding. He was not in favor of the President's proposal to present England with an ultimatum that the joint British-American occupation of Oregon must cease in a year. He was for peace. Polk said he too was for peace, but he was for maintaining our just rights.

On Calhoun's next visit, he suggested that Polk urge the Senators to hold an Executive session. Behind closed doors they could consider a resolution to advise the President to accept the forty-ninth parallel as the United States' Oregon border. McDuffie, Calhoun said, was ready to present such a resolution.

The President rejected the plan, which would have offended the more belligerent members of his own party. They were ably led by Lewis Cass, a Senator from Michigan, and were known by their slogan, "54-40 or fight." To offset their influence, Benton spoke to Secretary of State Buchanan and also called on the President saying that he, like Calhoun, also wanted to settle the Oregon question by accepting the forty-ninth parallel. He saw that if Britain would accept this line it would be an honorable compromise of the differences between the two countries.

Polk was intensely irritated, but ultimately he had to settle for the forty-ninth parallel because he could not disregard the Senate's willingness to accept it. That meant disappointing his most ardent followers, and someone had to prepare them for the blow by reminding them that the President was not committed against the forty-ninth parallel. Benton believed that Polk had assigned the task to Senator Haywood, who was both a personal and a political friend to the President.

After hearing Haywood speak, Benton anticipated that the way had been cleared for a peaceful settlement of the Oregon question.

Whether or not Haywood's words came from Polk, the Senators who wanted peace had indeed won. They had won because they were in a position to take a firm stand before events had progressed beyond control.

The Mexican situation, however, was quite a different matter. On May 11, 1846, the President sent a special message to Congress explaining his activities in that area.

"War Exists"

The May 11 message from the President included this explanation:

"On the 10th of November, 1845, Mr. John Slidell of Louisiana, was commissioned by me as envoy extraordinary . . . to Mexico . . . with full powers to adjust both the question of . . . boundary and of indemnification to our citizens."

The "indemnification" related to claims for injuries to American citizens or their property which the Government had been pressing for some time. At first, the President related, it looked as if Slidell was going to be courteously received, but unfortunately he had arrived on the eve of a successful military revolution. And the new Mexican Minister, "in terms that may be considered as giving just ground of offense. . ." had refused to receive the United States envoy.

Polk explained that after that, he had ordered an efficient military force to take a position that would allow it to intercept a threatened invasion of Texas, for that Republic had elected to accept the offer of annexation tendered to her by the United States Congress.

The President, it developed, had also ordered General Zachary Taylor to occupy the territory south of the Nueces River, which was claimed by Texas but not recognized as Texan by Mexico. As a result, the Mexican commander had notified Taylor that he had twenty-four hours to break camp and retreat, or hostilities would begin.

Two weeks later, on April 24, sixty-three American officers and men on a scouting expedition were surrounded. Some sixteen were killed or wounded, and the others surrendered. "Mexico," said the President, "has invaded our territory, and shed American blood upon American soil . . . the two nations are now at war. . . . [W]ar exists, and . . . exists by the act of Mexico herself . . ."

Having confronted the Congress with the established fact that war existed, the Commander-in-Chief proceeded to tell the legislators what he expected from them. He urged them to recognize the existence of war and to place at the disposition of the Executive the means of prosecuting the war with vigor.

Many Congressmen must have wished that they had not written the invitation for annexation in such broad terms as to encompass all "territory properly included within, and rightfully belonging to the Republic of Texas . . ." The geographic meaning of the phrase had obviously been dangerously vague.

Soon two Representatives from the House Committee on Military Affairs called on Polk to discuss the bill the President wanted. He wanted the authority to call for volunteers and funds to purchase supplies for the army.

Almost no one in Congress wanted to deny soldiers already in the field either supplies or reenforcements, but not everyone felt that the situation could be left at that. Representative Jacob Brinkerhoff of Ohio moved to add a preamble to the "supply bill." It began . . . "Whereas, by the Act of the Republic of Mexico, a state of war exists . . ."

To Benton's horror, this preamble formally recognizing the war was discussed in the House of Representatives for only two hours. Most of the members felt powerless to oppose it, since the decisions that had brought on the crisis had already been made. The forces friendly to the administration had thus been able to vote a two-hour limit on debate.

In no time at all, it seemed, Representative Brinkerhoff of Ohio demanded the previous question, and immediately Garrett Davis of Kentucky was on his feet. "I ask the House to

excuse me from voting," he announced. "This is a measure
... of very great importance, and yet no opportunity ... has been
allowed any Whig of this House to say one word upon it."

Davis objected to the preamble of the bill, "that this war was
begun by Mexico." He characterized that statement as utterly
untrue. "It is our President who began this war," he said. He
added that Congress, which was vested by the Constitution with
the war-making power, was not consulted.

He was loudly called to order for explaining why he was
against the bill and not why he should be excused from voting.
The Speaker upheld his right to state his position, and the
House upheld the Speaker. Then, subsequently, Davis withdrew his request to be excused. He had made his point and
would not refuse to vote for the supplies.

Sixty-six other Representatives were also against the preamble, but that was not enough to sever it from the supply bill.
When Davis sat down, they all had to answer the question,
"Shall this bill pass?" It passed the House 174 to 14, because the
country was already at war.

When the bill was received in the Senate, a number of Senators pleaded for time to study the question. But Senator Allen,
Chairman of the Committee on Foreign Relations, replied, "no
time can be afforded ... the urgency of the case requires instant
action ..."

Senator Mangum of North Carolina said he wanted more
facts and he could not see that any injury could come from
separating a declaration of war (the preamble) from a vote for
supplies.

Calhoun agreed. He could not affirm that war existed by act
of Mexico; he had no evidence to affirm it. He could not agree
to make war on our own Constitution by avowing the existence
of a war when no war had been declared by Congress.

Following his statement, another unsuccessful fight took
place to remove the preamble from the bill. Some eighteen members wanted it removed. Their opposition insisted that the bill
would become meaningless. The money and the supplies had to
be voted for some purpose.

To vote down the supply bill in order to get rid of the pream-

ble would have meant abandoning the troops already in the field. Almost no one was willing to do that, and soon the whole bill passed. The majority accepted the fact that it was now too late for action. Perhaps war could have been avoided when the treaties and resolutions of annexation were being worded. It could not be avoided now.

A Proviso

At first it was expected that the Congressmen who disliked the war would now be quiet and withhold their criticisms. But there was one closely related issue on which they did not intend to remain silent. That was the moral and political issue of slavery, and it became inseparably entwined with their objections to the war. The big political boulder that resulted was hurled into the House on August 8, 1846.

The members had called an evening meeting in order to finish the session's work and dispose of various bills from the Senate. These were passed, and the House then went into the Committee of the Whole to consider a motion proposed by James I. McKay of North Carolina.

Mr. McKay's motion formalized a request from the President into a bill. Polk wanted two million dollars for "extraordinary expenses." The members were expected to understand that Polk wanted to negotiate a peace with Mexico.

A resolution had been adopted limiting to ten minutes the time each member could speak on the matter when Hugh White of New York obtained the floor. "I have no confidence in this application for money; territory is what is sought after," he said, "and I cannot give my sanction to this appropriation . . ." He went on to call the war unnecessary and demanded that the bill be amended to specify that the funds were not to be used to extend the limits of slavery.

His remarks bore fruit. Representative David Wilmot of Pennsylvania presented his famous proviso that, as a condition attached to the use of the money to be appropriated, if any territory was acquired from Mexico, ". . . neither slavery nor involuntary servitude shall ever exist in any part of said territory . . ."

In a sense this was another declaration of war. It was a manifesto by the Northerners against the slavocracy.

Wilmot was immediately called to order. Slavery was not the subject of the McKay bill. In a previous Congress, that would have ended the Wilmot proviso. This time the Chair overruled the objection, and the House sustained the Chair. After that, the proviso was added to the bill.

By then, it was too late to send the bill to the Senate unless both Houses suspended their joint Rule Number 16. Number 16 forbade sending out measures from one House for the concurrence of the other during the last three days of the session. The suspension in such an instance required a majority vote. The Representatives gave it.

The next day was Sunday, but on Monday the Senators agreed to examine the proposal. As soon as he could get the floor, Dixon H. Lewis, of Alabama, an old-time States Rights Democrat, moved to strike the proviso from the bill.

The argument dragged on. Suddenly, it seemed, word came that the House had adjourned. The first session of the Twenty-ninth Congress was thereby at an end. With the session over, Polk did not get his funds and the appropriation bill was dead, but the impact from the Wilmot Proviso amended to it had only begun to live. The war did exist but there were still issues on which men of conscience felt compelled to differ. The spreading of slavery was such an issue.

"Not Another Inch"

The electric charge emanating from the Wilmot Proviso was stepped up by other factors that were changing the nation. Among them was the coming of a new age of transportation.

In 1842 the Baltimore and Ohio Railroad had extended its route all the way from Baltimore to Cumberland, Maryland. By 1852 it would reach Wheeling, West Virginia. By 1857 it would be possible to take the train to St. Louis. Obviously, the expectation of travel by rail added to the lure of the new West. Congressmen had to expect that the territories would be settled fast. The question whether a new territory was to allow slavery could not be left to the future, or it would be decided without the consent of the Northern Congressmen. As another indication of the changing times, the new telegraph clicked out the news when the Wilmot Proviso passed the House. The news spread fast and the reaction to it came quickly, even before the proviso was lost in the Senate.

In Indianapolis, one of the first to receive the word was the legislative correspondent and part owner of the *St. Joseph Valley Register*, the local Whig paper. The correspondent was Schuyler Colfax, a future Speaker of the House and Vice-President of the United States.

Colfax, excited by the news, was sure that the President must have used all of his influence and patronage to defeat the proviso in the House and it failed. Colfax told his readers: "Congress has ... given ... form to that public opinion of the Northern States which declares: 'Not another inch of slave territory.'"

He may not yet have known the extent to which the Whig Party was being split, dividing those who still wished to placate the South from those who did not. To help men in doubt, he would have been justified in writing that slavery had existed in Louisiana, Florida, and Texas before they came into the Union; but by contrast, it had been abolished in Mexico years back and so did not exist in the territory that the President hoped to acquire with the appropriation to which the proviso was attached. When this was pointed out, numbers of Northerners resented seeing human bondage spread to once-free soil.

Their Congressmen were awed by the vastness of the territory about to be acquired. The treaty of Guadalupe-Hidalgo, which would not be signed for another two years, would do more than settle the northwest boundary of Texas. It would add to the United States an area that would one day make up the

States of California, New Mexico, Arizona, Nevada, and Utah, as well as parts of Colorado and Wyoming. Senator Clayton of Delaware estimated that civil government would be needed for 1,004,492 square miles, an area about one third the size of Europe.

If enough of this space became part of the slavocracy, the Northerners in Congress could find themselves dominated by the slaveholders. With these anxieties in mind, Colfax spelled out the hopes of the anti-war protesters.

"If it is positively known that all the territory our army can wrest from Mexico is to come into the Union as free States, thus girding the Slave States with a belt of freedom, our Southern President will himself begin to consider the war as useless . . ."

Back in the White House office, President Polk felt the pressure of this new attitude. In January, 1847, when the second session of the Twenty-ninth Congress was already six weeks old, the exasperated President complained to his diary, "Nearly half the session has passed and they are engaged in debates about slavery and party politics, and have passed none of the essential measures which I have recommended as indispensible to the vigorous & successful prosecution of the war."

Polk did not yet realize how completely the war issue had merged with the slavery issue. He attributed the agitation in Congress to the next Presidential campaign, but whatever was causing it, Congressional behavior made the President eager to negotiate for peace.

As it happened, Congressmen were excited partly because of the previous fall election, which had changed the balance of power in the House. The Whigs, now the minority party, would outnumber Polk's Democrats 115 to 108 in the next Congress.

Meanwhile, in February of 1847, a measure was again brought forward to give the President an appropriation with which to negotiate for peace or territory. This time the measure called for granting him three million dollars.

Once again the Wilmot Proviso was attached to the appropriation. Once again the Proviso passed the House, this time by a vote of 115 to 105. Here was the flag of defiance brandished at Southern threats to dissolve the Union.

It was a tense moment, but soon the Senate would once more refuse to concur in the Proviso. It would, in a short time, pass its own bill; and after much urging from Senator Lewis Cass, the members of the House would reluctantly drop the proviso from their measure.

Not all of them, however, dropped it from their plans. By the end of the year, Polk had made a tactical error and the forces of protest had gained a most significant recruit.

The President had equated the voting of supplies with endorsing the war, and in January of 1848 Representative Abraham Lincoln brought the matter to the attention of the House. In a lawyerlike fashion he explained that President Polk had told the truth but not the whole truth. The President had ignored the futile attempt to disconnect the supply bill from the declaration of war written into the measure's preamble. Lincoln said that he had not previously expressed himself, but now he felt compelled to speak out and prevent this kind of misrepresentation, and he joined the chorus of men who blamed the war on Polk.

Unfortunately, Lincoln was not the only advocate in the chamber to clarify his position with new firmness. The listening Southerners realized that if anything like the Proviso succeeded, a host of free States would deprive them of all influence. Led by Calhoun and Rhett of South Carolina, and by Robert Toombs and Alexander Stephens of Georgia, Southerners demanded the right to carry their slave property into the new territory. Anything else was an illegal denial of a Southerner's "equal rights" to enjoy national assets, they said.

They, too, could feel that the times were changing. For years they had been placated by the Northern members of their own party. Now, in 1848, Congressman Collins could boast that the legislature of thirteen States had instructed their Senators and requested their Representatives to oppose the further extension of slavery.

This change was only partly due to the efforts of the abolitionists and to the new transportation, which shrank distances. The fact that the new lands were Federal property, and hence everyone's responsibility, had made once-indifferent men and women feel that the slavery issue was a part of their lives. In ever-increasing numbers they were ready to say "Not another inch!" and as they had changed, so had the Congress.

The Speakership, the Committees and the Compromise

By now a surge of animosity swept the chamber at the beginning of each session when a Speaker was to be elected. He alone —unbridled by any considerations of seniority or by the will of any organized group in the House—appointed the committees.

In 1847 Giddings persuaded Representative Palfrey to write to Robert C. Winthrop, the candidate from Massachusetts, asking whether if elected he would so arrange the committees as to assure a respectful reception for the antislavery petitions. They did not even receive the courtesy of an answer. As yet, they were not strong enough to defeat anyone, and in December Winthrop was elected. That gave them two years to wait and gather their forces for the next Speakership contest. Meanwhile, each passing day made it obvious that the contest of 1849 was going to be crucial.

There was one crisis which most noticeably contributed toward that realization. It began when the House attached an antislavery proviso to the bill to provide Oregon with a territorial government. The Senate removed the proviso after Mississippi's Jefferson Davis, the future President of the Confederacy, reiterated the South's position.

As the tension mounted, President Polk called for a compromise. Senator John M. Clayton, an antiwar Whig from Delaware, proposed and then headed a Senate compromise committee. But the committee only widened the crisis by trying to decide what should be done not only about Oregon, but also about California and New Mexico. In the end, it failed to propose anything the House would accept. Clayton was afraid the

Union was facing dissolution and civil war. It was mid-August of 1848 before any bill passed, and it dealt only with the organization of the Oregon territory; but at least Oregon's soil was to be free of slavery.

The members left the California question unsettled and went home to run their election campaigns. Those campaigns splintered and hardened the warring political factions that divided the nation and the Congress. Even Congressmen who thought they knew their constituents found new and disturbing forces becoming more prominent.

Of course, not all sections were alike. In Lancaster, Pennsylvania, there was a young attorney named Thaddeus Stevens who had participated in his State's constitutional convention, campaigned for Harrison for President, and served as a member of the State Legislature.

Stevens had received a letter from Salmon Chase, Ohio's next Senator, who would one day be a Chief Justice of the United States. Chase, knowing that Stevens was vehement in his hatred of slavery, hoped Stevens would join the Liberty Party, which sought to regulate slavery in areas under congressional control and, as he saw it, to deliver the Federal Government from the slave power. He asked Stevens to bring the old Anti-Masonic party of Pennsylvania on the Liberty platform and to persuade William Seward, New York's Whig Governor, to lead the movement.

Stevens delayed answering, then wrote to another friend. He had given the problem considerable thought and decided that more could be accomplished by electing a good Whig who respected the rights of freedom of speech and petition than by going down to defeat sponsoring a more extreme antislavery candidate.

It was a practical, not an ideological, decision, and for the moment Stevens was committed to it. When he reached Congress in 1849 as a Representative ready to participate in the battle over the Speakership, he was still known as a Whig, but the other antislavery factions eyed him hopefully.

In Massachusetts the picture was different. The older Whigs, including Webster, Caleb Cushing, and Edward Everett, had always considered themselves helpless to interfere with slavery in the States that wanted it. Moreover, they were repelled by the wild abolitionist troublemakers. To them, the most important of all considerations was to preserve the Union. On this basis, they hoped to retain the loyalty of their juniors.

Their hopes received a severe setback when Winthrop voted for the Supply Bill, with its damning preamble declaring war on Mexico. His vote became a burning issue for the State's young idealists. At last, four of them took the course that had been taken so often by their political forebears. They met and established a newspaper. Two of these men were Charles Sumner and Charles Francis Adams, the son of John Quincy Adams.

Sumner had begun his political career not by holding local office but by supporting various campaigns. He was for prison reform, for world peace, and—along with Horace Mann—for more and better public education. He and Charles Adams and Giddings' friend John Palfrey went to the next Whig convention and demanded that the party support no men for office unless they were known to oppose the spread of slavery.

When this failed, Sumner helped organize the Free Soil party, formed to resist the spread of slavery into the territories. "Free Soil, Free Speech, Free Labor and Free Men" was their slogan. They ran Martin Van Buren for President, Charles Francis Adams for Vice President, and Sumner for Congress. Unlike Stevens, they preferred to fight for the most glorious, if still unobtainable, results. All three of them were beaten.

Thus Sumner was not on hand to fight Winthrop's bid to retain the Speakership. To reach Congress, Sumner would have to wait for 1851, when Democrats and Free Soilers in the Massachusetts State house would be deadlocked for three months and finally select him to be their United States Senator.

Though defeated, Sumner was corresponding with Giddings, and the very existence of his party added to the bitterness and division in the House in 1849. Giddings had become a Free Soiler, and so had David Wilmot and Horace Mann. There were in all nine members of that party present in the chamber, and they were determined that no one would get their votes unless he agreed to organize committees that would give Free Soilers a fair hearing.

On top of that, the California question that had defied solution in the last Congress had since become more complicated. Following the discovery of gold, a mass of people had rushed to California. They had now organized and written a constitution and were asking to have California admitted to the Union as a free State. There was no slave State waiting to be admitted to offset her. The soon-to-be-determined fate of California— which, of course, would have to be taken up in the Committee on Territories—added to the urgency of the 1849 contest for the Speakership.

All this, and the possibility of a civil war over the issues, was in the minds of the men in the chamber as they looked over the candidates. Winthrop was running for reelection, having appointed committees which Giddings said favored the South. But while ten candidates opposed Winthrop, the front runner among them was Howell Cobb of Georgia, a zealous spokesman for the slavocracy. Time after time the members cast their ballots, and still no candidate received a majority. For nearly three weeks, the House was paralyzed. When a Democrat named William J. Brown came within two votes of being elected, someone noticed that the Free Soilers were also voting for Brown. With that, his Southern supporters deserted him.

At last the House resigned itself to not obtaining a majority for any candidate. Reluctantly, members agreed to have as Speaker a man who could win a mere plurality. After that, on the sixty-third ballot, a Georgian, Howell Cobb, became Speaker of the House.

The Whigs blamed the Free Soilers. By withholding their support from Winthrop, they had placed an advocate of slavery in the Chair to pick the committees. And these were the committees that were to consider the Clay compromise of 1850.

The Whigs thought the Free Soilers could not have picked a worse time to be stubborn. The Free Soilers felt that the Whigs had not made a sufficient effort to safeguard the rights of the friends of abolition. In short, there had been no compromise between the nonslaveholding factions. Hence, the committees Clay had to please were geared to guard the South from losing anything the South thought was its due.

By then, it was more obvious than ever before that only another compromise could save the Union. While designing it, Clay relied on the help of Democratic Senator Stephen Douglas, who was chairman of the Senate Committee on Territories and a wholehearted expansionist. Douglas wanted the Federal Government to make appropriations of land for internal improvements and to facilitate the construction of a transcontinental railroad. Maintaining the peace was an important prerequisite to his plans for national growth. He and Lewis Cass thought they had found the solution to the slavery issue—let each territory decide for itself whether it would permit slavery. The influence of Douglas's program (to which he gave the eyecatching name of "popular sovereignty") as well as Clay's awareness of who sat on the committees Cobb picked, can be seen in the compromise Clay wrote.

California had already written a free Constitution; so be it. But let Congress form a territorial Government for New Mexico and Utah without mentioning the issue. The rest of the resolutions proposed by Clay in the Senate on January 29, 1850, are well known. Texas was to be paid for ceding territory to New Mexico. Slavery was to remain in the District of Columbia, but the slave trade was to be forbidden. The Fugitive Slave Act of 1793 for the recapture of escaped slaves was to be strengthened and enforced. Finally, Congress was not to interfere with the slave trade between the slave States.

What Clay wanted was an omnibus bill lumping all these provisions together to make a package compromise. The House then had a rule, which is still in effect, forbidding its members from offering nongermane amendments. But it had no rule against openly putting unrelated topics in the same bill. The statesmen of 1850, however, refused to have this list of seemingly unconnected matters all voted on together in one measure. (Their present-day descendants are still arguing whether to outlaw the omnibus-type bill, at least in some areas). As it turned out in 1850, splitting the compromise into a series of measures made little difference.

Thaddeus Stevens snatched the opportunity to object to the obnoxious Fugitive Slave Law. "The distinguished Senator from Kentucky," he said, "wishes . . . to make it the duty of all

bystanders to aid in the capture of fugitives; to join the chase
. . . This is asking more than my constituents will ever grant."

It made little difference what he said. He himself knew the
compromise was gaining support from the public, because it
was advocated by the great men in whom the people were accustomed to place their trust. Senators Chase and Seward stood by
helplessly while the giants of the dying era pushed through all
the parts. Webster, in his famous seventh of March speech,
instead of fighting Clay, had urged the North to submit. His
words "I speak today for the preservation of the Union; hear me
for my cause," made an appeal that was hard to reject.

Nothing could stop the compromise after that but a Presidential veto. Some thought President Zachary Taylor would veto
the bill, but that hope vanished when Taylor became ill and died
early in July. His successor, Millard Fillmore, signed each of the
compromise bills before Congress adjourned.

When the Whigs and the Free Soilers did not join forces, they
both lost. Clay lost the influence that could have come from
strongly antislavery committees, and Northerners who were
forced to swallow another distasteful compromise suffered the
most from this proliferation of ineffective factions.

The Aftermath of the Compromise

The full implications of the Clay Compromise of 1850 did not
become evident until after December of 1853, when Augustus
Dodge of Iowa asked and obtained leave in the Senate to introduce a bill to organize the territory of Nebraska. His proposal was referred to the Committee on Territories, chaired by
Stephen Douglas of Illinois.

Douglas was delighted. He had already obtained Federal land
grants for the Illinois Central Railroad and was eager to see
more done to organize and open up the central west. He was also
aware that earlier attempts to organize the Nebraska territory
had been resisted by Southern Senators. In order to avoid a

recurrence of this, the bill came out of committee containing the Chairman's favorite solution, popular sovereignty—known also as squatter sovereignty—letting settlers in a territory decide for themselves whether they wanted to permit slavery. Indirectly this repealed the Missouri Compromise, and the Northern press was quick to notice it.

Massachusetts abolitionist Senator Charles Sumner was well aware that to fight the bill he must contend with Douglas. The Illinois Senator wanted to be President. Sumner must have thought that ambition had led Douglas into trying to hand the South this new plum. With the initiative that Douglas exercised as chairman of one of the most important committees, with the respect he commanded on the floor of the Senate, and with the approval he enjoyed from President Pierce, Douglas must have seemed to Sumner almost as powerful as the President.

It was another case of leadership coming from where the leader was. Douglas, who was hardly five feet tall, was an adroit leader and tried to calm the angry verbal battles in the chamber. Sumner, on the other hand, was large and aggressive. He had once asked the Senate's consent to make a speech against the Fugitive Slave Act at a time when other statesmen, who hoped the question was finally settled, were unwilling to renew the agitation. Contrary to their usual courteous habit, their consent was denied.

Sumner waited until Senator Hunt of Virginia, the ex-Speaker of the House, reported a bill to pay the expenses of officers executing the laws. Then Sumner immediately offered an amendment, "Provided that no such allowance shall be authorized for expense incurred in executing the Act of September 18, 1850 [the Fugitive Slave Act], which act is hereby repealed."

"The amendment which I now offer proposes to remove one . . . of these extraordinary expenses. Beyond all controversy or cavil it is strictly in order," he announced with evident satisfaction, "And now, at last . . . I am to be heard; not as a favor but as a right." He had the satisfaction of knowing there was nothing the others could do to silence him, but he made no impression on the Fugitive Slave Act.

The episode was part of the background when he rose on January 17, 1854, to try to reinstate the Missouri Compromise in the Douglas bill. He failed.

A week later, Douglas arrived in the Senate fresh from a Sunday conference with President Pierce and Secretary of War Jefferson Davis. The chairman then formally introduced a revision of his own bill that now provided for two territories, Kansas and Nebraska. It also flatly declared that the compromise of 1850 had canceled forever the earlier Missouri Compromise, and that henceforth squatters in a territory could decide the slavery question for themselves.

No sooner had copies of the new bill been laid on the desks than Douglas pressed for its passage. After some debate, Sumner and others managed to get it postponed. Their next move was to call together a small group of Senators and Representatives, who signed their names to an appeal to the country entitled, "Shall Slavery Be Permitted in Nebraska?"

In strong language—Sumner was good at that—it exposed the "wickedness" about to be perpetrated. The signers described themselves as "Independent Democrats," but that made it impossible for men who did not want to be known as Democrats to add their names. However, as Seward explained later, in no case would they have been able to offset Douglas. "All that we could hope to do," he said, "was to organize and prepare the issue for the House of Representatives and awaken the country."

Sumner was convinced that the trouble was that Douglas was not allowing enough time for people to learn about the bill. Instead, Douglas pushed the matter forward until it passed.

On March 4 it went to the House. There the proposal to declare the Missouri Compromise repealed was as controversial as it had been in the Senate, but in the House the opposition had even greater problems. With the passage of time and the emergence of controversies the rules had become stricter and more numerous.

With all these rules Alexander Stephens of Georgia had familiarized himself, and like many of his present-day equivalents, he knew how to use his parliamentary skill to baffle his opponents.

When he moved to strike out the enacting clause in the Kansas-Nebraska bill, he had made a privileged motion. Until the Representatives voted it down, which Stephens knew they would, this motion to destroy the bill took precedence over any motion for amendments. It thus served to deprive other orators of the time they needed to win support for vast revisions of the measure.

The House members finally had to vote on a bill much like the Senate bill. And the minority which had hoped to change the act materially was not strong enough to block it. Back it went to the Senate, where it again passed and provided the basis for a bloody contest between the slavery and antislavery forces in Kansas. That bloodshed served as a preamble to the Civil War.

Reading the measure, Sumner made his prophetic announcement. The bill constituted a breach of the agreement between North and South. "[I]t annuls all past compromises with slavery and makes any future compromise impossible," he said.

Unfortunately, Sumner did not stop there. He also went to great lengths to express contempt for the bill's authors, Douglas and South Carolina's Senator Andrew Butler. He infuriated Preston S. Brooks, Butler's relative in the House. Brooks found Sumner late one afternoon sitting at his desk in the Senate chamber. Occupied as he was, Sumner did not see Brooks come up from behind him with a raised cane. The Senator was so badly beaten that he had to be carried from the hall. It took him three years to regain his health fully.

When the assault charges went to court, Brooks was fined so small an amount that the foes of slavery considered it an insult. Psychologically the District was a Southern city.

Meanwhile, the House had to consider Brooks' conduct from its own point of view. The members failed to muster the necessary strength to expel him, but they did censure him. At the same time, a few members took the occasion to express their "disapprobation of the use of language in debate of a character personally offensive to individual members of Congress or any State of this Union."

It was a noble endeavor, but the Civil War was too near at hand for any mere resolution to keep the peace. Justin Morrill, a freshman Congressman, wrote home to Vermont, "The excitement here is intense. The Northern men are determined to submit to no further outrages, and scenes of great turbulence are expected."

A Leader Develops

In 1855 Justin Morrill was one of those newcomers whose arrival in the House of Representatives signaled the beginning of the next era. John Quincy Adams had died seven years before. Calhoun had been gone for five. Clay and Webster had both died in 1852. Morrill, a freshman Representative in the Thirty-Fourth Congress, was destined to serve his country until nearly the end of the century.

He came from Vermont, where on the occasion of the opening of a village library he gave the crowd a picture of his boyhood.

"It may be asked what will the town profit by a library? . . . Ask the boy, taken perhaps by his parents reluctantly from the schoolhouse to the field or the workshop at the age of fifteen, feeling as I once felt, as though youthful ambition and hopes had been nipped by an early frost . . ."

It was years before he outgrew the feeling that a lack of formal training had blighted his future. During those years he first clerked in a village store and later became a director of the local bank. As early as 1844 he was chairman of the Whig county committee, and he was at the Whig convention of 1852, which was deadlocked for five days seeking agreement on a presidential candidate. He saw General Scott reluctantly nominated and watched the delegates leave Baltimore divided, disorganized, and headed for defeat. Morrill never forgot it. Later in life he did his best to smooth over dissension in the Republican Party.

When he took his seat in the House of Representatives on the first Monday of December, 1855, he learned that the session would begin with another battle over the Speakership. Never having held a legislative office before, he admitted that he felt inadequate. Nevertheless, he was already enough of a politician to try to assess the relative strength of the contesting factions. He noticed that in addition to the larger parties, there were the Know-Nothings (who wanted only native Americans to hold office), and the anti-Nebraska Democrats, and—most important to Morrill's future—members of the new Republican party.

The repeal of the Missouri Compromise, Morrill decided, had ruined the Democrats in the North without giving them any new strength in the South. The policy of Northern men upholding Southern measures, he felt sure, was gone forever and should be.

Then the endless balloting got under way and he saw that not everyone in the room agreed with him, for the members insisted, often belligerently, on explaining their votes when the clerk called their names. This continued until finally, on the one hundred and thirty-third ballot, on February 2, 1856, the House elected a Speaker. Much to Morrill's satisfaction, he was Nathaniel Banks, an antislavery man from Massachusetts.

Banks was escorted to the chair and sworn into office by Giddings, the oldest—and that day the proudest—member of the House. It was a scene that would take its place in Morrill's memory along with the spectacle of old Sam Houston, the former President of Texas, sitting in the Senate whittling on a piece of wood; and the times when a few members had a little too much to drink; and above all, those terrible chaotic occasions which the chamber was still to see.

The Democrats sat on one side of the House and their opponents on the other. But late one night a Republican gentleman from Pennsylvania named Grow wandered over to the Democratic side and was told by a cursing Southerner, "Go home, you black Republican, to your own side . . ." Grow snapped out an answer, and within minutes blows were being exchanged. Members from all sides rushed into the battle. The Speaker's gavel pounding for order had as little effect as if it had been bidding the thunder to be still.

Speaker James Orr of South Carolina, who had succeeded Banks, ordered the Sergeant-at-Arms to arrest those making the

On February 2, 1856, after two months of repetitive balloting, as the 133rd rollcall vote ended, Nathaniel Banks was declared Speaker of the House. The Northerners who cheered from the visitors' gallery rightly expected that Banks would place antislavery majorities on the key committees. It is the memory of contests like this one that have kept our present seniority system going.

House of Representatives Scene   *Culver Pictures* disturbance, which Morrill said included nearly the whole House. One man was set against two hundred and forty.

Moreover, since the Sumner affair, there were Northerners who had banded together determined to give blow for blow. And it was not unheard of for a member to have a revolver on his person.

Without arguing, Sergeant-at-Arms Adam J. Glossbrenner lifted the ponderous mace and carried it into the mob. Morrill was impressed as he watched the tumult subside.

He was not as favorably impressed on another occasion. Alexander Stephens, who Morrill said looked as if his skin were glued to his bones, came and sat by Morrill, saying, "Your people are making a great fuss about the State of Kansas coming in as a slave State, but you will all submit."

When Morrill denied the prediction, the Georgian refreshed his memory. "You said as much when Texas was annexed . . . and yet you all submitted."

Like Giddings, Morrill was determined that this time would be different. In this, as in other matters, he admired Giddings both for his ability and for his integrity. Giddings had made himself an expert in the area of claims against the Government. He was hated by the slaveholders, but when he reported a bill from the committee on claims, his judgment was accepted by them and by all others. A claim favored by him was sure to pass, and one he disapproved of had no chance.

Morrill, who felt thwarted by his own lack of education, was impressed to see Giddings lead other men by virtue of his expert knowledge. It must have occurred to Morrill at this point that he also had a field of competence. In business and in the bank he had acquired an expert knowledge of finance.

In 1856, when he was reelected, he had an opportunity to use his business training when the tariff bill was discussed. Nevertheless, the Speaker put him on the Committee on Territories. He was thus a member of the conference that met with Senators on the bill to admit Kansas. The House did not recognize the proslavery constitution, which had been prepared by a segment of the territory's population. Instead, the Representatives wanted the document resubmitted to all the voters in Kansas.

Morrill advised his fellow Representatives not to yield on this point. By now Colfax was in the Senate fighting with them not to have slavery forced on the Kansas settlers. To his great credit, Stephen Douglas agreed. The Lecompton Constitution, as it was called, was therefore resubmitted to the voters. They rejected it, and Kansas waited until 1861 to come into the Union as a free State.

In March of 1857, the Republican Party watched the inauguration of Democratic President Buchanan with great misgivings. Actually, a worse blow to their cause came two days after inauguration. The Supreme Court announced its Dred Scott decision. The Court held that the Missouri Compromise was unconstitutional, and that Congress could not exclude slavery from the territories. If the Court thought it had put an end to the discussion, it was mistaken. The Republican Party stood for arresting the spread of slavery. It could not accept this decision and exist.

All around Morrill, tempers flared. In the midst of the excitement he somehow managed to make his presence felt without becoming embroiled in an incident. Perhaps it was well that he was not a dramatic orator. Instead, he had acquired the habit of speaking clearly and precisely and of planning ahead what he wanted to say or do.

While the country was about to face its greatest tragedy, Morrill was planning to convert one of his favorite dreams into reality. On December 16 of 1858, he introduced a bill to grant land to States and territories to aid them in establishing public colleges.

He wanted the measure sent to the Committee on Agriculture, of which he was a member. It went instead to the Committee on Public Lands, which kept it several months and then reported it out unfavorably. When the bill was attacked and about to be recommitted to its death, Morrill quickly offered a carefully revised substitute. His substitute bill had never been in committee, but he knew he could count on enough votes to get it passed. When it came to a vote, it passed, 105 to 100.

When the measure reached the President's desk, Buchanan, who was a States Rights Democrat and against giving land for local purposes, quickly vetoed it. There matters stood until Abraham Lincoln became President. Morrill then reintroduced his measure and had the satisfaction of seeing it become law. His triumph was a strong demonstration of the dwindling opposition to congressionally financed improvements. In part, it was another triumph for the late Henry Clay.

It was not, however, the only step that Morrill took during these years toward his goal of becoming a man respected for his competence. When because of the financial panic of 1857 there was not enough revenue to meet Government expenses, Congressmen turned their attention to the problems of loans, taxes, and tariffs. Few could forget how ably the gentleman from Vermont discussed the tariff. In May, 1858, Morrill wrote home that he had been promoted to membership on the Ways and Means Committee. Placed on the tariff subcommittee, he painstakingly used his knowledge of goods and prices to work out a schedule.

Then he called on Thaddeus Stevens, urging the Pennsylvanian to use his colorful style to win support for the measure.

Stevens gave the bill his effective endorsement, and the Chairman of the Ways and Means Committee, John Sherman, guided it through to passage. The Republicans pointed to it as one of their achievements, and it helped elect Abraham Lincoln.

Before the returns were in, the Southerners, accompanied by both hisses and applause, had announced on the floor of the House that they would never submit to the inauguration of a Republican President.

After Lincoln was elected, their States seceded and they left the halls of Congress. Morrill was one of those who was greatly shaken. Because of his tariff, he was also one of those attacked in the newspapers as part of a last futile drive to reach another compromise.

The war silenced that attack. And Congress turned to Morrill for help as the Union faced the gigantic problems of financing the war.

As the war progressed, he was offered the chairmanship of the Ways and Means Committee. But he wrote his wife, "the work is very great and I dare not undertake it." The fact was that the

Ways and Means Committee chairman was still, by and large, the floor leader of the House. Thus, most of the work of timing the presentations of measures and whipping up support for them fell on his shoulders. Thaddeus Stevens undertook that chairmanship. And it was not until 1865, when the House split the Ways and Means Committee into two committees, Appropriations and Ways and Means, that Morrill had to accept the Ways and Means chairmanship in order to continue the work in which he excelled. He was then what Giddings had been, a man whose leadership had sprung from his area of competence.

The Reversal of a Trend

The war began, and Congress meekly upheld the President—for a while. Few Congressmen dared to oppose the Commander-in-Chief.

That did not mean that they were not provoked. When the guns opened up on Fort Sumter, Lincoln called for the State militia, enlarged the Army and made rules for its conduct, suspended the right of habeas corpus, and without authority spent public funds for use in the emergency. All these were acts which normally required the prior consent of Congress, but Lincoln had not even called it into session until July 4, 1861, eleven weeks after the hostilities began.

Once belatedly in action, the Senate confirmed Lincoln's appointments. Congress delayed but ultimately consented to his extralegal acts in regard to the armed services and to his expenditures. The members then debated the matter of his having suspended the great writ of habeas corpus. Many felt that this was a power expressly given to Congress. Instead of settling the question, they passed, but with provisos, an act which gave the President the power he had already seized. A civilian suspect could be held in a military prison, but only until the local grand jury met. If the jury failed to indict, the prisoner could be released by a local judge.

Congress then did investigate the awarding of military contracts. It did set up a committee which made recommendations
on the conduct of the war. But in all this, the Congressmen acted
with caution in their relation to the President. A radical Republican caucus decided to tell Lincoln that they were dissatisfied
with Secretary of State William H. Seward, whose enthusiasm
for the war they questioned, but they simultaneously decided
that this was not the time for a fight between themselves and the
President. They did not carry the issue to the public, and
Seward remained in the Cabinet.

Not surprisingly, before Lincoln was gone from the scene the
radicals in Congress were at war with his plans for reconstruction. It was not only that they wanted a harsher peace than he
did; they also intended to have a say in shaping affairs in the
postwar years.

Executive assertiveness had been rising since Jackson's day.
Lincoln's use of his war powers was the climax of that spiral. As
President, he had refused, in July of 1864, to sign a reconstruction bill and had then announced that he would implement only
those parts of the measure that met with his approval. As a result
of this unheard-of conduct Lincoln was denounced for carrying
on "a Government of personal will' instead of "a Government
of law." The words came from the reconstruction bill's author,
Representative Henry Winter Davis of Maryland, and they
came after Davis and Senator Benjamin F. Wade of Ohio had
issued a manifesto to the press against the President's actions.
The manifesto reflected the changing mood in Congress.

Lincoln would have been satisfied to have the Southerners
merely swear allegiance to the Union and agree to abide by its
laws. He wanted to permit the citizens of a vanquished State
who would take a loyalty oath (be they only ten percent of the
population) to participate in a State constitutional convention
and elect their men to Congress. His successor, Andrew Johnson, wanted the Southerners readmitted to Congress in 1865.

Instead, Senators and Representatives from former Confeder-
ate States found that their credentials were either laid on the
table and not considered or referred to a committee on reconstruction. Their presence was not acceptable to Thaddeus Ste-

vens. And Stevens and Davis led the House and shared the same viewpoint.

The Constitution vested in Congress the supreme authority over territories and new State Governments. Therefore, as they saw it, the decision rested with Congress when and under what conditions the vanquished were to be readmitted into the Union. In short, the time had come to check the enlarged influence of the Executive over the authority of Congress.

By then, the hostilities and bloodshed had changed something else. Congress had at first intended to prosecute the war for the sole purpose of preserving the Union and maintaining the Constitution as they were originally. Then it became evident that slavery was a source of strength to the enemy. At the very least, the slaves could grow food while their masters fought the North. Stevens and his radical Republican followers maintained that this alone justified emancipation.

To those who feared to tamper with the Constitution they replied with contempt that the South had forfeited its old constitutional protection. They led Congress into freeing the slaves on Federal territory. They and their abolitionist followers wanted Lincoln to use his war power to issue his emancipation proclamation long before he did. But the President weighed the sentiments of the border States and waited until he thought the time was right. His proclamation of January, 1863, then, freed only the slaves in the rebel States.

By 1864, Congress was exploring methods of freeing the others. It was then that they decided once again, as they had in 1787, that "the fundamental difficulty was a want of power in Congress."

Since the Constitution recognized slavery, the Constitution would have to be amended if Congress was to have the authority to compel the once-independent States to respect human rights. Early in 1865, the Thirteenth Amendment was proposed to the States. It was only the first of the three so-called "Civil War Amendments." Its primary purpose was to forbid slavery or involuntary servitude to exist in the United States. But it was also the first amendment to contain the words that changed forever the nature of this Union and the authority of Congress over the States. Like the Fourteenth and the Fifteenth Amendments, it ended with the words "Congress shall have the power to enforce this article by appropriate legislation." Congress had gained the power to enforce these civil rights within a State.

It would be a long time before Congress exercised all the new might given to it by these three amendments. The old ways and old attitudes died slowly, particularly among the vanquished. In the postwar years as before, not only Congress as an institution but also the geographic groups within Congress would seek to exercise their influence. But that is part of another tale, which has as its prelude the history of reconstruction. To examine it, one must first question whether Congress could have handled reconstruction more wisely if executive-legislative relations had been more cordial; if the vanquished Southerners had behaved differently; if the people had elected different Congressmen. It is a tale long enough to fill another volume.

At this point it is enough to say that Congress had proved that it would not be manacled and frustrated indefinitely by the Executive or by the States. As the Civil War ended, it checked them both and interrupted a trend that was eclipsing the prerogatives of the legislature.

Future legislators working in a world in which crisis and problem would never end could thank the past. They had been left the structure of the legislative process and more. Congress not only had the tools to assert its legislative might; it had a tradition of having done so.

Conclusion

The Congress of the United States started as a small, informal body faced with problems as forbidding as our own, and manned by men who clung to their conflicting views.

To broaden its knowledge of the issues, Congress put the committees into operation. Through the committees, it applied its right to investigate. While coping with the nation's problems, it altered its own procedures. It replaced its initial informality with rules to protect itself from being dominated or disrupted by a bully. As its membership grew, it replaced long orations with limited debate. In short, its procedural rules were responses to its functional needs, making it more effective.

Simultaneously, Congress learned to be flexible. To meet the country's needs, it broadly interpreted its own powers, establishing the bank and financing improvements. When the people so demanded, it changed its decisions. It lifted Jefferson's embargo. It altered its stand on slavery. In the process it gleaned its leadership from many sources: from Hamilton when he was Secretary of the Treasury; from Madison when he was a Congressman; from Jefferson as a popular President; from Clay when he was Speaker and when he was Senator. The majority followed Van Buren and Benton when they spoke for Jackson. The members listened to Adams when he pricked their consciences, to Stephen Douglas when he was Chairman of the important Committee on Territories, and to Giddings and Morrill because of their expert knowledge.

Among the great contributions left by these giants were their biographies, diaries, and memoirs. With a frankness that has rarely, if ever, been excelled, statesmen of this period laid bare their approach to the problems of providing a legislative government. Their firsthand accounts provide an essential understanding of their world which no one can afford to miss who hopes to influence the nation's course by electing, petitioning, or serving as a member of Congress.

Appendix

THE PRINCIPAL SOURCES

Part I

Books

Bowen, Catherine D., *Miracle at Philadelphia*, Boston, 1966.

Elliot, Jonathan, *Debates in The Several State Conventions on the Adoption of The Federal Constitution*, Philadelphia, 1836,

Franklin, Benjamin, *The Complete Works of Benjamin Franklin*, John Begelow, ed. New York, 1887.

Farrand, Max, (ed.) *Records of The Federal Convention*, Conn., 1911, 1934.

Hamilton, Alexander, James Madison and John Jay, *The Federalist*, Jacob Cooke edition, Conn., 1961.

Hamilton, Alexander, The Works of Alexander Hamilton, Henry Cabot Lodge ed., New York, 1904.

Madison, James, *Writings of James Madison*, Galliard Hunt, New York, 1905.

Madison James, The Journal of the Debates in the Convention which Framed The Constitution of the United States as Recorded by James Madison Gaillard Hunt ed., New York, 1908

Madison, James, *Letters and Other Writings of James Madison.* Published by order of Congress, 1865.

Morris, Richard B., *Alexander Hamilton and the Founding of the Nation.* New York, 1957.

Van Doren, Carl., *The Great Rehearsal*, New York, 1948.

United States Federal Records.

Journals of the Continental Congress, 1774 to 1789.

Part II

Books

Adams, Henry, *The Life of Albert Gallatin,* Philadelphia, 1879.
Adams, Henry, *John Randolph,* Boston, 1898.
Ames, Seth, *Fisher Ames Works,* Boston, 1854.
Anderson, Dice R., *William Branch Giles.* Wisconsin, 1914.
Beard, Charles A., *Economic Origins of Jeffersonian Democracy,* New York, 1927.
Bowers, Claude G., *Jefferson and Hamilton,* Boston, 1933.
Boyd, George Adams, *Elias Boudinot,* New Jersey, 1952.
Fribourg, Marjorie G., *The Bill of Rights: Its Impact on The American People,* Philadelphia, 1967.
Hamilton, Alexander, The Works of Alexander Hamilton, Henry Cabot Lodge, ed., New York, 1904.
Harlow, Ralph V., *The History of the Legislative Method in the Period Before 1825,* Conn,., 1917.
Jefferson, Thomas, *The Works of Thomas Jefferson,* Ford, ed., 1904
Irving, Washington, *The Life of George Washington,* New York, 1865.
Madison, James, *The Writings of James Madison,* Gaillard Hunt, ed. New York, 1905.
Maclay, William, *The Journal of William Maclay,* New York, 1927.
Malone, Dumas, *Jefferson and The Ordeal of Liberty,* Boston, 1962.
Rives, William, *History of the Life and Times of James Madison,* 1859.
Schachner, Nathan, *Thomas Jefferson,* New York, 1951.
Washington, George, The Writings of George Washington, U.S. Printing Office, 1939.

United States Federal Records

Annals of Congress, Volume 1–10.
History of the United States House of Representatives (By George B. Galloway), House Document No. 250, United States Printing Office, Washington, D. C. 1965.
History of the George Washington Bicentennial Celebration, Vol. II. Printed by order of Congress.

Manuscripts

Jefferson Papers Library of Congress

Part III

Books

Adams, John Quincy, *Memoirs of John Quincy Adams*, Charles Francis Adams, ed., Philadelphia, 1874.

Adams, Henry, *History of the United States of America*, New York, 1891.

Anderson, Dice R., *William Branch Giles*, Wisconsin, 1915.

Baldwin, Joseph G., *Party Leaders*, New York, 1855.

Bowers, Claude G., *Jefferson in Power*, Mass., 1936.

Bruce, William Cabell, *John Randolph of Roanoake*, New York, 1922.

Cunningham, Noble E., *The Jeffersonian Republicans*, North Carolina, 1957.

Fribourg, Marjorie G., *The Supreme Court in American History*, Philadelphia, 1965.

Garland, Hugh A., *The Life of John Randolph of Roanoke*, New York, 1859.

Jefferson, Thomas, *The Writings of Thomas Jefferson*, H. A. Washington, ed., Philadelphia, 1869.

Jefferson, Thomas, *The Works of Thomas Jefferson*. Ford, ed., 1904.

Madison, James, *Letters and Other Writings of James Madison*, Published by the order of Congress, 1865.

Malone, Dumas, *Jefferson and the Ordeal of Liberty*, Mass., 1962.

Morison, Samuel Eliot, *Harrison Gray Otis; The Urban Federalist*, Mass., 1969.

Plumer, William, Jr., *Life of William Plumer*, Mass., 1857.

Schachner, Nathan, *Thomas Jefferson*, New York, 1951.

Wilson, Edwin Mood, *The Congressional Career of Nathaniel Macon*, North Carolina, 1900.

Wilmerding, Lucius, Jr., *The Spending Power*, New Haven, 1943.

United States Federal Record

Annals of Congress, Volume, 10 to 20.

The Sixth Congress to the Twelfth.

Marbury v. Madison, 1 Cranch 137, 1803.

Part IV

Books

Adams, Henry, *The History of the United States,* New York, 1891.
Adams, John Quincy, *Memoirs of John Quincy Adams,* Charles Francis Adams, ed., Pennsylvania, 1874.
Alexander, De Alva, *The History and Procedure of the House of Representatives,* New York, 1916.
Beirne, Francis F., *The War of 1812,* New York, 1949.
Brant, Irving, *James Madison,* 5 Volumes New York, 1941–1956.
Bruce, William C., *John Randolph of Roanoke,* New York, 1922.
Capers, Gerald M., *John C. Calhoun, Opportunist.* Florida, 1960.
Calhoun, John C., *The Papers of John C. Calhoun,* South Carolina, 1959.
Clay, Henry, *The Papers of Henry Clay,* James Hopkins, ed., Kentucky, 1951
Clay, Henry, *The Works of Henry Clay,* Calvin Colton, ed., 1904.
Clark, Joseph, *The Sapless Branch,* New York, 1964.
Colton, Calvin, *The Life and Times of Henry Clay,* New York, 1846.
Dangerfield, George, *The Awakening of Nationalism,* New York, 1965.
Eaton, Clement, *Henry Clay and The Art of American Politics,* Boston, 1957.
Fuller, Hubert Bruce, *The Speaker of the House,* Boston, 1909.
Fribourg, Majorie G., The *Supreme Court In American History,* Philadelphia, 1965.
Gallagher, Hugh Gregory, *Advise and Obstruct,* New York, 1969.
Hulbert, A.B., *The Path of Inland Commerce,* Yale, 1920.
Hunt, Gaillard, *John C. Calhoun,* Philadelphia, 1908.
Jackson, Andrew, *Jackson's Correspondence,* Volume 1; J. S. Bassett, Washington, 1935.
King, Rufus, *The Life and Correspondence of Rufus King,* New York, 1894.
Mallory, Daniel, *The Life and Speeches of the Honorable Henry Clay,* New York, 1843.
Meigs, William M., *Life of John Caldwell Calhoun,* New York, 1917.
Morison, Samuel Eliot, *Oxford History of the American People,* New York, 1965.
Morison, Samuel Eliot, Frederick Merk and Frank Freidel., *Dissent in Three American Wars,* Mass., 1970.
Poore, Ben Perley, *Reminiscences of Sixty Years in the National Metropolis,* Michigan, 1886.
Quincy, Edmund, *Life of Josiah Quincy,* Boston, 1867.
Richardson, James, *Messages of the Presidents,* Washington, D. C., 1897.

Revenel, Harriott, *The Life Times of William Lowndes*, Boston, 1901.
Smith, Margaret Bayard, *The First Forty Years of Washington Society*, New York, 1906.
Schurz, Carl, *Life of Henry Clay*, Boston, 1887.
White, Leonard D., *The Jeffersonians*, New York, 1951.
Webster, Daniel, *Private Correspondence*, Vol. 1, Boston, 1857.
Wilmerding, Lucius, Jr., *The Spending Power*, Connecticut, 1945.
Wiltse, Charles M., *John C. Calhoun, Nationalist*, Indianapolis, 1944.
Wiltse, Charles M., *John C. Calhoun, Nulifier*, Indianapolis, 1949.
Winthrop, Robert C., *Memoirs of Clay*, Massachusetts, 1880.
Young, Jeremiah S., *A Political and Constitutional Study of the Cumberland Road*, Chicago, 1902.

Periodicals

Follette, Mary Parker, "Henry Clay as Speaker of the United States House of Representatives," *American Historical Association Report*, 1891.
New York Evening Post
National Intelligencer

United States Federal Records

Annals of Congress, and Register of Debates the Ninth Congress to the Twenty-First.

Manuscripts

The MacBride Papers Library of Congress.
New York Historical Society Letters quoted with their kind permission
The Papers of James Monroe, Library of Congress
The Samuel Smith Papers

Part V

Books

Adams, John Quincy, *Memoirs of John Quincy Adams*, Charles Francis Adams, ed., Philadelphia, 1874.
Benton, Thomas Hart, *Thirty Years View*, New York, 1854.
Bowers, Claude G., *Party Battles of the Jackson Period*. Boston, 1922.
Buchanan, James, *The Works of James Buchanan*, John Bassett Moore, ed., Philadelphia, 1908.

Calhoun, John C., *Correspondence of John C. Calhoun*, American Historical Association Report of 1899, Washington, D. C., 1900.

Calhoun, John C., *The Works of John C. Calhoun*, Richard Craille, ed., New York, 1854.

Catteral, Ralph, *The Second Bank of the United States*, Chicago, 1903.

Clay, Henry, *The Works of Henry Clay*, Calvin Colton, ed. New York, 1904.

Curtis, George T., *Life of James Buchanan*, New York, 1883.

Hunt, Gaillard, *John C. Calhoun*, Philadelphia, 1908.

Jackson, Andrew, *Correspondence of Andrew Jackson;* J.S. Bassett, ed., Washington, D. C., 1935.

McCormac, Eugene I., *James K. Polk a Political Biography*. California, 1922.

Meigs, Willam M., *The Life of Thomas Hart Benton*, Philadelphia, 1904.

Meigs, William M., *The Life of John Caldwell Calhoun*, New York, 1917.

Polk, James K., *Diary of James K. Polk;* Milo M. Quaife, ed., Chicago, 1910.

Richardson, James (Compiler), *Messages and Papers of the Presidents.* Washington, D. C., 1897.

Schlesinger, Arthur M., Jr., *The Age of Jackson*, New York, 1945.

Tyler, Lyon G., *The Letters and Times of the Tylers*, Richmond, 1884.

Webster, Daniel, *The Writings of Daniel Webster*, National Edition. Boston, 1903.

Wilson, Woodrow, *History of the American People*, New York, 1918.

Wiltse, Charles M., *John C. Calhoun, Sectionalist*, Indianapolis, 1951.

Wise, Barton H., *Life of Henry A. Wise*, New York, 1899.

Wise, Henry A., *Seven Decades of the Union*, Philadelphia, 1872.

Van Buren, Martin, *Autobiography of Martin Van Buren*, American Historical Association Report of 1918, Washington, D. C., 1920.

Periodicals and Newspapers

Democratic Review
National Intelligencer
New York Herald

United States Federal Records

Biographical Directory of the American Congress, 1950.

History of Congress, Congressional Globe, and Gales and Seaton Register of Debates in Congress for the Eighteenth Congress to the Twenty-Fifth.

Executive Journal of the United States Senate, Vol. 4, No. 199. March 2, 1833.

House Executive Document, No. 300, Twenty-Second Congress, First Session, 1831.

Part VI

Books

Adams, John Quincy. *Memoirs of John Quincy Adams;* Charles Francis Adams, ed., Philadelphia, 1874.

Alexander, De Alva S. *History and Procedure of the House of Representatives,* Boston, 1916.

Benton, Thomas Hart, *Thirty Years View,* New York, 1854.

Calhoun, John C., *Correspondence of John C. Calhoun; American Historical Association Report of 1899,* Washington D. C., 1900.

Calhoun, John C., *The Works of John C. Calhoun,* Richard Craille, ed., New York, 1854.

Clark, Bennett Champ, *John Quincy Adams, Old Man Eloquent,* Boston, 1932.

Curtis, George T., *The Life of James Buchanan,* New York, 1883.

Jackson, Carlton, *Presidential Vetoes,* Georgia, 1967.

Polk, James K. *Diary of James K. Polk,* Milo M. Quaife, ed., Chicago, 1910.

Richardson, James (compiler), *Messages and Papers of the Presidents,* Washington, D. C., 1897.

Tyler, Lyon G., *Letters and Times of the Tylers,* Richmond, 1884.

Wilson Woodrow, *History of The American People,* New York, 1918.

White, L. A., *Robert Barnwell Rhett; Father of Secession,* New York, 1931.

Wise, Henry A., *Seven Decades of the Union,* Philadelphia, 1872.

Periodicals and Newspapers

New York Herald.
Jonesborough Whig
National Intelligencia

United States Federal Records

Biographical Dictionary of the American Congress
Congressional Globe

Gales and Seaton Register of Debates in Congress; the Twenty-Second
     Congress to the 28th.
Hinds Procedents of the House of Representatives
House Report no. 75, 27th Congress, 28th Session, May, 1842.

Part VII

Books

Adams, Charles Francis, *Charles Francis Adams by his son.* Boston, 1900.
Benton, Thomas Hart, *Thirty Years View,* New York, 1854.
Binkley, W. E., *Powers of the President,* New York, 1937.
Fite, Emerson David, *The Presidential Campaign of 1860,* New York,
     1911.
Fribourg, Marjorie G., *The Bill of Rights: Its Impact on the American
     People,* Philadelphia, 1965.
Julian, George W., *The Life of Joshua Giddings,* Chicago, 1892.
Moore, A. Y., *The Life of Schuyler Colfax,* Philadelphia, 1868.
Parker, William Belmont, *The Life and Public Services of Justin Smith
     Morrill,* Boston, 1924.
Polk, James K., *The Diary of James K. Polk,* Chicago, 1910.
Sandburg, Carl, *Abraham Lincoln The War Years,* New York, 1939.
Sumner, Charles, *The Works of Charles Sumner,* Boston, 1871.
Tyler, Lyon G., *Letters and Times of the Tylers,* Richmond, 1884.
Wilson, Woodrow, *History of the American People,* New York, 1918.
Woodburn James Albert, *Life of Thaddeus Stevens,* Indianapolis, 1913.

Periodicals

Niles' National Register

United States Federal Records

Biographical Dictionary of the American Congress
The Congressional Globe The Twenty-Eighth to the Thirty-Ninth
     Congress.

Index

273